Modern
Botanical
Watercolor

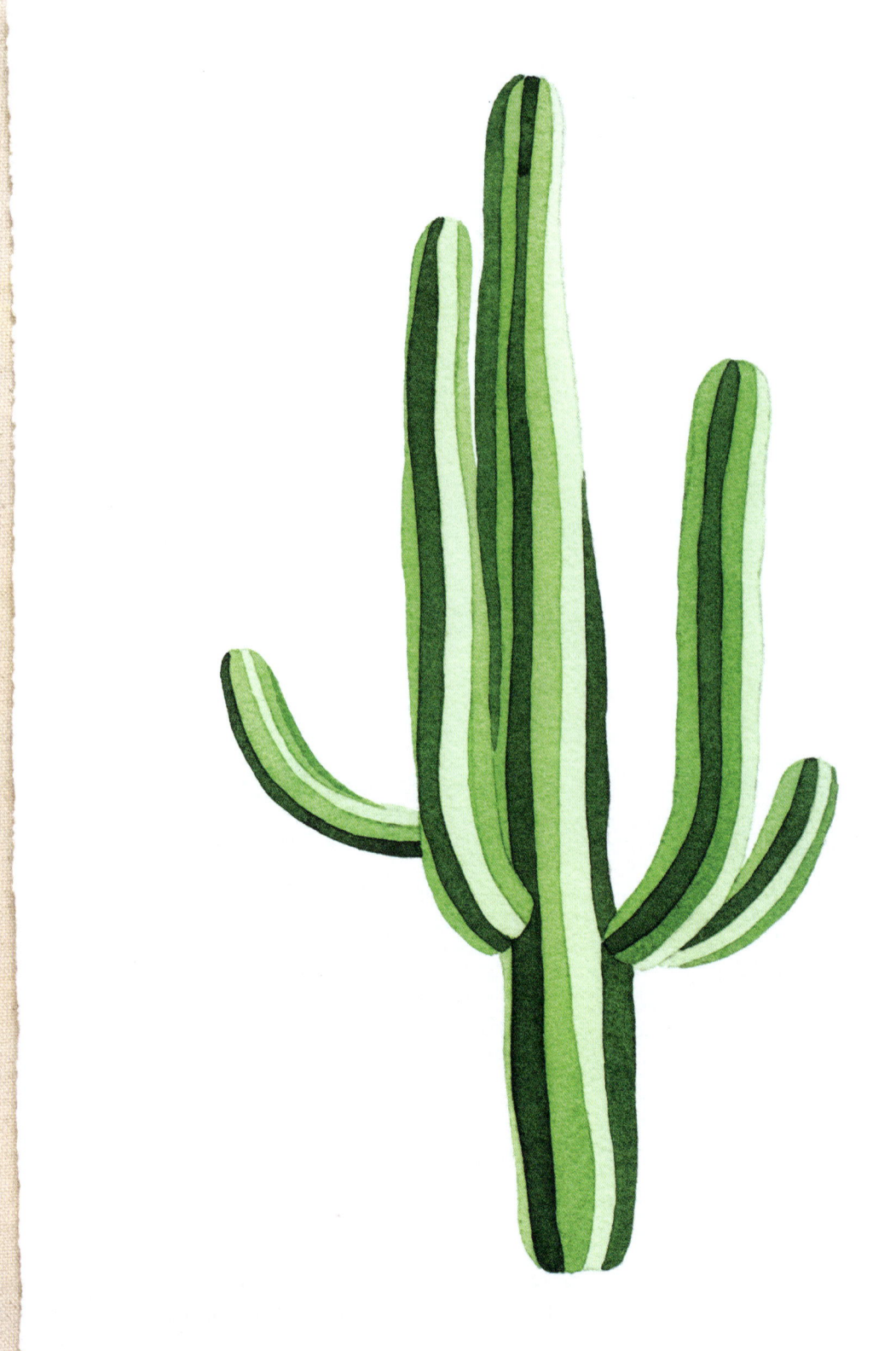

Jenny K

Modern Botanical Watercolor

Easy & expressive painting techniques

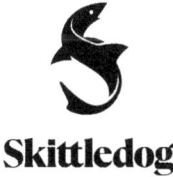

Skittledog

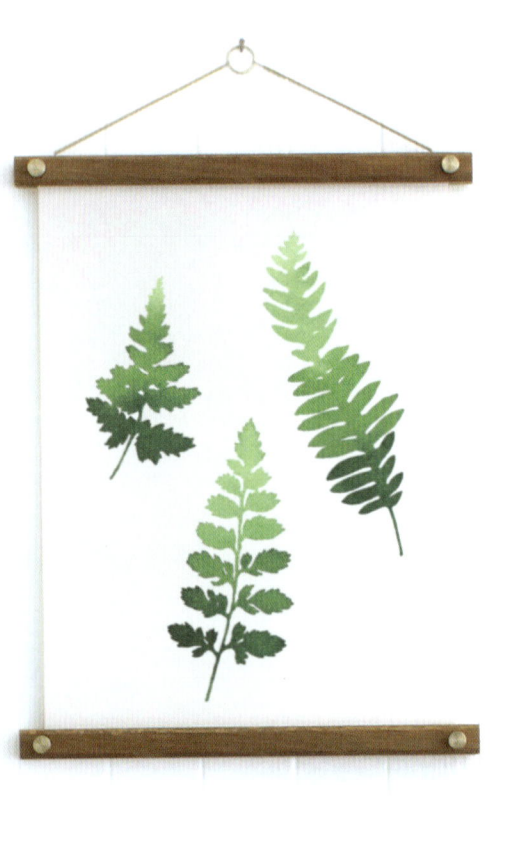
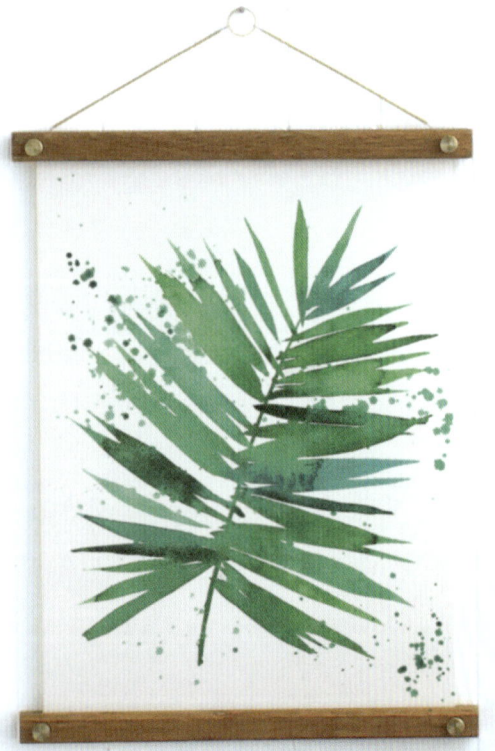
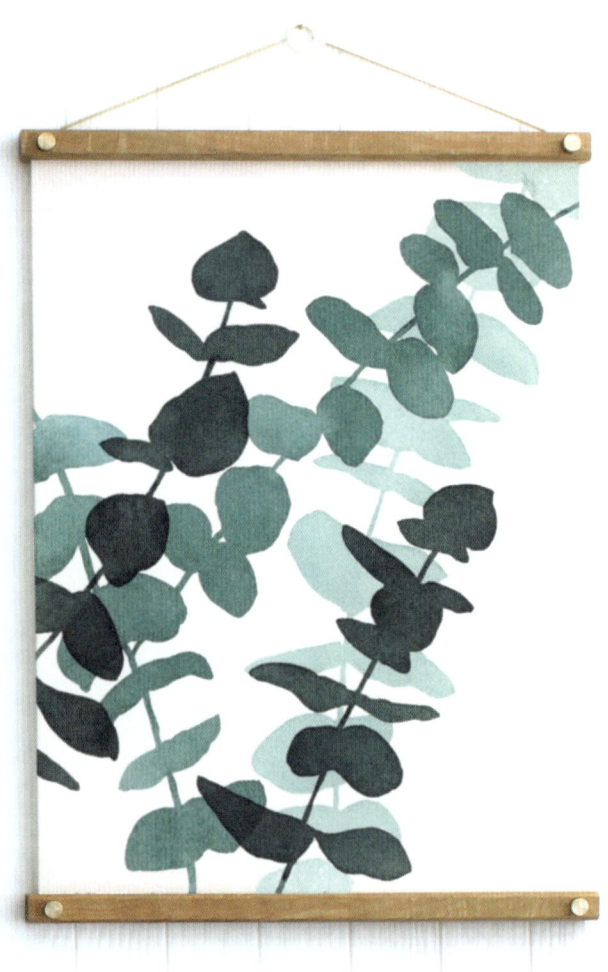
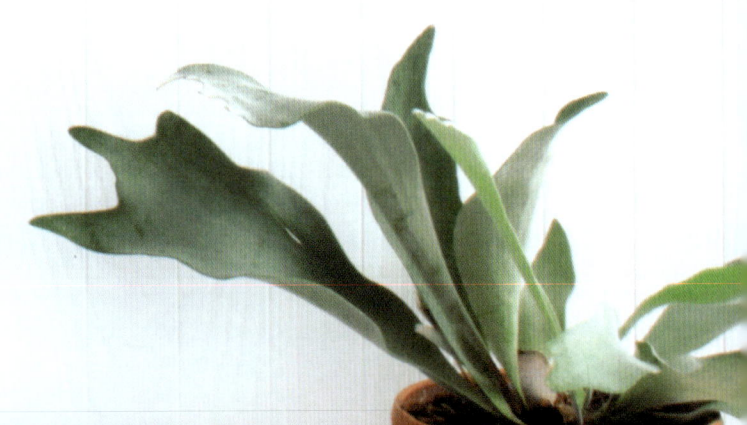

Contents

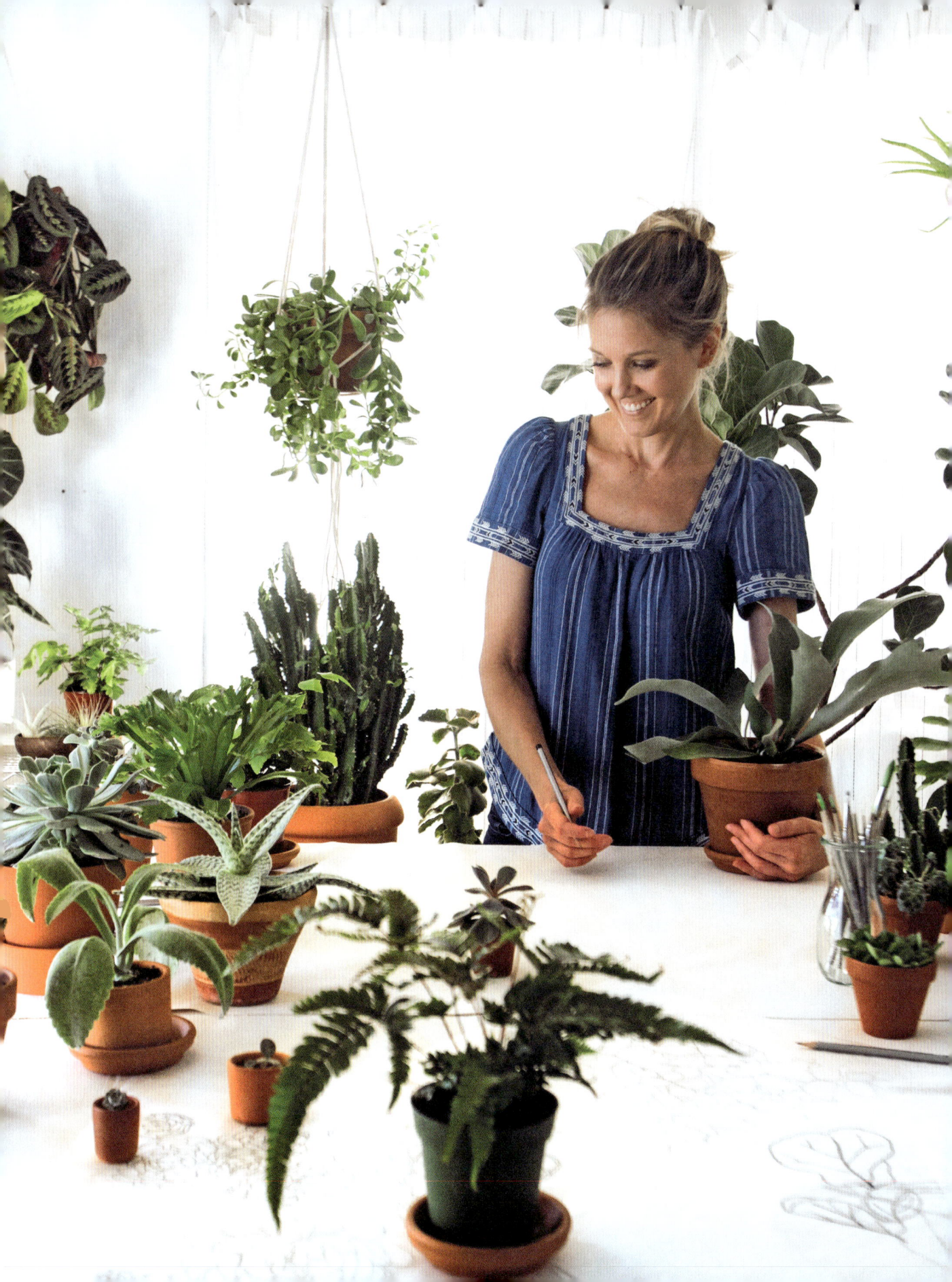

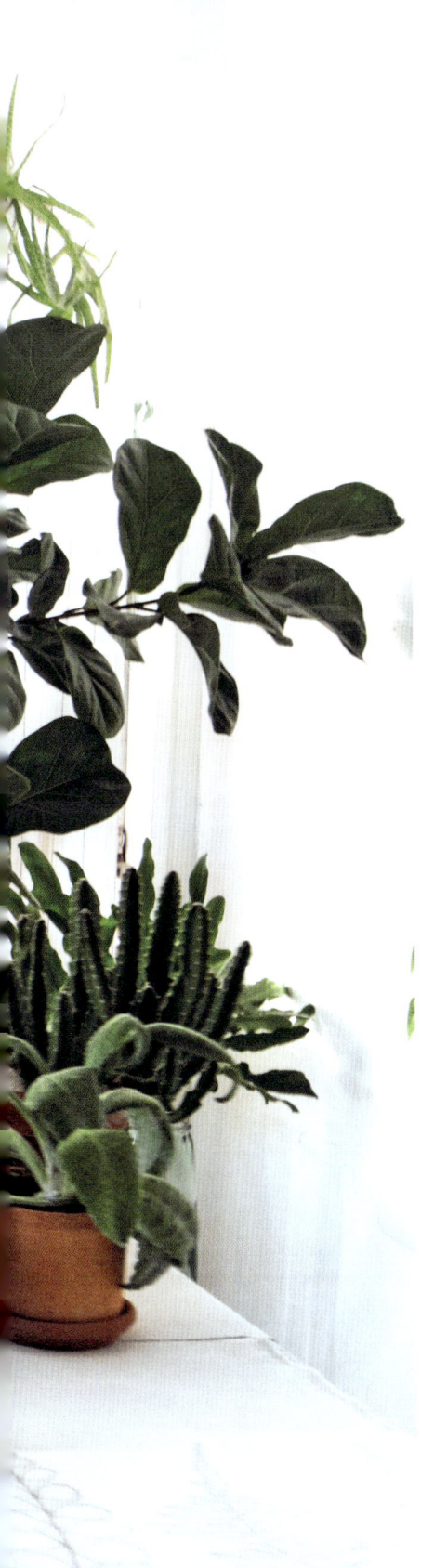

Introduction

Welcome to this joyful journey into the art of capturing nature's beauty. I'm Jenny K, also known by my pen name Living Pattern, and I'm thrilled to be your guide on this colorful adventure.

Whether you've never held a paintbrush or you've been dabbling in watercolors for years, this book is for you. As an artist and teacher based in the lush landscapes of South Florida, I've spent years developing a style that captures the essence of plants in vivid, flowing watercolors.

The capacity for artistic expression lies within each of us—sometimes it just needs a gentle nudge. This book is that nudge. From my studies at the Savannah College of Art and Design to my work as a textile designer and creative display designer, I've cultivated a love of pattern and design that I'm excited to share.

Within these pages you'll discover the fundamentals of color theory, essential materials, and techniques tailored to bringing leaves, flowers, and plants to life on the page. We'll explore everything from basic washes to intricate textures and the unique characteristics of a variety of botanical subjects.

This book is about more than just technique. It's an invitation to slow down, observe the natural world, and translate that beauty onto paper. Whether you're painting a simple leaf or a complex tropical arrangement, you'll develop skills to capture not only the form, but also the spirit of your botanical subjects.

So gather your supplies, open your eyes to the wonders of the plant world, and let's embark on this transformative journey together. With practice and patience, you'll soon be creating gorgeous contemporary watercolor artworks that reflect the beauty of nature.

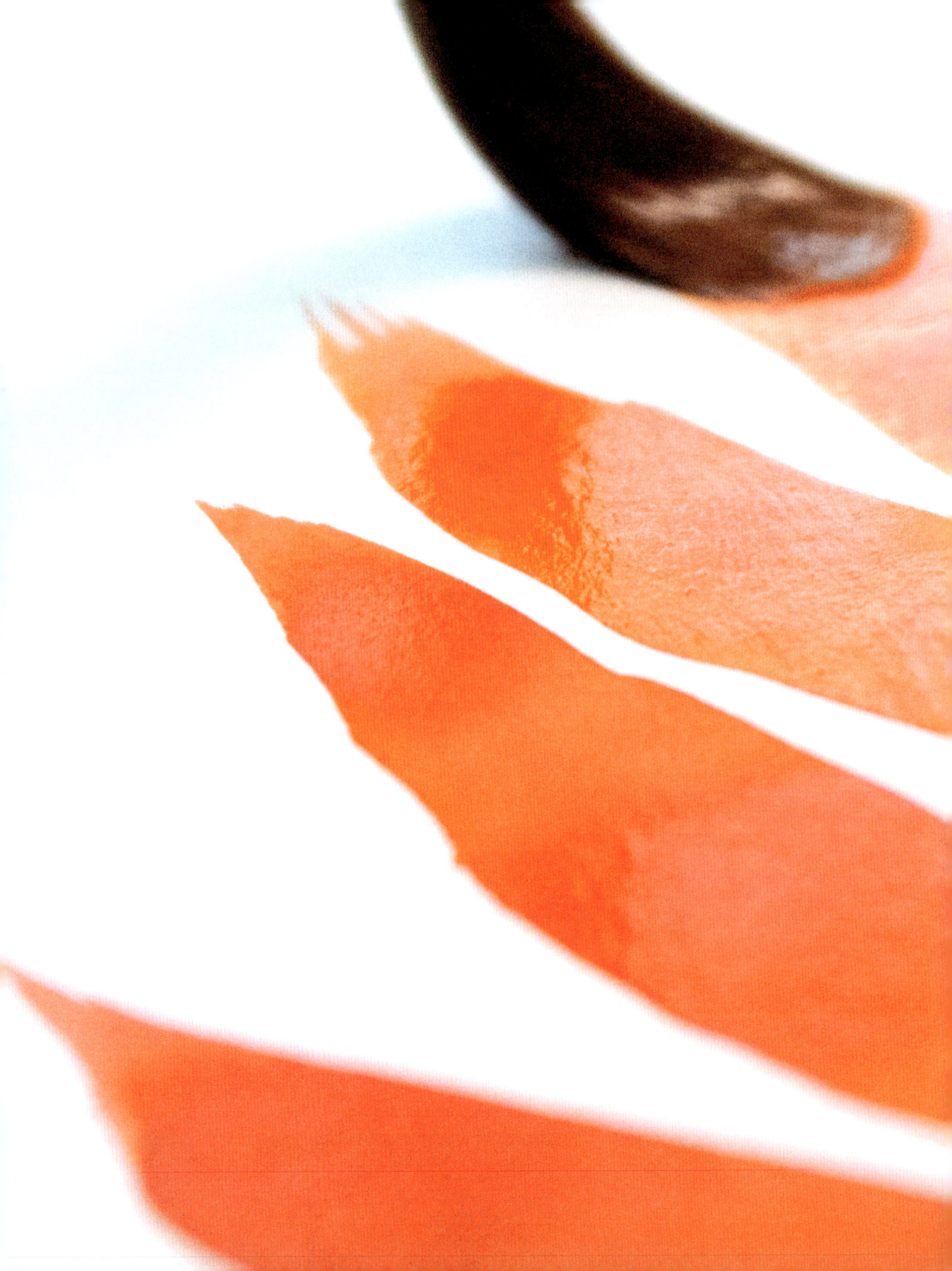

Color Theory & Watercolor Paints

The Color Wheel

The color wheel can be seen as an artist's compass, guiding us through the vast spectrum of available hues. It is the foundation of color theory, helping us mix and organize colors effectively.

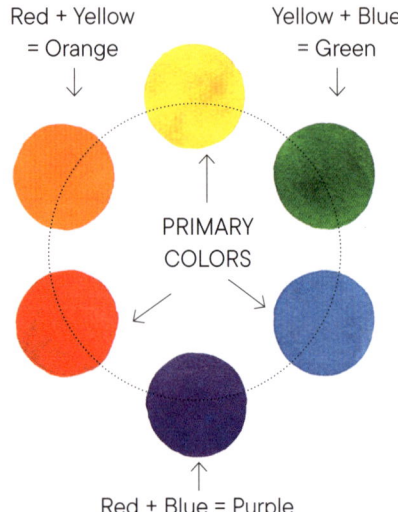

Red + Yellow = Orange

Yellow + Blue = Green

PRIMARY COLORS

Red + Blue = Purple

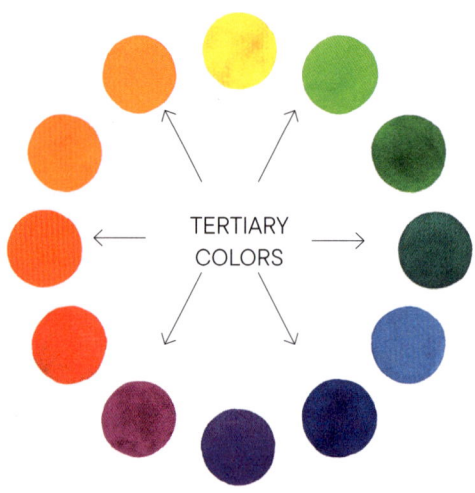

TERTIARY COLORS

Primary colors

At the heart of the color wheel are three primary colors: red, yellow, and blue. These are the building blocks with which all other colors are created. They are pure colors, meaning they cannot be made by mixing other colors.

Secondary colors

When we mix two primary colors, we create secondary colors:

- Red + Yellow = Orange
- Yellow + Blue = Green
- Blue + Red = Purple

Tertiary colors

These are formed by combining a primary color with its neighboring secondary color. The six tertiary colors are:

- Red-Orange
- Yellow-Orange
- Yellow-Green
- Blue-Green
- Blue-Purple
- Red-Purple

Warm & Cool Colors

Color is the essence of watercolor painting, evoking particular feelings and setting the mood of our artwork. It's crucial to understand the distinction between warm and cool colors.

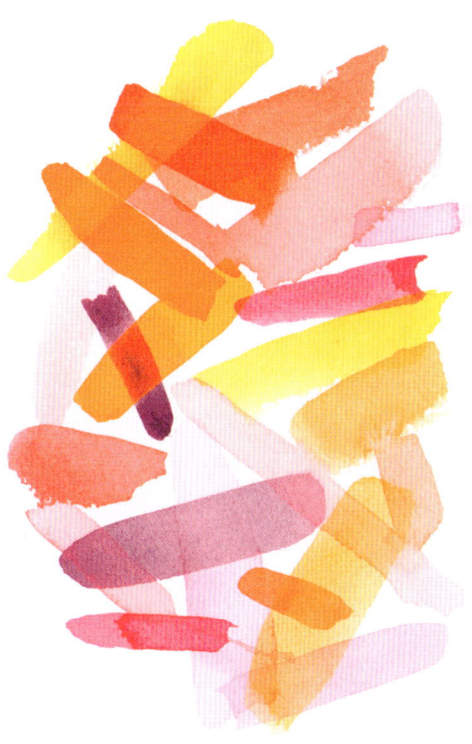

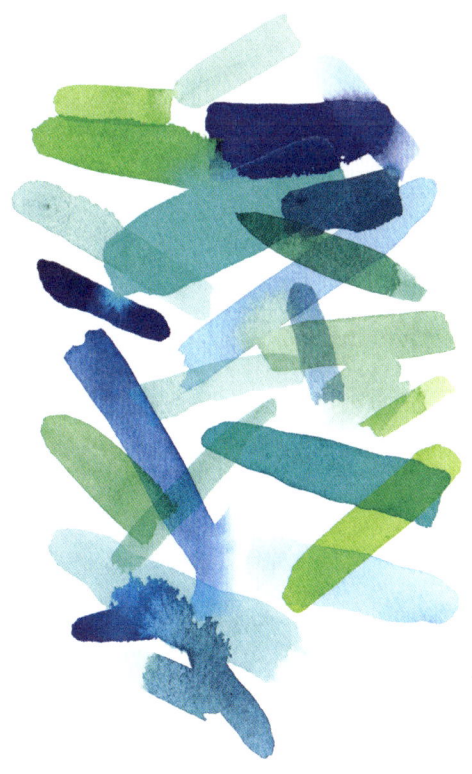

Warm colors
Reds, oranges, and yellows remind us of sunlight and fire. They tend to advance in a painting, drawing the viewer's eye.

Cool colors
Blues, greens, and purples evoke water and sky. They often recede in a composition, creating a feeling of depth.

Using warm and cool colors together
Don't be afraid to use both warm and cool colors together in a single piece: the interplay between them can breathe life into your botanical subjects.

The Emotional Impact of Color

When choosing colors, consider the feelings you want to evoke as your starting point.

Warm colors

- Red: passion, love, energy
- Orange: vitality, creativity, enthusiasm
- Yellow: happiness, optimism, cheerfulness

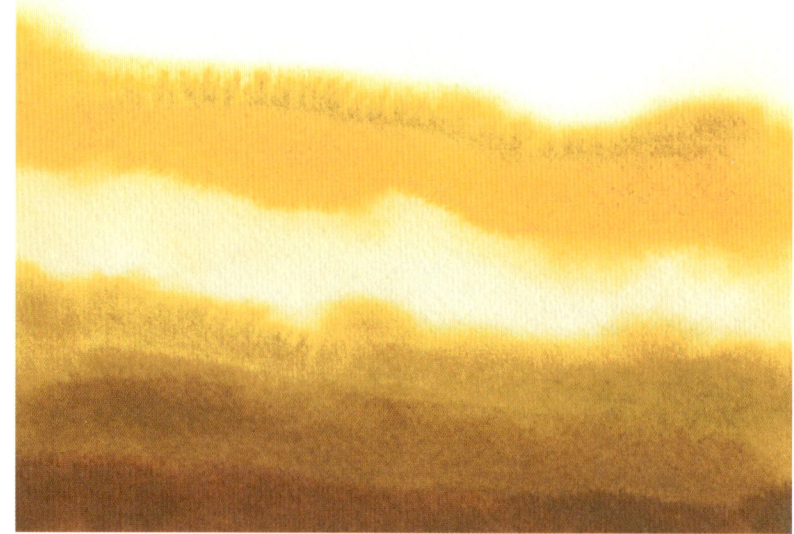

Cool colors

- Green: growth, nature, harmony
- Blue: calmness, serenity, trust
- Purple: royalty, mystery, spirituality

Tip: Remember, these categories aren't absolute. A yellow-green might feel cool next to a true yellow, but warm when placed beside a blue-green.

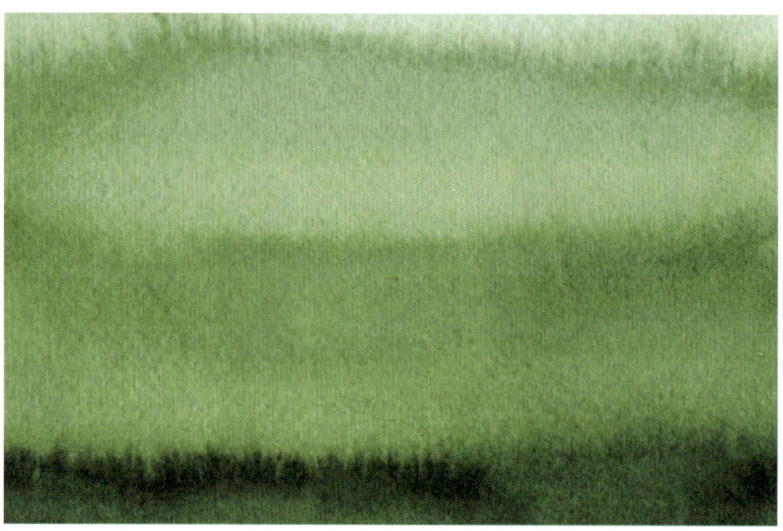

Warm and cool colors

The combination of warm and cool colors can produce dynamic botanical paintings. Placing warm-colored flowers amid cool-colored leaves creates visual contrast and enhances the three-dimensional appearance of your artwork. For instance, the striking combination of orange and peach blossoms against green foliage results in a vibrant, eye-catching composition full of depth.

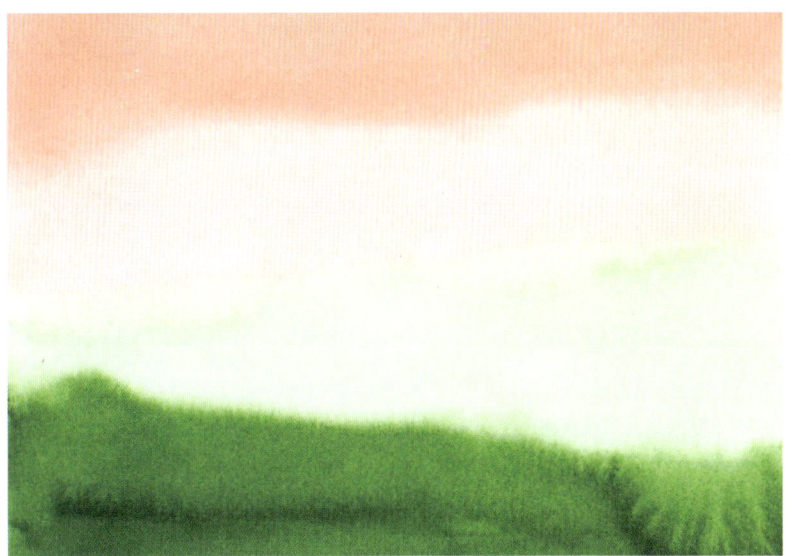

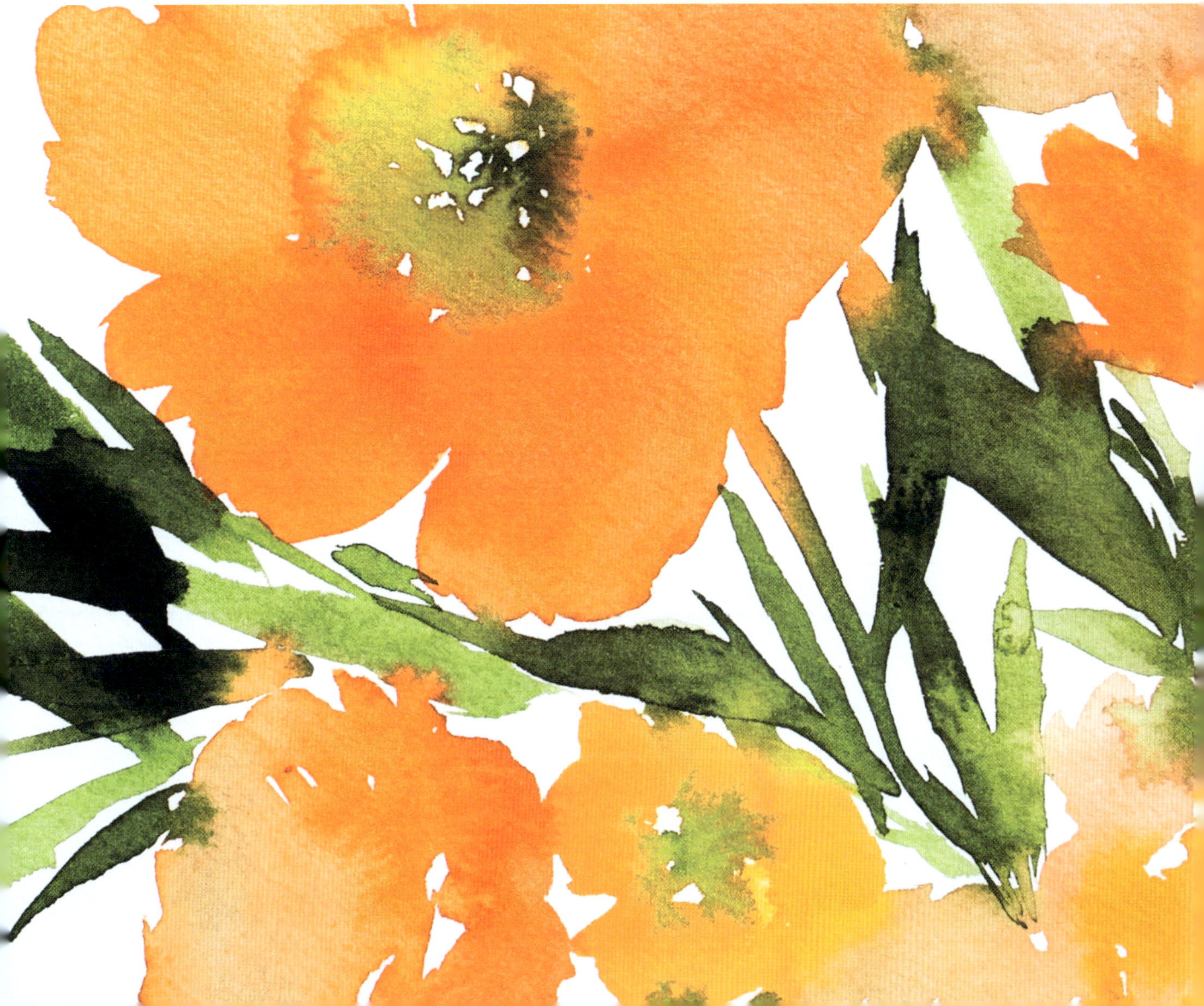

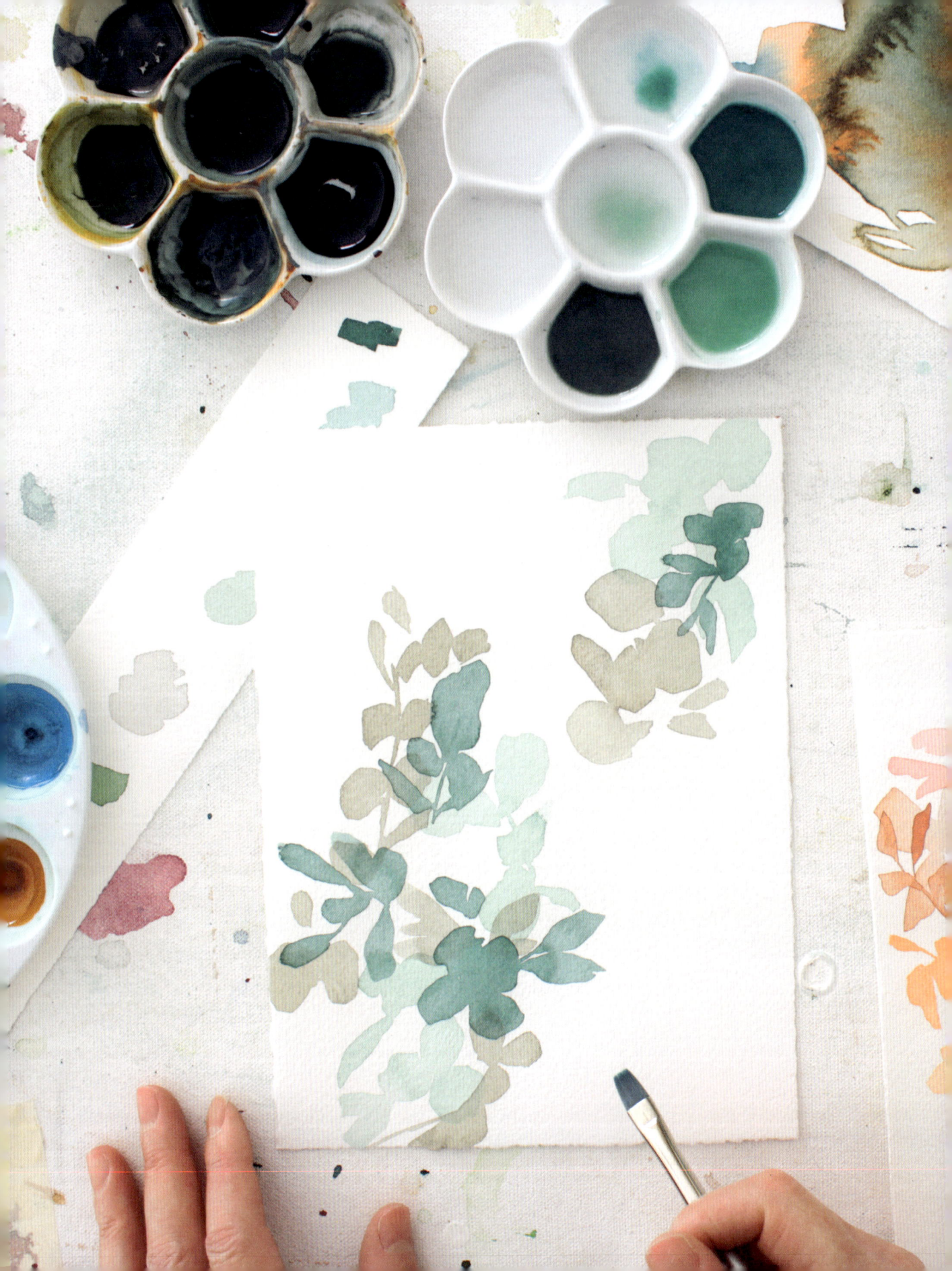

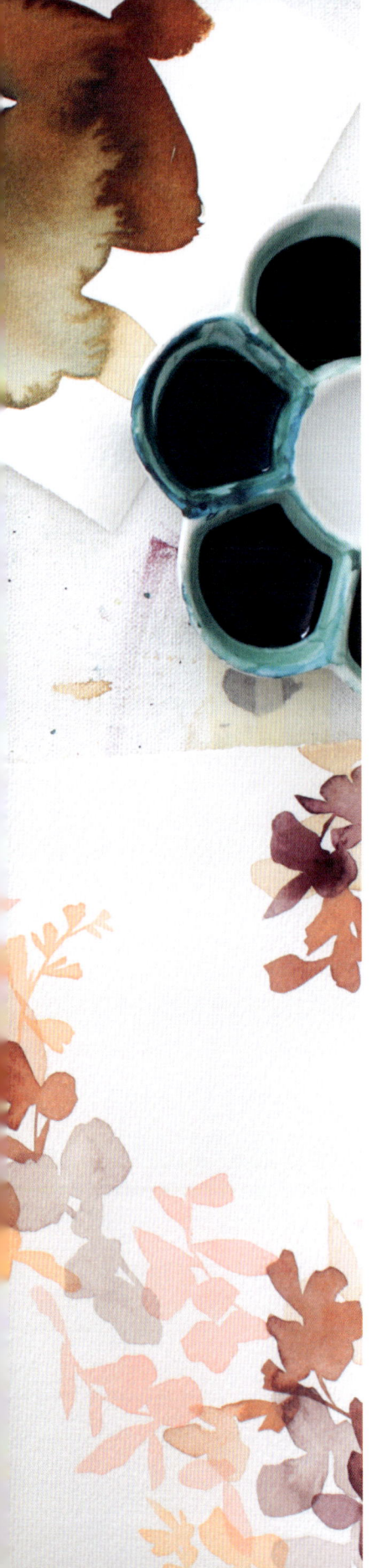

Color Palette Harmony

Just like a beautiful piece of music, a stunning watercolor painting needs harmony. Let's explore how to create color palettes that sing, no matter your subject.

By understanding and practicing these principles, you'll be well-equipped to create watercolors that resonate, whether you're painting delicate botanicals, sweeping landscapes, or expressive abstracts.

Color schemes

Referencing the color wheel on p.10, see how colors can be used together in the following ways to create a variety of visual effects, moods, and levels of harmony or contrast.

Complementary: opposites attract and make each other seem brighter. Pair colors from opposite sides of the wheel for dramatic accents and balanced compositions (e.g., blue and orange for sky and earth landscapes).

Analogous: neighbors that play well together. Use 3–5 adjacent colors (e.g., yellow, yellow-green, and green for spring botanicals).

Triadic: three is the magic number, so choose colors evenly spaced around the wheel for vibrant effects (e.g., red, yellow, and blue for primary color abstracts). Try using one dominant color and the other two as accents for balance.

Split-complementary: a softer version of complementary; one color plus two adjacent to its complement (e.g., yellow with violet-blue and red-violet for dynamic florals).

Tetradic: create lively compositions with two pairs of complementary colors (e.g., yellow-orange, blue-violet, red-orange, and blue-green for more complex landscapes).

Choosing & Using Colors

Understanding how to intentionally select and place colors can help balance your composition, draw the viewer's attention, and create depth, contrast, and mood.

Remember that color harmony is a powerful element of your artistic toolkit, but it's not a rigid rulebook. Don't be afraid to break the "rules" to create your own unique color stories. Embrace the unpredictable nature of watercolor by allowing colors to mix on paper and viewing "mistakes" as creative opportunities. As you progress on your watercolor journey, you'll develop an intuitive sense of color.

Palette

- Use a limited palette (usually 3–5 colors) to produce cohesive, harmonious paintings; mix these colors to create a range of hues and values.
- Muted colors can create a feeling of nostalgia or melancholy.
- Bright, saturated colors can be used to express joy or excitement.
- Neutrals balance bright colors, add depth, and can be created by mixing complementary colors.
- Consider the visual weight of different colors: warm, dark, and highly saturated colors feel more dominant and may need to be balanced with cooler or lighter tones for depth and harmony.
- Use warm and cool colors intentionally.

Placement

- Create paths for the eye using color.
- Use contrasting colors for focal points.
- Try using one color to dominate, one to support, and one or more as accents to avoid cluttering your composition.

Tip: Try painting a simple subject multiple times using different color schemes, and reflect on how each changes the piece's overall feel.

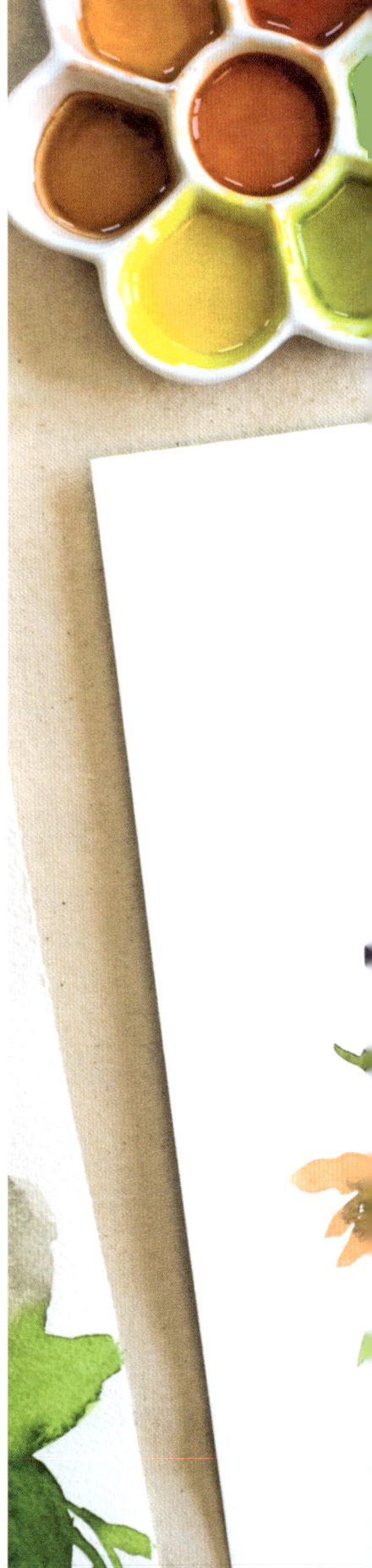

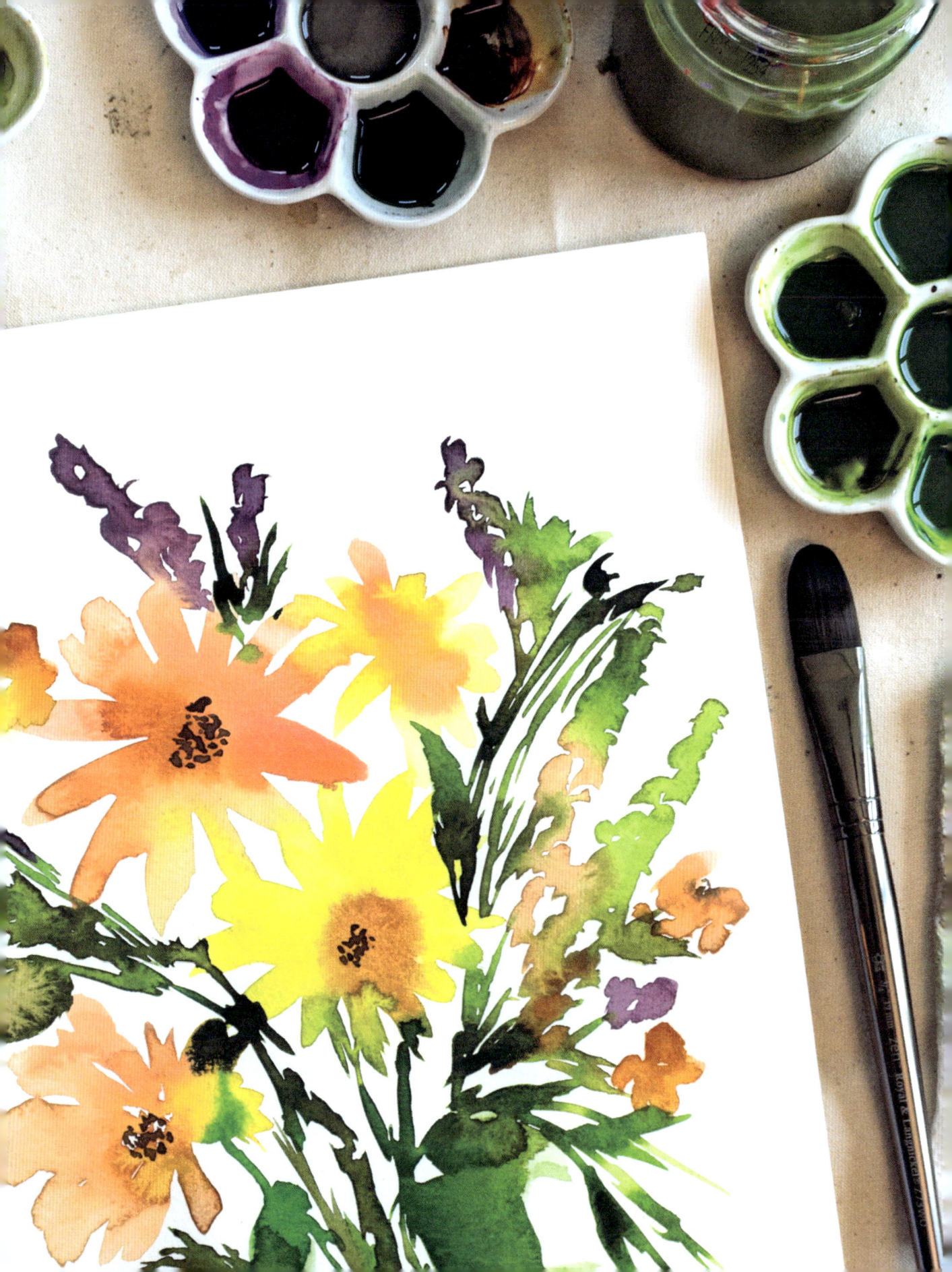

Watercolor Paints

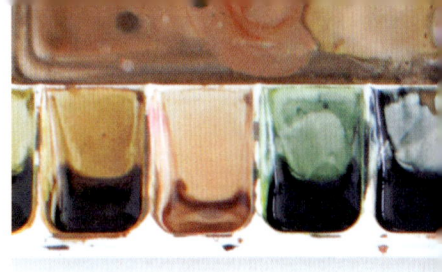

While watercolors come in several forms, I primarily use professional-grade tube watercolors in ceramic palettes for their versatility and rich mixing potential.

These concentrated pigments offer unmatched control and excellent value when filling palette wells. Remember that generous wells of tube paint will reward you with months of consistent color, making them an excellent investment for serious botanical work.

Grades and properties of watercolor paint

Artist-grade tubes are most expensive but offer pure, vibrant pigments, superior lightfastness, and excellent mixing capabilities. Student-grade paints are cheaper and work well for learning, but provide less intensity.

Understanding pigments improves your mixing success. Single-pigment colors create cleaner mixes, while multi-pigment ones offer convenience but can become muddy when combined. While I prefer tubes, other options include pan watercolors (in ready-to-use blocks, so perfect for traveling), and liquid watercolors (fluid consistency, so good for flowing washes).

Most brands will indicate the following properties on the tube labels or on color charts you can find online or in store.

Transparency: refers to how much light can pass through, with higher transparencies revealing underlying layers and creating luminous effects. Paints will usually be marked as transparent, semitransparent, or opaque.

Staining power: how much a pigment penetrates and binds to the paper, denoting how difficult it is to remove once dry. Nonstaining paint is easy to lift or lighten, so good for softening edges. Staining is good for building rich layers.

Granulation: the visual texture created when pigment particles clump together rather than settling evenly, creating a mottled, grainy effect. Heavy granulating pigments are good for creating texture, but not so great for smooth, flat washes.

Lightfastness: indicates how resistant the color is to fading over time—an important consideration if you are looking at selling your work.

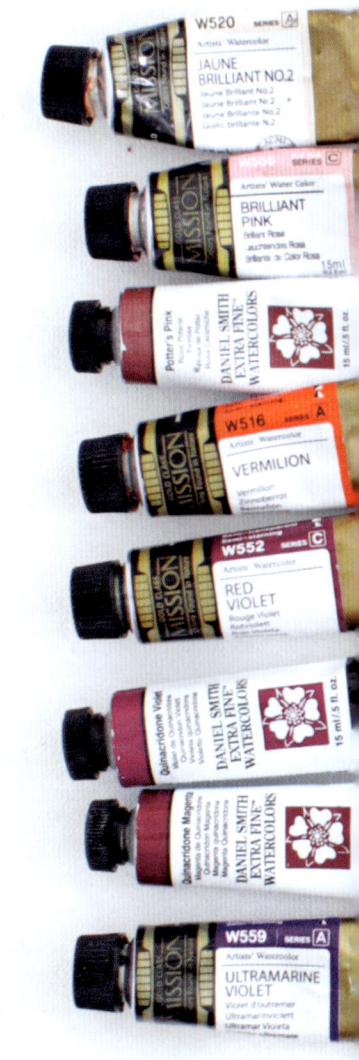

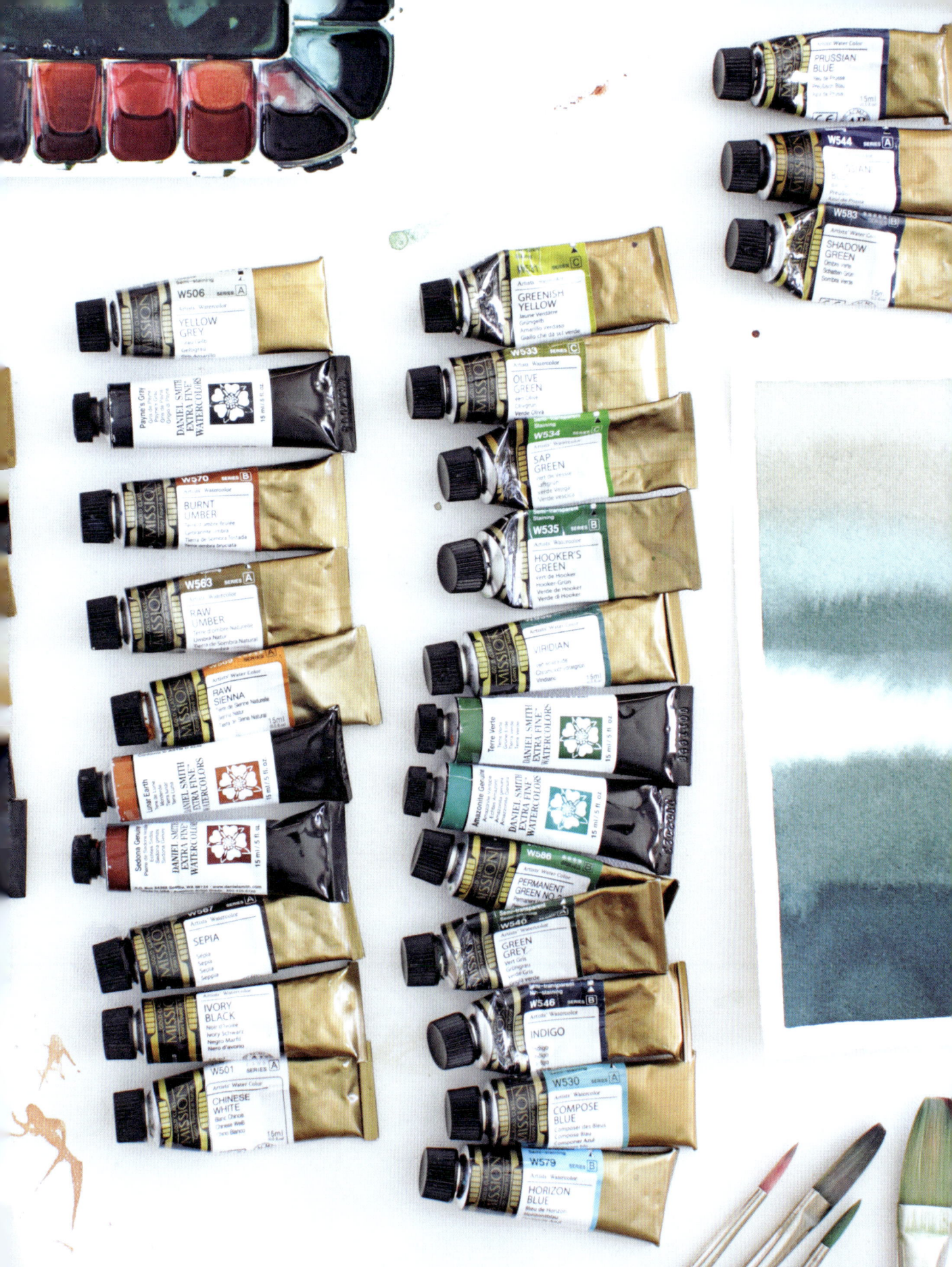

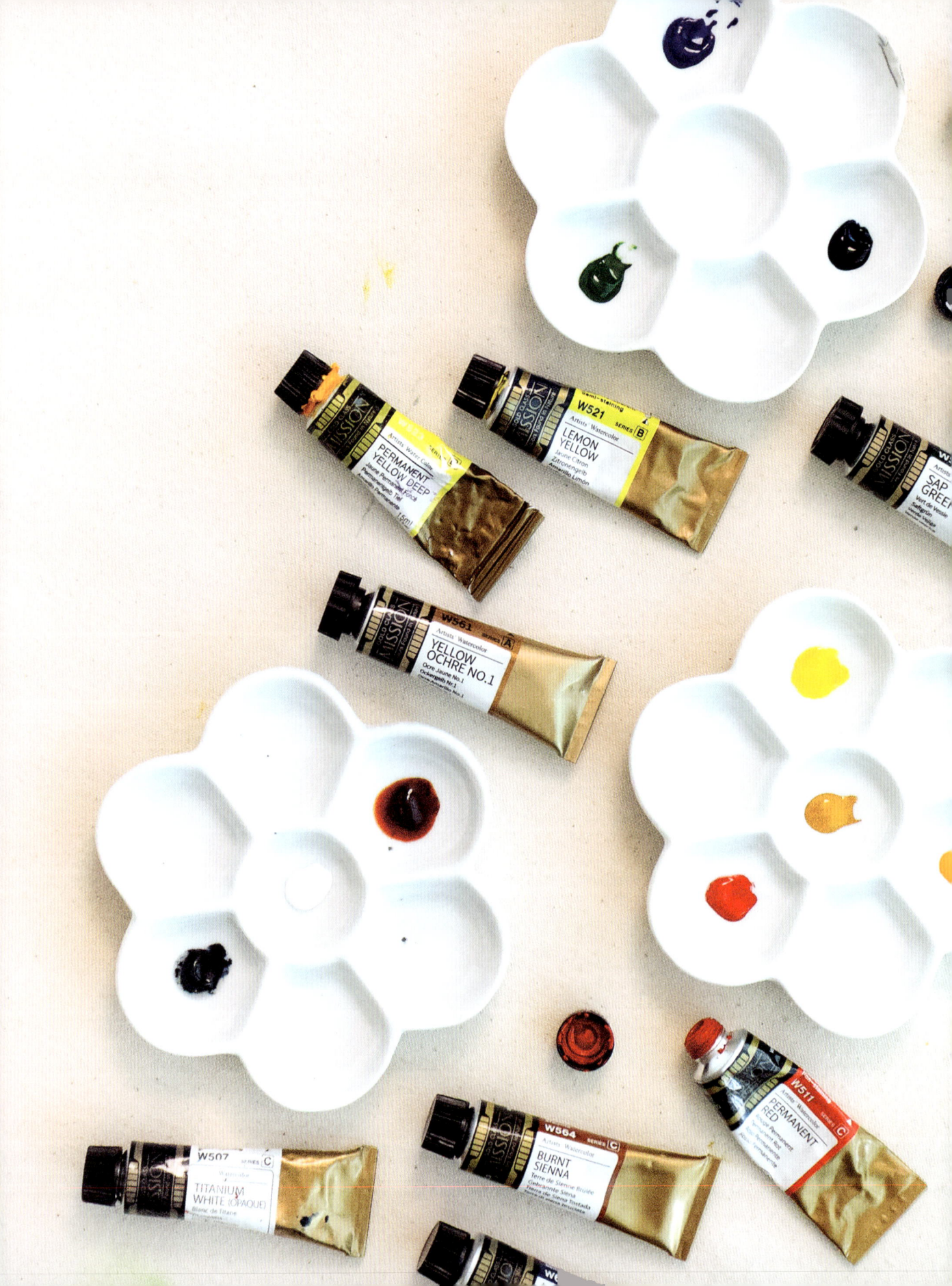

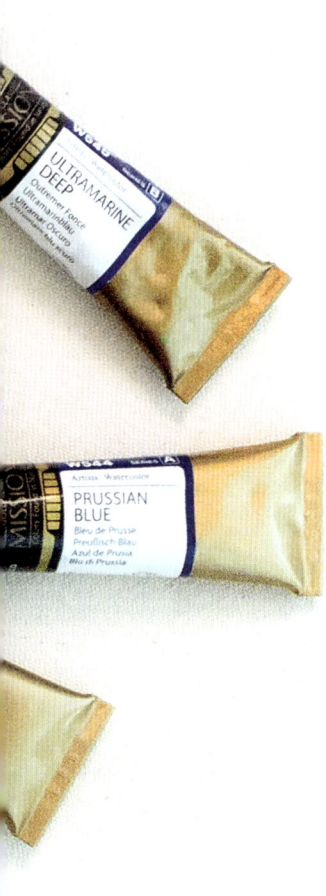

Creating a *Basic Palette*

To build a basic watercolor palette for botanical art, choose colors that mix well, reflect natural hues, and support plant detail.

Throughout the book I'll demonstrate how to use a range of popular pigments, but you don't need to go out and buy dozens of paints in order to get started. The following tube colors will serve as the foundation of your palette.

- Ultramarine Deep
- Prussian Blue
- Sap Green
- Lemon Yellow
- Permanent Yellow Deep
- Yellow Ochre
- Permanent Red
- Burnt Sienna
- Payne's Gray
- Titanium White

Setting up your ceramic palette with tube colors is simple:

1. Arrange colors around the edges, leaving center wells for mixing.

2. Squeeze generous amounts into each well.

3. Begin working immediately, or allow to dry and reactivate the colors with water when you come to paint.

Optional additional mediums
These special additions can transform your paintings in wonderful ways, no matter your subject or style.

Watercolor ground: like a magical primer that lets you paint on almost any surface. Use it to fix mistakes or add texture to your paper.

Masking fluid: a protective shield for your white paper, perfect for preserving highlights, creating intricate patterns, or saving white spaces. Allow it to dry before painting, then remove when your artwork is fully dry.

Gum arabic: this increases transparency and flow, ideal for layering techniques, and helps colors spread more evenly. Mix a little in with your paint for beautifully smooth washes in large areas.

Iridescent medium: gives a pearlescent sheen to your watercolors, great for highlighting details. Add to light colors for subtle sparkle, or to dark colors for dramatic effects.

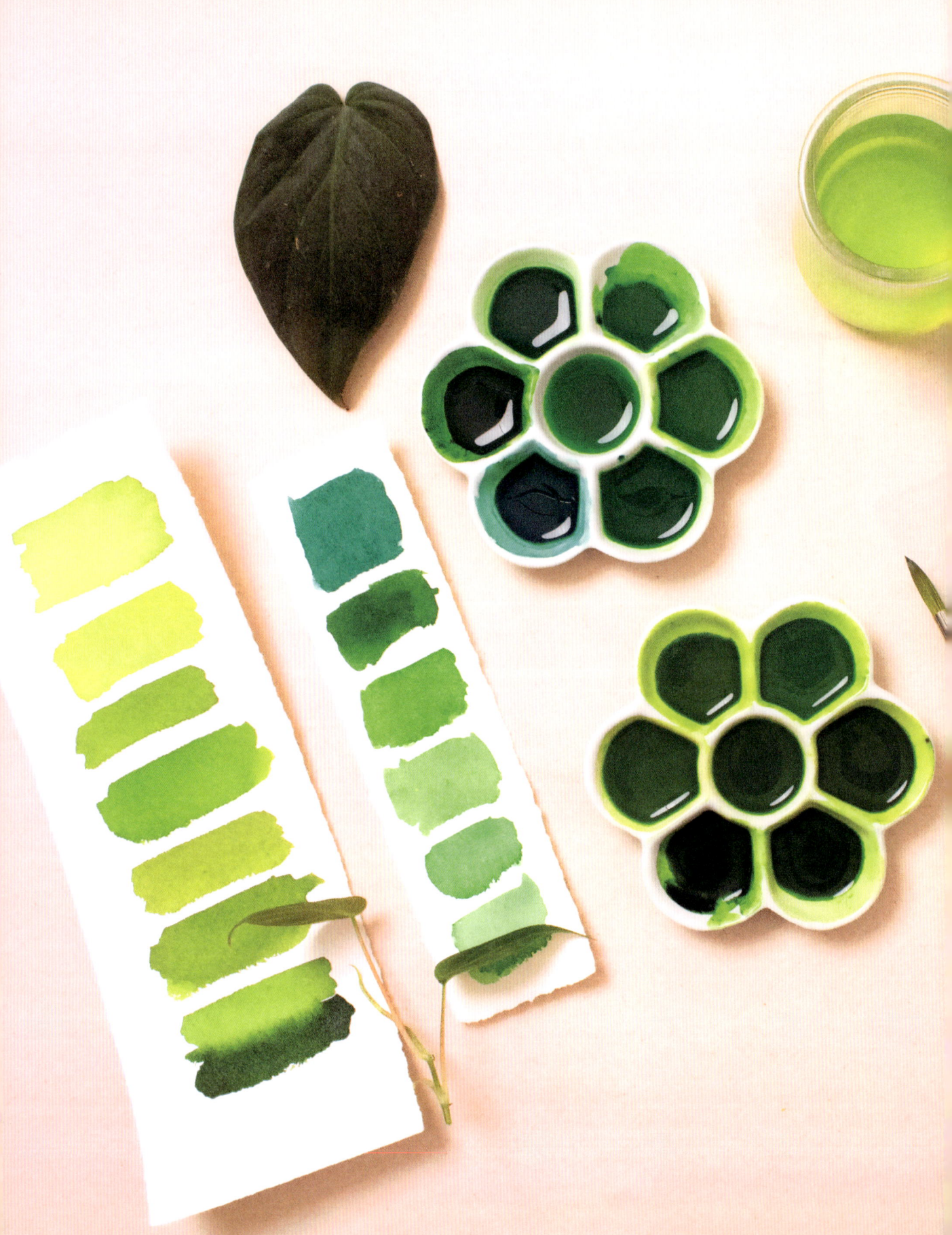

The Art of Color Mixing

Using the palette from the previous page, it's possible to create thousands of beautiful tints and shades. Let's explore the fundamentals of mixing watercolors.

Basic technique

1. Sweep a damp brush gently over your tube color to lift some pigment: less pigment is often better than overloading your brush.
2. Transfer to a clean mixing well on your ceramic palette.
3. Clean your brush thoroughly between colors.
4. Add your second color and mix with controlled amounts of water.
5. Test on a scrap piece of paper.

Essential color recipes for botanicals

I find the following mixes create wonderfully realistic and evocative hues for use in botanical paintings. Remember that experimentation leads to discovery, so don't be afraid to play around with different combinations and ratios of pigment/water to find your perfect mix. Label and note down successful combinations and mix more than you think you'll need.

Fresh greens: Sap Green + Lemon Yellow (70/30)
Deep greens: Ultramarine Deep + Lemon Yellow + touch of Burnt Sienna
Rich browns: Burnt Sienna + Ultramarine Deep (60/40)
Warm grays: Ultramarine Deep + Burnt Sienna + Permanent Red (equal parts pigment and water)
Natural blacks: Prussian Blue + Burnt Sienna (50/50)

Adjusting colors

Lighten: add water gradually to Increase transparency.
Darken: increase pigment concentration to make a color more saturated and opaque.
Desaturate: add a tiny touch of complementary color to decrease the intensity.
Brighten: mix with a purer, cleaner pigment.

Materials &
Preparation

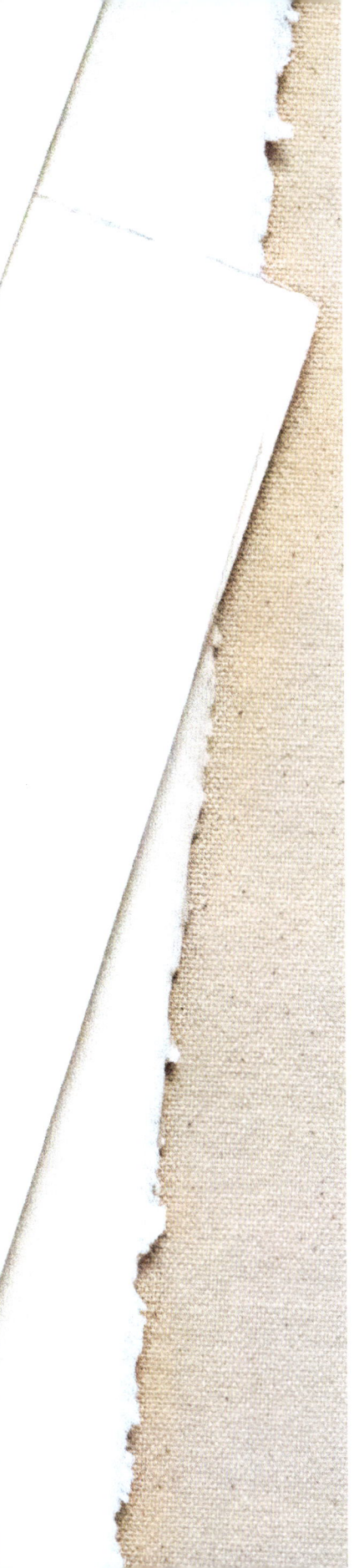

Watercolor Paper

Botanical watercolor art requires paper that allows precision for fine details, color vibrancy for subtle hues, and layering capacity for depth.

When selecting paper, consider your subject matter and preferred techniques: some highly detailed work might benefit from hot pressed paper, while textural subjects could shine on more textured surfaces. Cold pressed paper is a great starting point due to its versatility, and is often the most adaptable choice for a wide range of watercolor techniques and subjects.

The paper's absorbency, which is affected by composition and sizing (a treatment applied to watercolor paper to manage its absorbency), influences how pigments behave on the surface. Experiment to find what best captures your botanical subject's essence. When selecting paper, consider the key characteristics below.

Texture
Cold pressed: slightly textured, suitable for a wide range of subjects. This balances detail and texture and handles layering and lifting well, making it the go-to choice for most artists.
Hot pressed: smooth satin-like surface, ideal for highly detailed work and controlled techniques. Allows for crisp edges and fine lines.
Rough: the pronounced, bumpy texture creates interesting effects in loose landscapes and abstract pieces. Adds character and can give interesting effects to bark or textured leaves but may be too prominent for detailed work.

Weight
Medium (300gsm/140lb): versatile for most botanical subjects. It handles multiple washes without buckling, crucial for layering techniques.
Lightweight (190gsm/90lb): thin and prone to buckling when wet, so doesn't handle heavy layering or water-intensive techniques well. Ideal for quick sketches and studies, and cost-effective for practice.
Heavy (638gsm/300lb): thick, durable, and highly absorbent. Best for very wet techniques or large-scale work. Resists buckling even under heavy washes, so suits large pieces with rich backgrounds.

Format
Sheets: flexible in size and can be stretched; ideal for larger works.
Blocks: pre-stretched and convenient for outdoor painting.
Rolls: economical for large-scale work or series.
Sketchbooks: perfect for on-the-go studies and daily practice.

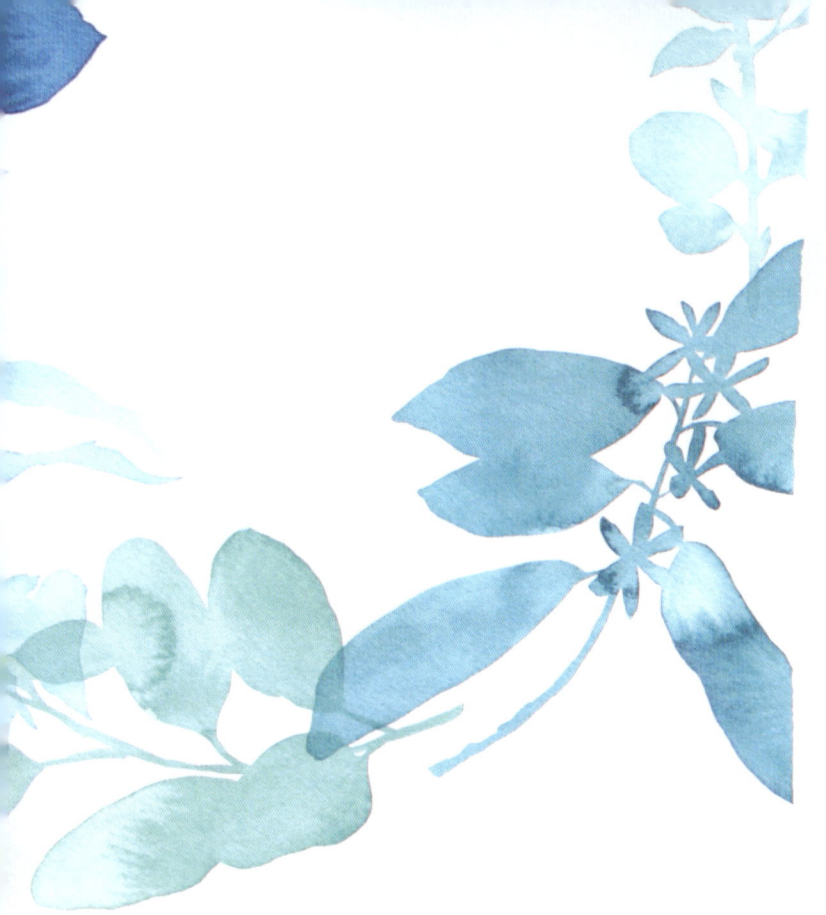
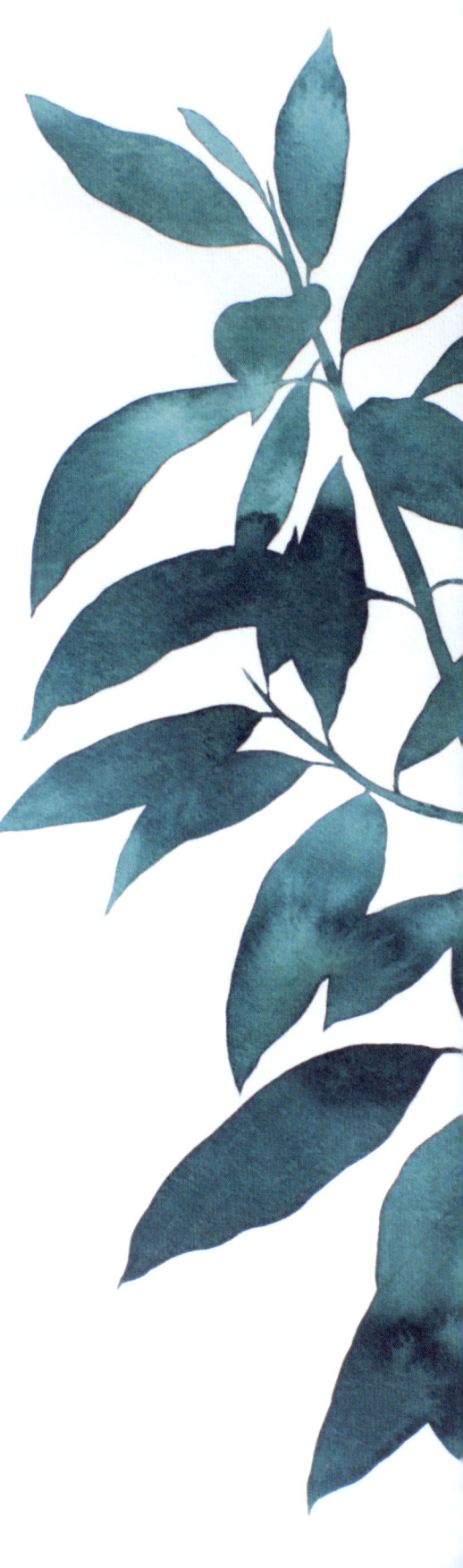

Composition

100% cotton: the most expensive, high-quality choice preferred by professionals. Paint flows smoothly, and it offers superior color vibrancy and longevity, essential for archival-quality illustrations.

Wood pulp: these are more affordable and readily available, suitable for practice. However, they are less absorbent, can warp easily, and may yellow over time.

Cotton/cellulose blends: these mid-range options balance cost and performance, containing 25–50% cotton and the remainder is wood pulp.

Sizing

Sizing prevents water and pigment from soaking in too quickly, allowing for better color vibrancy. Well-sized paper allows for lifting and creating soft edges, useful for depicting delicate petals and leaves. Over-saturated or poorly sized paper can cause blotchy results.

Recommended brands include Arches, Fabriano Artistico, and Saunders Waterford. These perform well for detailed botanical work, offering the right balance of absorbency and surface texture. Canson Heritage excels for precise petal work, while Stonehenge Aqua is a good budget option.

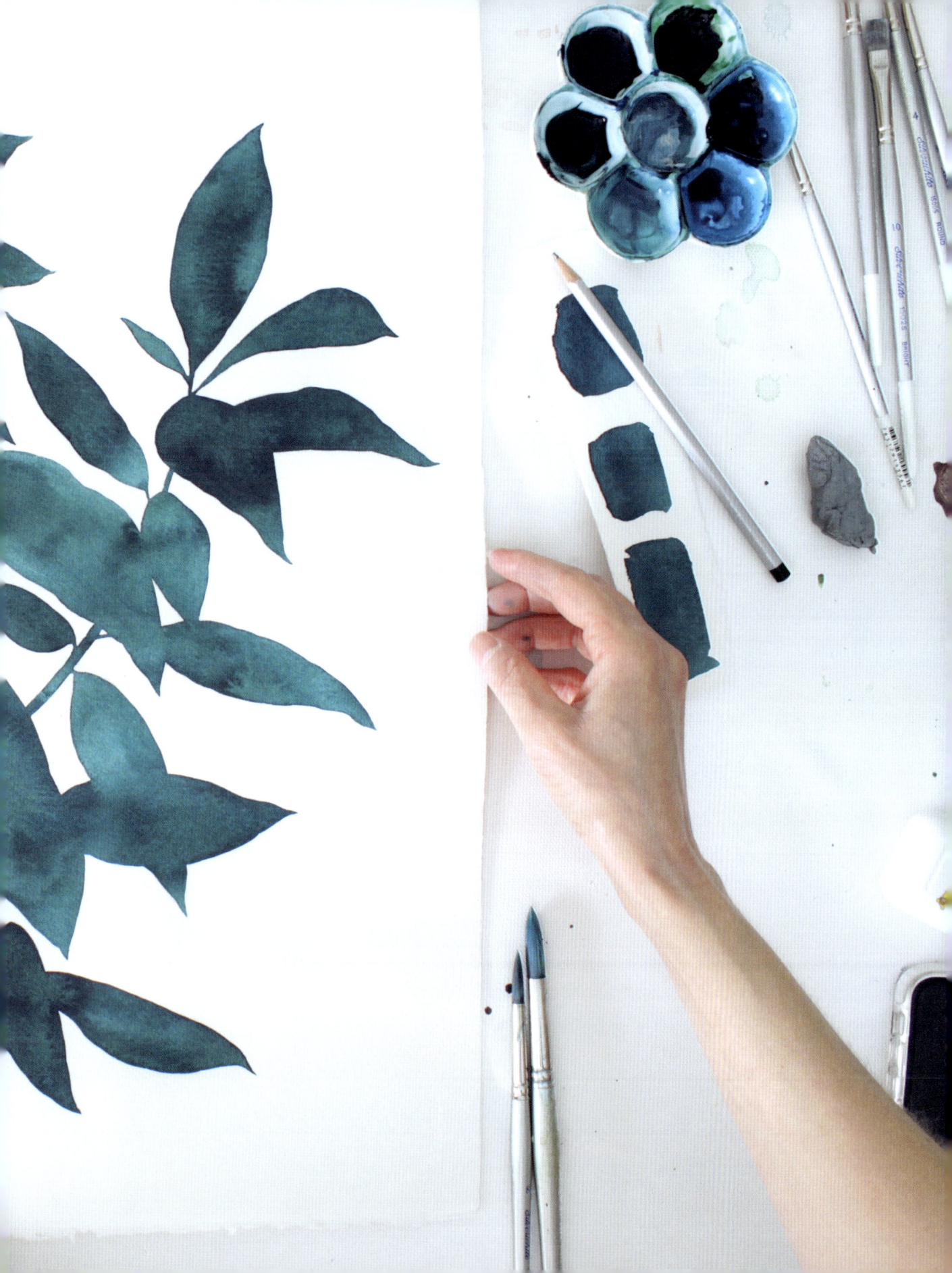

Choosing Brushes

The right brush can make all the difference in botanical watercolor painting. Experiment with using different brushes on the same subject to see varied effects. Don't be afraid to use what might be considered the "wrong" brush intentionally for interesting textures (for example, a fan brush for petals).

Brush materials

Watercolor brushes are available in a variety of materials, affecting water retention and precision. While natural materials were traditionally favored, many brands now offer high-quality synthetic brushes that work beautifully for botanical work. Look for eco-friendly options with sustainable wood handles and minimal packaging; some brands use recycled materials.

Natural hair
(e.g., sable, squirrel, pony)
- Pros: excellent water retention, fine points
- Cons: expensive, not vegan-friendly
- Best for: detailed work, soft washes

Synthetic
(nylon and polyester blends)
- Pros: affordable, durable, vegan-friendly
- Cons: may hold less water than natural hair
- Best for: general use, animal-free option

Synthetic/natural blends
- Mix synthetic fibers with natural to balance affordability, durability, and water control

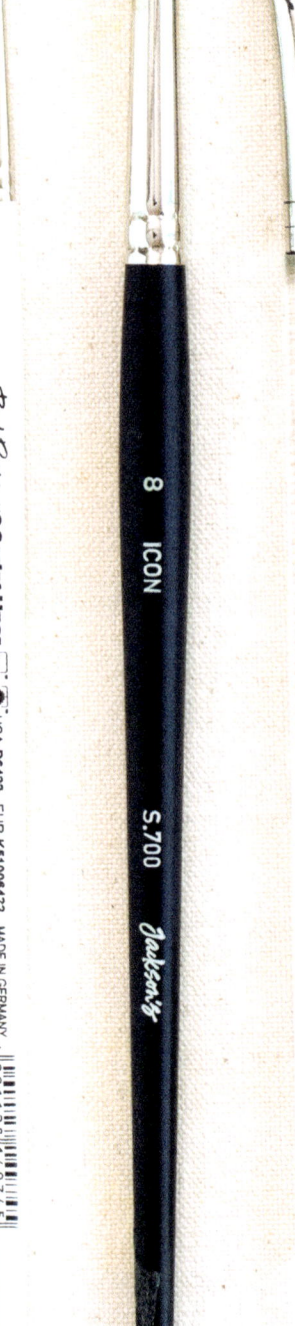

Shapes and sizes

Sizes are usually marked by numbers like 000, 00 (often expressed as 3/0 and 2/0), 0, 1, 2, 4, 6, 8, 10, 12, 16, 20 (the larger the number, the larger the brush tip). Some are sized in inch increments: ⅛, ¼, ½, ¾, 1, 2, and so on. It's worth noting that different brands' sizing may vary, and a size 4 in one brand may differ slightly from another.

Size	Description
000–0	Very fine detail
1–3	Fine details, thin lines
4–6	Medium-sized strokes, small washes
8–12	Good for general painting and washes
14–20+	Large washes and broad strokes

Liner: long, thin tip, for fine details and branches.
Round: with a tapered point, versatile for most botanical elements.
Flat: for broad leaves and background washes.
Filbert: perfect for natural-looking petals, for blending and curved strokes.
Fan: for textural foliage effects, blending, and dry brush work.
Quill: round with a fine point, good for washes and details; these come in non-standardized sizes. 10/0 is equal to the smallest standard brush, and size 6 is the largest (similar to a standard 12 or 14).

Brush selection by subject

Delicate flowers: small rounds (0–4), liner brush.
Large flowers: medium rounds (6–10), filberts.
Leaves: rounds for most shapes, flats for large leaves.
Stems: liner for thin stems, rounds for thicker ones.
Succulents: small flats for angular leaves, rounds for rosettes.

Caring for your brushes

- Clean thoroughly after each use.
- Shape bristles when wet, and lay to dry horizontally.
- Store brushes flat or standing with bristles up.
- Avoid soaking brushes in water.
- Invest in a brush restorer to maintain the fine points of your detail brushes.

Tip: Start with a set of round brushes in various sizes (000 to 12), then add specialty brushes as needed.

Tools & Materials

Here are some other essential items for your kit. Try to invest in quality supplies within your budget. Better materials often lead to better results and a more enjoyable painting experience.

1. Selected paints: see p.20 for info on building a basic palette.

2. Paint pipettes: versatile tools for adding details to your artwork, mixing colors, and applying liquid watercolors.

3. Color wheel: handy reference for understanding color relationships and mixing schemes.

4. Pencils and erasers: soft pencil (HB or 2B) and kneaded eraser for sketches and removing guidelines. Staedtler white erasers for stubborn pencil marks.

5. Foam brush: good for laying down large background washes or wetting paper for wet-on-wet blending.

6. Squirt bottle: useful for wetting both your palette and paper.

7. Water containers: two are ideal—one for rinsing your brush and one for clean water. Simple jars are fine.

8. Palette: white plastic or ceramic tray with wells for colors. The white surface shows colors accurately. Alternatives are old jars or ceramic plates.

9. Paper towels or clean cloth: indispensable for blotting excess water and cleaning brushes. Recycle rags, cutting them into 12 x 12-in squares.

10. Masking tape: (not shown) low-tack artists' tape for securing your paper and creating clean edges.

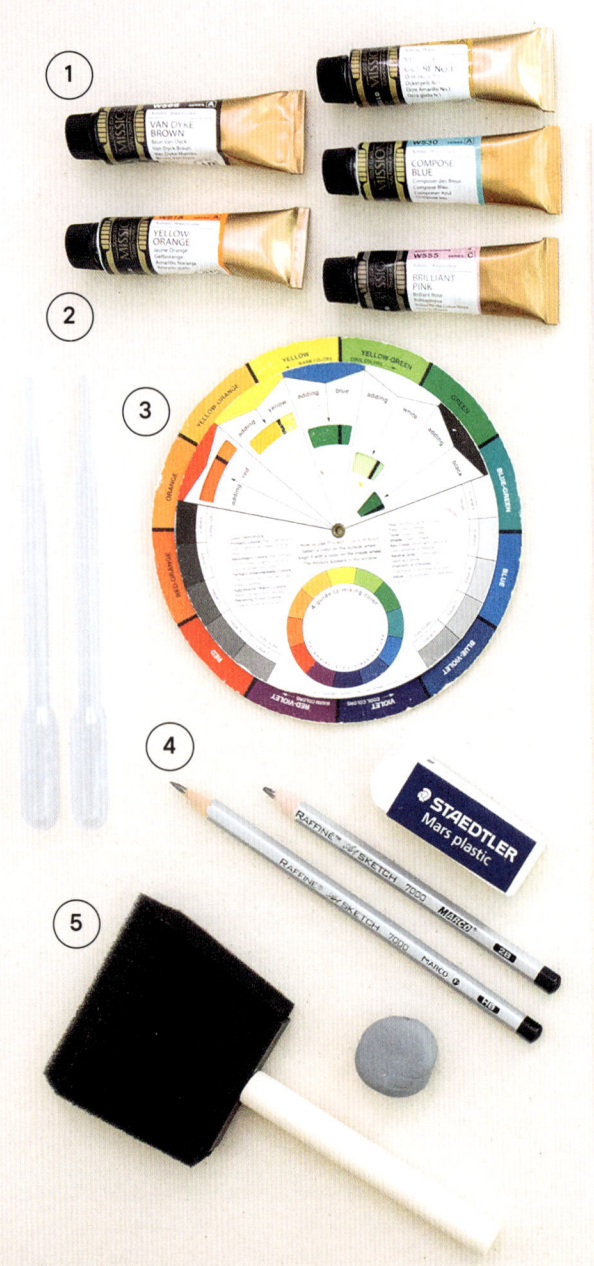

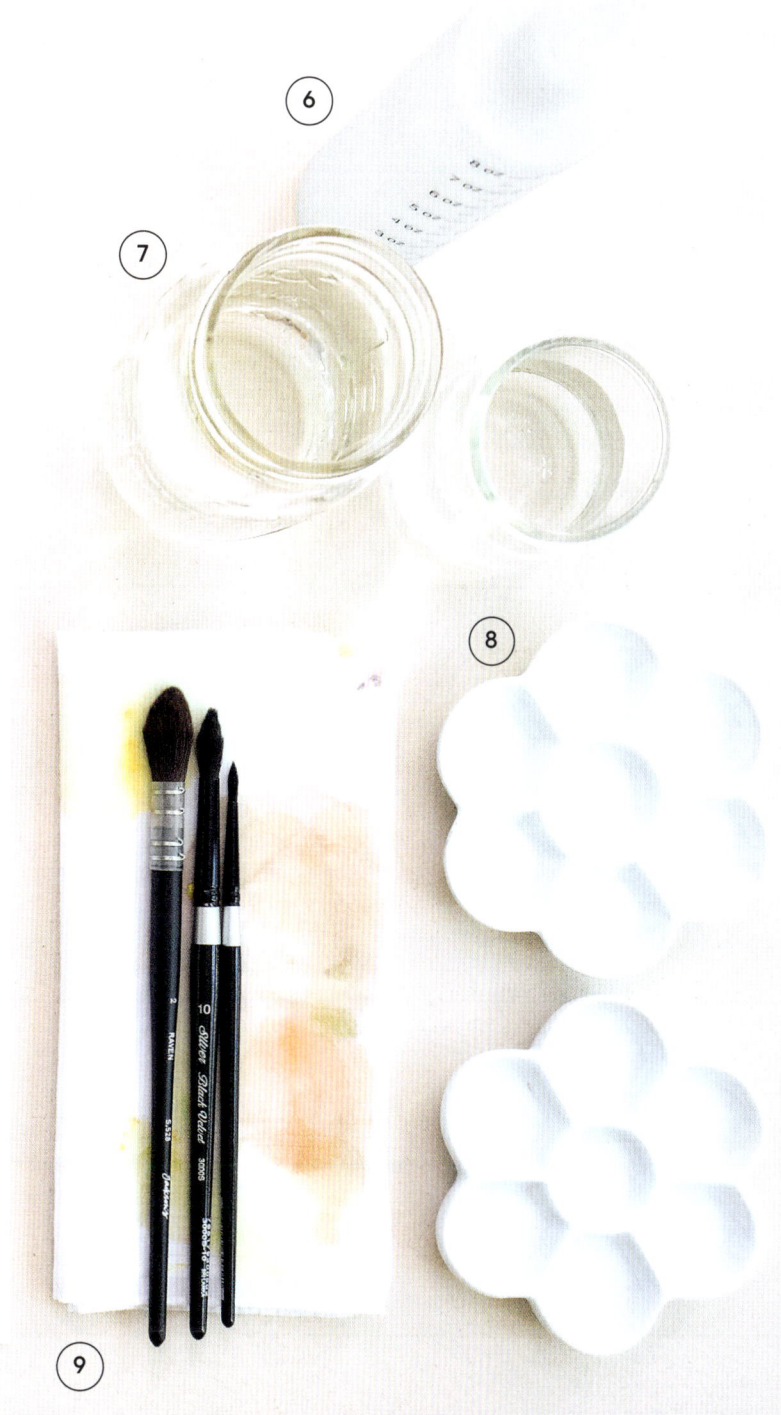

Setting Up Your Studio Space

It's time to create a space where your creativity can run wild, whether you have a dedicated room or just a cozy corner. Make it a place you love, and it will show in your art.

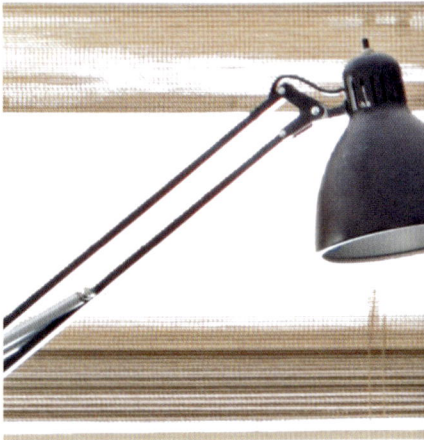

Your ideal space should be:

- Well-lit (natural light is ideal).
- Comfortable and inviting.
- Free from major distractions.
- Have enough room to store supplies and inspiration.

Lighting matters

Good lighting is crucial for accurate color mixing and detailed work, and different light affects color perception.

- Natural light: north-facing windows provide consistent indirect light; add a sheer curtain to soften the light and reduce glare.
- Task lighting: use adjustable desk lamps for focused work.
- Overhead lighting: ensures even illumination of your workspace, but can cause glare on wet paper. Invest in a daylight lamp for late-night sessions or gloomy days.

Tip: Create an "inspiration station" with plants and cuttings to keep your creativity growing year-round.

Work surface

Options include a dedicated art table, an easel with a side table, or a converted desk. Your main work area should be:

- Spacious enough for paper, palette, and reference materials.
- At a comfortable height for long painting sessions.
- Easy to clean.
- At a slight tilt to help prevent water pooling—a propped board works well.

Organizing your space

Keep supplies accessible but tidy, and make space for storing and displaying your botanical inspiration.

- Use jars for brushes (store tip-up to protect bristles).
- Organize paints by color family or frequency of use.
- Store paper flat to prevent warping.
- Use a pin board for sketches and dried specimens.
- Have shelves for plant and art books.
- Keep vases for fresh flowers or cuttings.

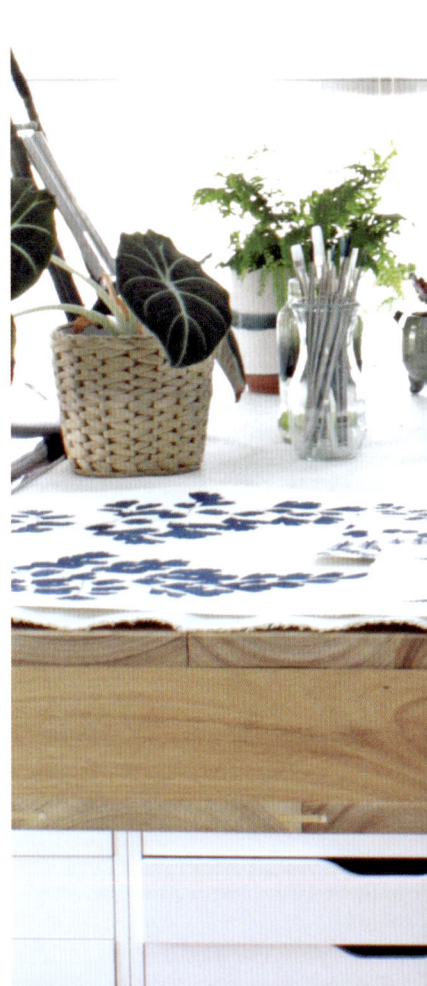

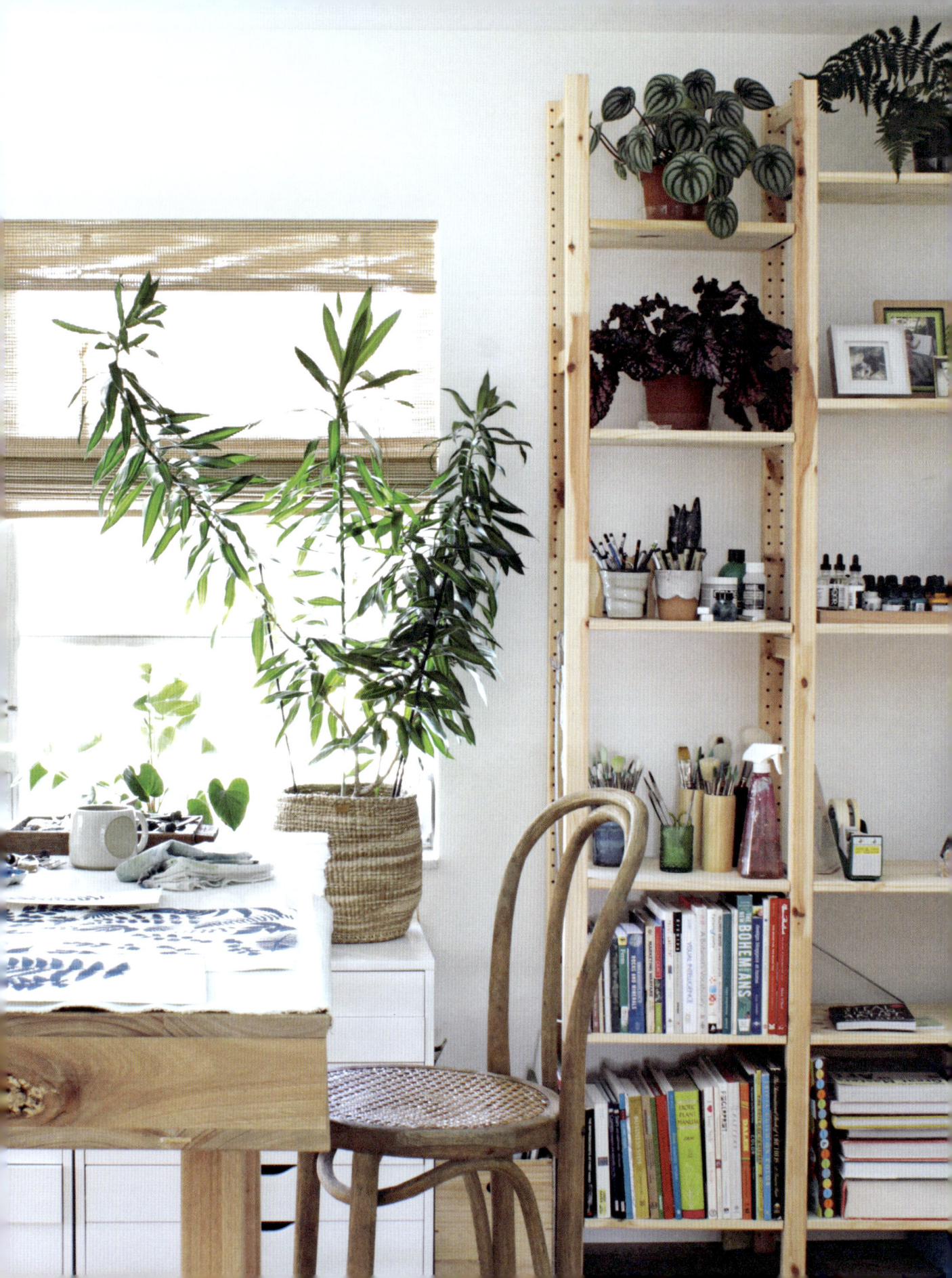

Gathering Botanical Inspiration

Inspiration is everywhere—from a crack in the sidewalk to a carefully tended garden. Keep your eyes open and your sketchbook handy. Challenge yourself to find beauty in overlooked plants: the "weeds" that most people pass by unnoticed might just become the star of your next piece.

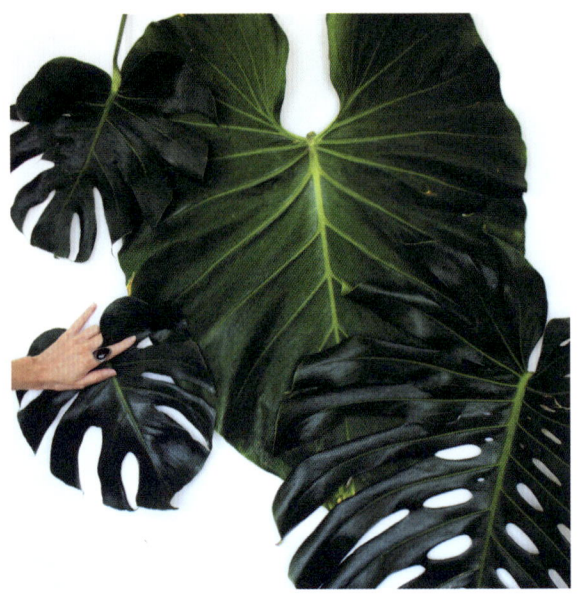

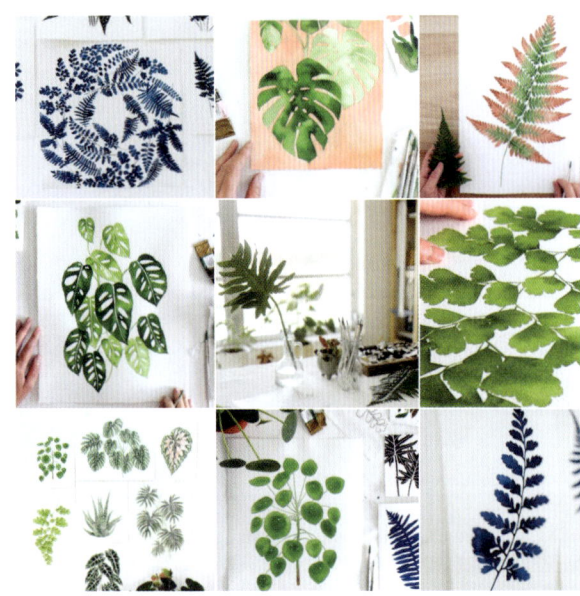

Nature walks and urban exploration

- Take regular walks in nearby parks and green spaces.
- Observe seasonal changes in plants.
- Look for plants thriving in unexpected city spots.
- Notice how light interacts with leaves and flowers in urban settings.
- Create an "inspiration walk" route in your neighborhood, revisiting the same plants throughout the year to capture their changing beauty.

Digital resources

- Follow botanical artists and gardens on Instagram and Pinterest.
- Join online communities for plant lovers and artists.
- Explore world-famous gardens through virtual online tours.
- Screenshot interesting compositions or plant combinations.

Develop your botanical eye

Start by slowing down during daily routines. That morning walk becomes an opportunity to notice how light filters through leaves. Even houseplants on a windowsill offer lessons in form, shadow, and subtle color variations.

Keep a small sketchbook with you always. Quick gesture drawings, color notes, or simple observations about how plants respond to different lighting will build your visual library. Press interesting leaves in a journal, organize photos by color families, and start a "color diary" recording interesting combinations you encounter in nature. These observations will strengthen your paintings with authentic natural color relationships.

Seasonal opportunities

Each season brings many possibilities for different approaches to botanical art. Spring brings delicate colors, perfect for wet-on-wet techniques. Summer provides bold, saturated hues, ideal for vibrant approaches. Fall offers rich tones, showcasing gradient techniques, while winter reveals structural beauty, perfect for segmented linework.

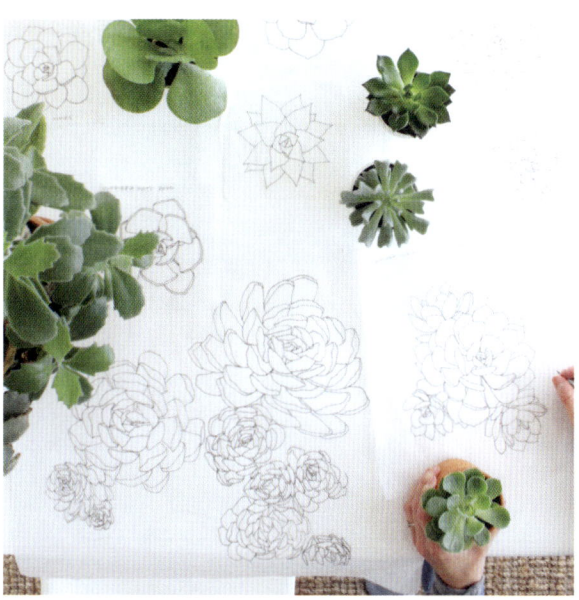

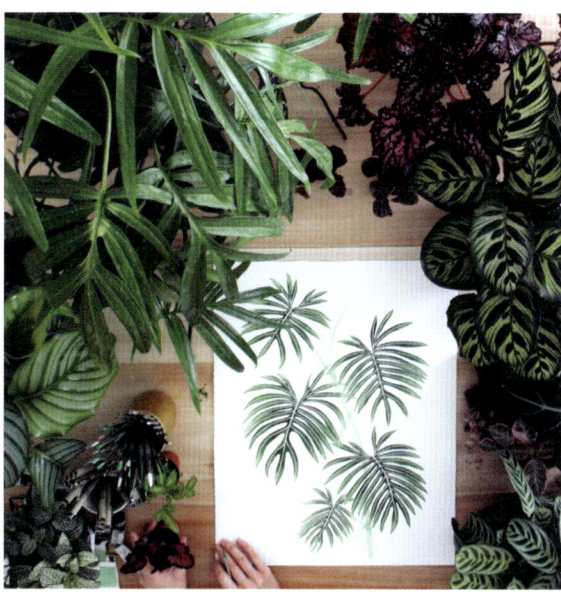

Other sources

- Botanical prints and vintage illustrations: visit local libraries or secondhand bookshops for old botanical books.
- Textile patterns: look at floral fabrics for interesting color combinations, observing how plants are stylized in different cultural textile traditions.
- Local flower markets: sketch quick studies of flower arrangements, or buy small bunches to practice painting from life at home.

Build a reference library

- Sketch or photograph interesting specimens.
- Press flowers and leaves in a dedicated sketchbook.
- Collect interesting seed pods, pine cones, or bark samples.
- Organize your plant photos in albums by species or color.
- Use apps like PlantNet to identify and learn about new plants.

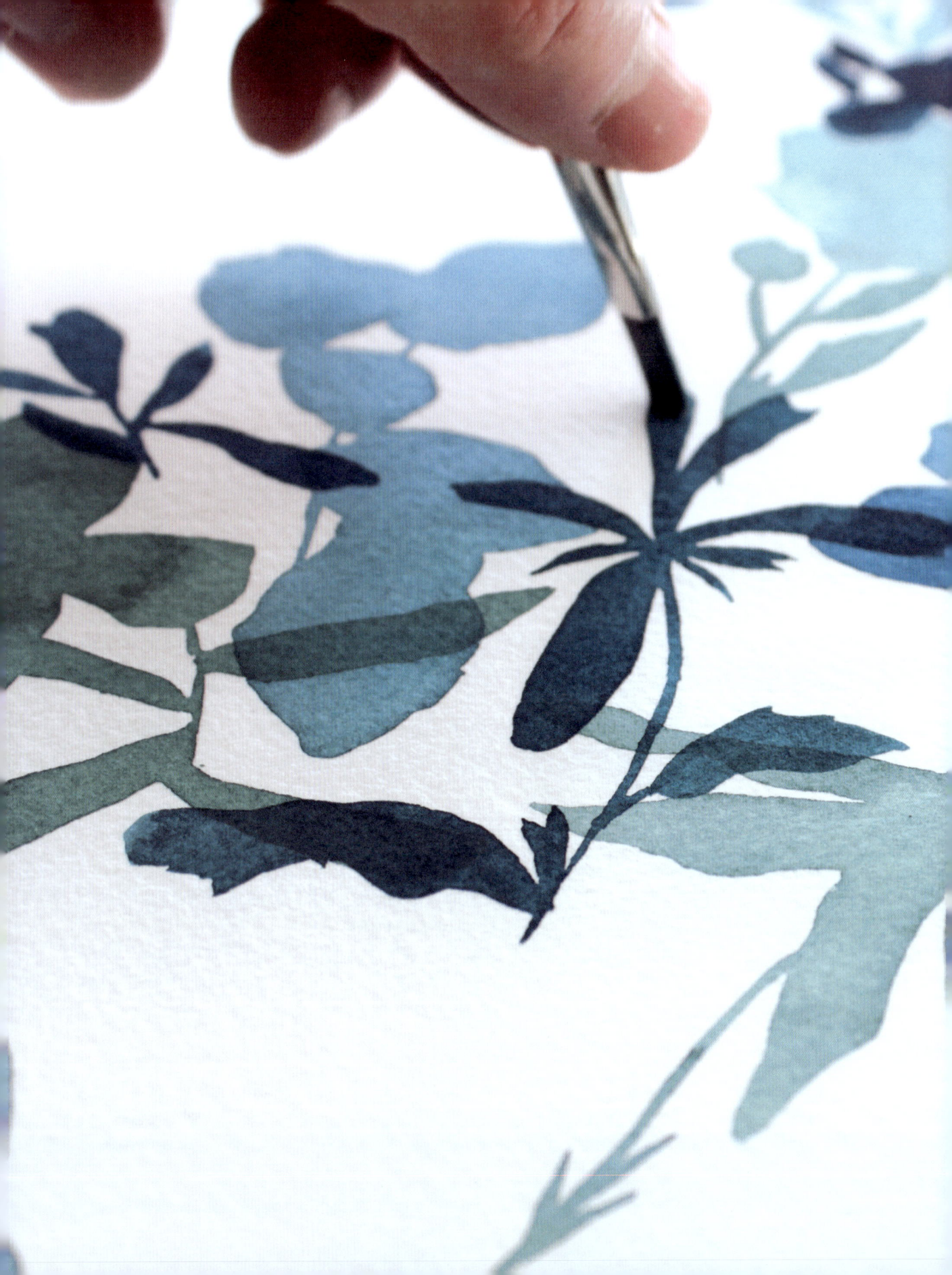

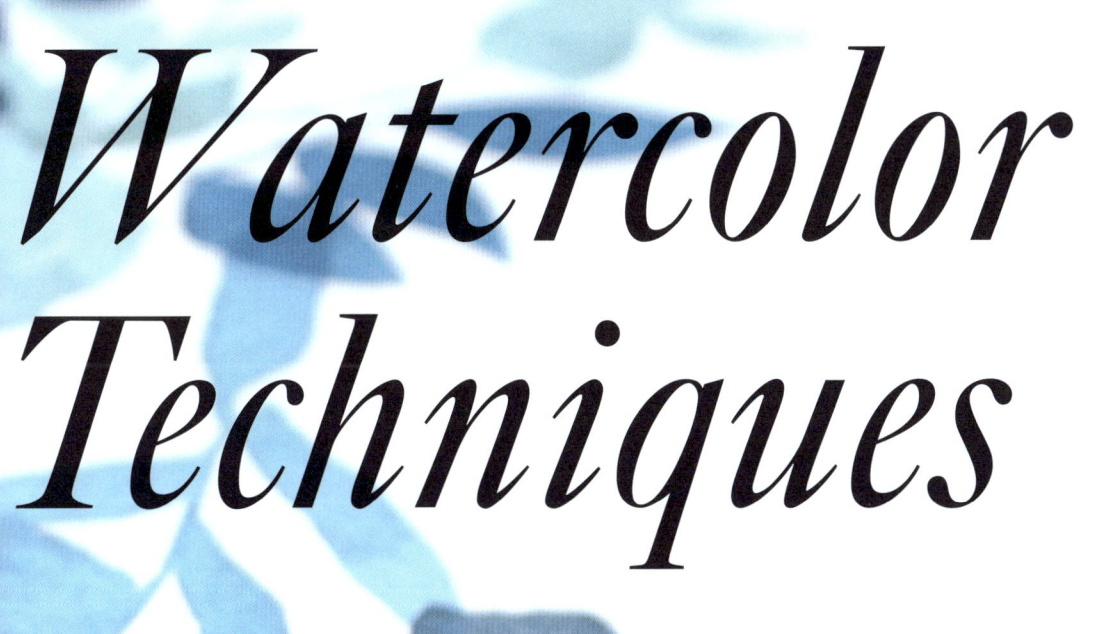

Watercolor Techniques

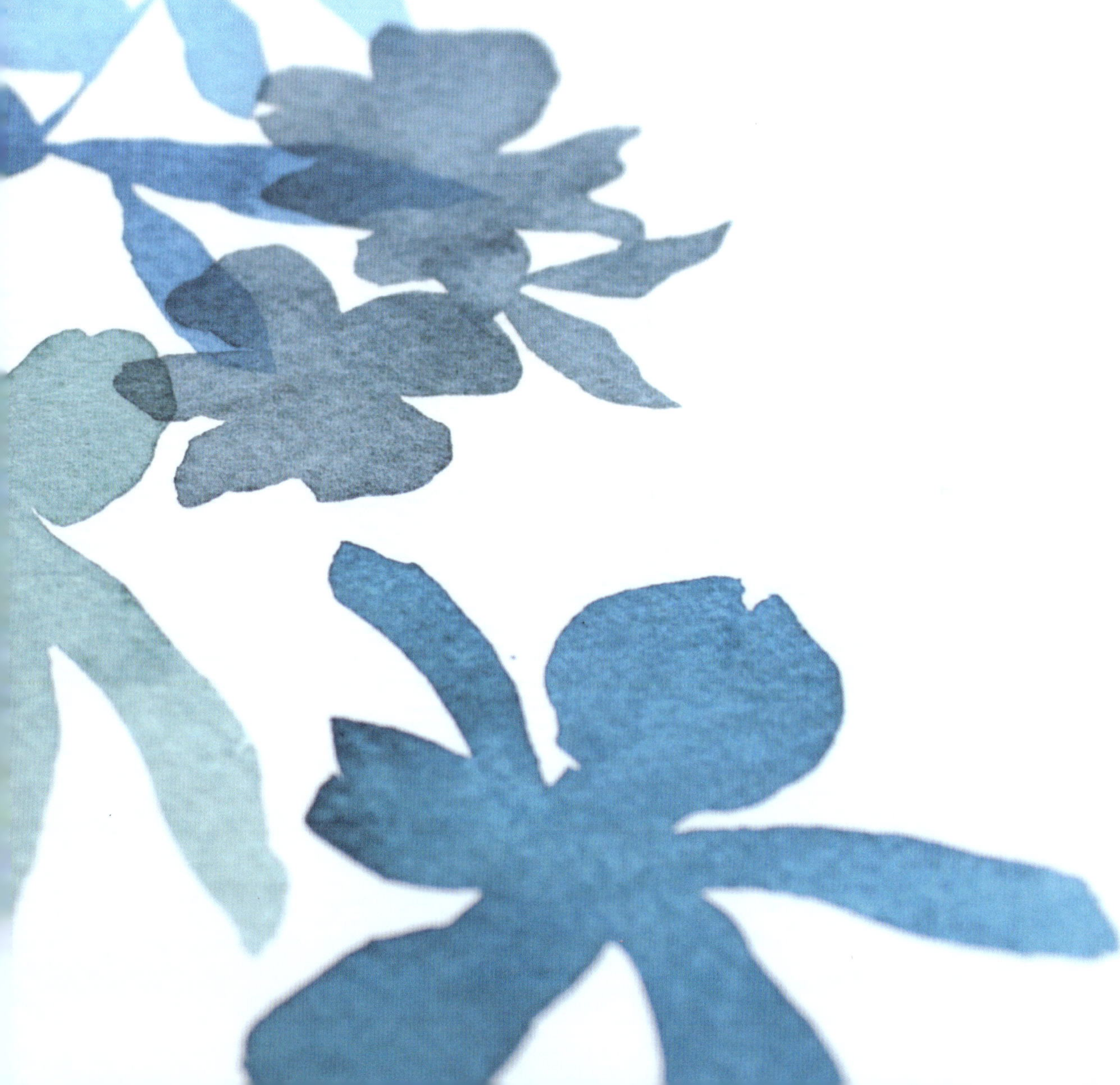

Pigment & Water Control

The key to great work is mastering the dance between pigment and water. Too much water and your colors become pale; too little and you'll lose those dreamy, fluid effects. Remember that watercolor is about embracing "happy accidents" as much as control.

Pigment-to-water ratios

Think of consistency as your paint's personality type, each with its own unique charm. These ratios are guidelines, not strict rules, so feel free to experiment and find what works best for your particular style.

Tea consistency (light wash): 1:4 pigment to water
This is a transparent, delicate color, ideal for underpainting and soft backgrounds. Load your brush with this watery mix and let it flow freely on the paper.

Milk consistency (standard mix): 1:2 pigment to water
A balance of intensity and transparency, good for mid-tone layers and controlled washes, and the main body of leaves, flower petals, and stems. Apply with confidence, allowing colors to mingle and blend on the paper.

Cream consistency (intense color): 2:1 pigment to water
Strong color with minimal transparency, perfect for details such as veins in leaves and flower centers, textures, and shadows. Apply with a light touch for precise, bold lines and textures.

Don't be afraid to play mad scientist and mix up your consistencies:
- Start with a watery wash for the base of a flower.
- Layer milky paint for petal definition.
- Finish with creamy paint for fine details and depth.

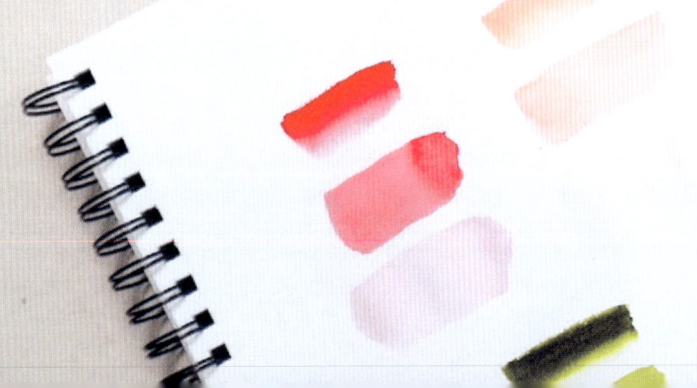

Water control and pigment play

- Thirsty Brush: squeeze out excess water on a paper towel for more control.

- Touch and Go: lightly touch your brush to create organic shapes.

- Bead Master: keep a "bead" of water and pigment at the stroke's edge for seamless painting.

- Gradient Guru: start pigment-heavy, gradually adding water for smooth transitions.

- Color Cocktail: mix colors on paper for vibrant, unexpected hues.

- Dry Brush Dash: use pigment-heavy paint for adding texture.

Tip: Create a "consistency chart" in your sketchbook with swatches of your favorite colors at different ratios.

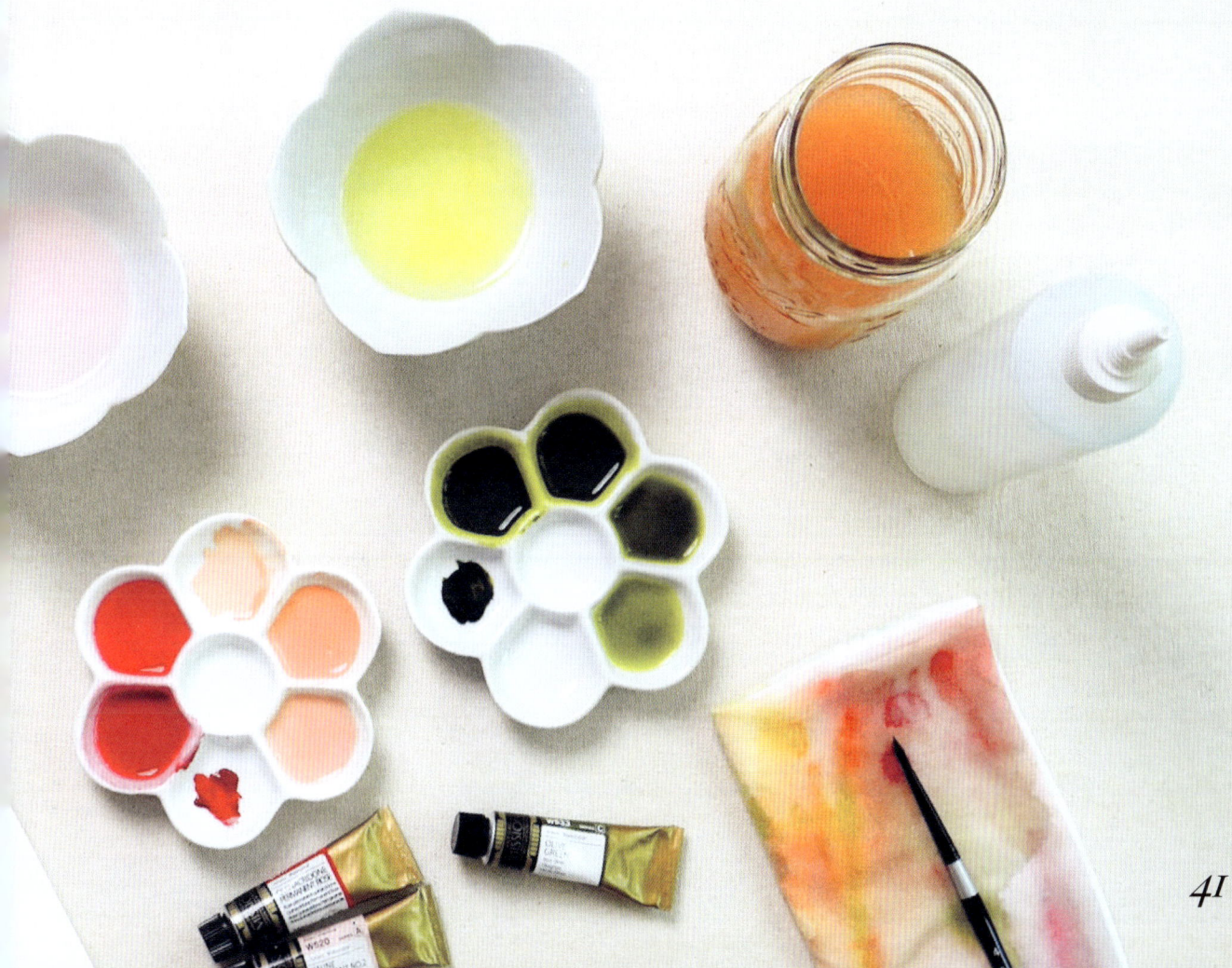

Brushwork & Mark-Making

Transform your watercolors from simple studies into expressive artworks with thoughtful brushwork and mark-making techniques.

Botanical watercolor brushwork emphasizes precision and fluidity, with controlled strokes, varied pressure, and brush angles creating naturalistic forms. These methods add personality and depth to your paintings while highlighting the unique characteristics of your subjects.

The key to mastering these techniques is practice and patience. Don't worry if your first attempts aren't perfect—every stroke is a step toward finding your unique style. Create a "technique sampler" in your sketchbook by making a small swatch for each technique and labeling it. It's like building your own personal watercolor dictionary.

Tip: Practice these techniques with different brush sizes. A round brush is versatile, but don't be afraid to experiment with flat or fan brushes too.

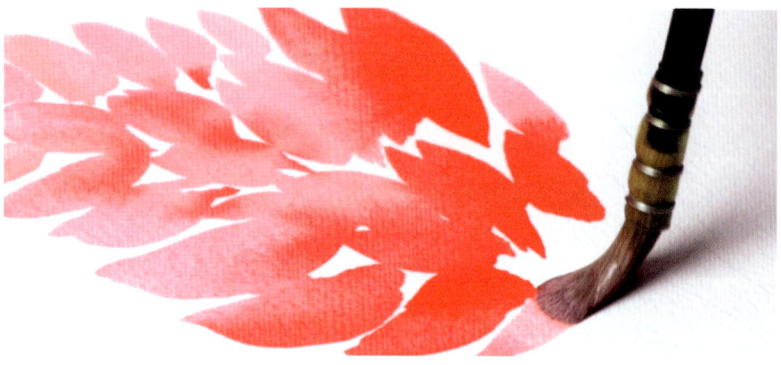

Classic stroke
What it is: your go-to move for clean lines and shapes.
How to do it: hold your brush at a 45-degree angle and apply even pressure.
Perfect for: outlining leaves, creating stems, and defining petal edges.

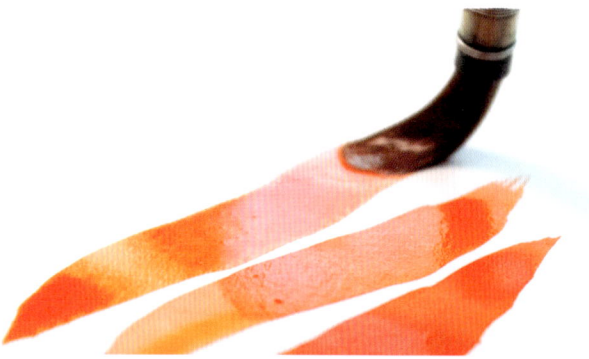

Gestural brushstroke
What it is: confident strokes capturing plant movement.
How to do it: vary pressure and angle of brush; focus on overall form and energy.
Perfect for: capturing energy and emotion rather than fine detail.

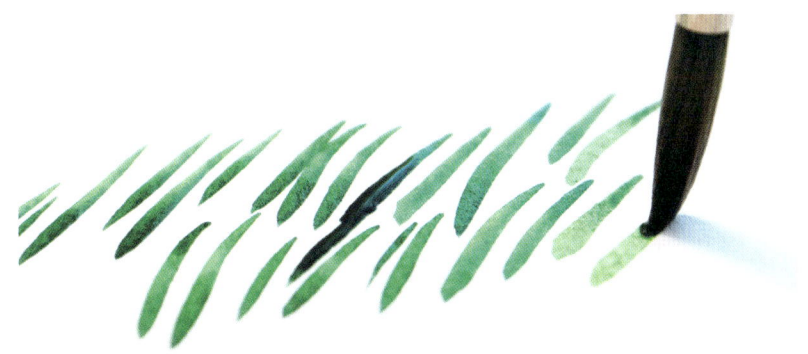

Flick

What it is: a quick, directional stroke.

How to do it: hold your brush loosely and flick your wrist.

Perfect for: creating grass, adding movement to leaves, or painting wispy flower stamens.

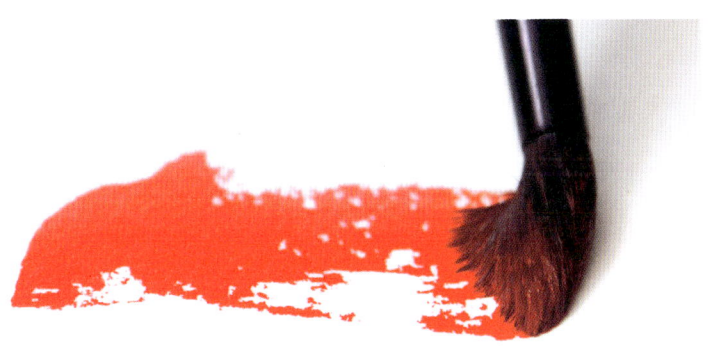

Dry brush

What it is: a textured stroke using minimal water.

How to do it: use a fairly dry brush with thicker paint, applying light pressure.

Perfect for: adding texture to bark, creating fuzzy leaf surfaces, or wispy flower centers.

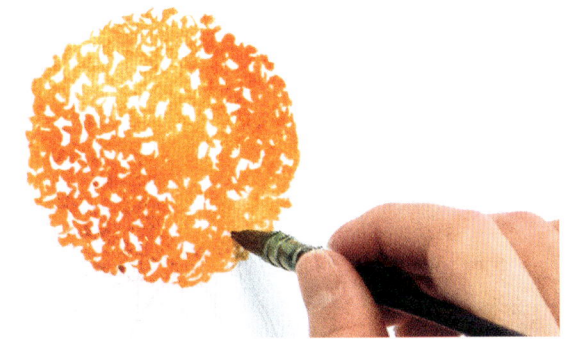

Stipple

What it is: a series of small dots or dabs.

How to do it: gently tap your brush perpendicular to the paper; vary pressure and density to produce different effects.

Perfect for: adding texture to flower centers, creating leaves on distant trees, and adding subtle shadows.

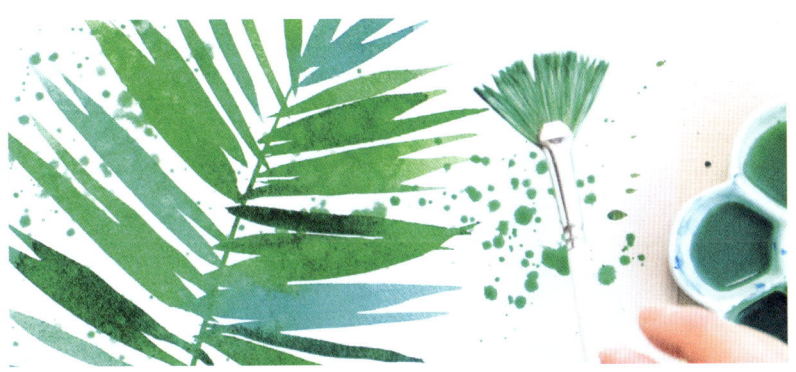

Expressive splattering

What it is: watery paint flicked onto paper for spontaneous effects.

How to do it: load a brush or toothbrush with watery paint and tap it to release splatters, or flick the bristles toward the paper.

Perfect for: suggesting dew drops or dappled light.

43

Washes & Bleeds

These add life and softness to botanical watercolor art by allowing colors to merge naturally. Apply color when the paper is damp, not soaked. Mastering these techniques adds depth, luminosity, and interest to your work.

Washes

These are smooth, thin, transparent layers of color applied evenly across the paper. They're used to build color, create atmosphere, and add depth.

Layered gradients use multiple transparent washes in sequence, creating subtle color transitions within individual elements. Patience is key—each layer must be completely dry before adding the next to maintain crisp, clean gradations.

Basic layered gradient: start with your lightest wash, applying it across the entire area. While still damp, introduce a slightly darker tone to one end, allowing the colors to blend naturally. Once completely dry, apply a second transparent layer, focusing on the shadow areas only. This builds up color intensity gradually while preserving luminosity.

Specific botanical applications: for flower petals, begin with a pale base wash of your lightest color. Add deeper tones near the flower center where petals attach, letting colors merge while wet. After drying, apply selective darker washes to create shadow areas and suggest a petal's curved form.

Flat wash: uniform layer of solid color, great for base layers and backgrounds.

Graded wash: gradually changes from dark to light; creates depth and subtle transitions, mimicking how sunlight hits a plant.

Variegated wash: blends two or more colors; use for florals and abstract effects (my personal favorite!)

Water drips

Lightly drip water from your brush onto wet paint to produce a mottled textured effect. This technique can be used to create atmosphere and add visual interest.

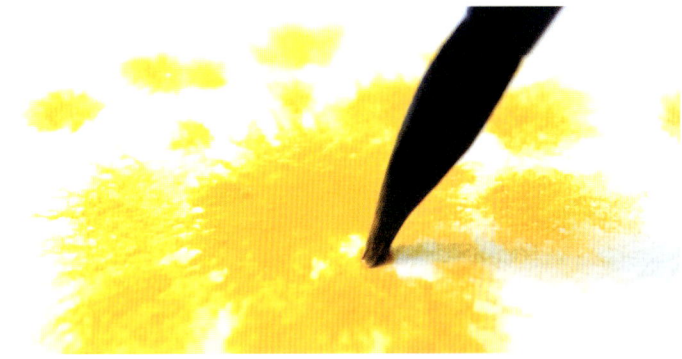

Lifting

Remove paint while it's still wet using a clean, damp brush or paper towel. You can use this technique to create highlights on petals and leaves, blend the edges between color transitions, soften petal edges, create texture, and correct mistakes.

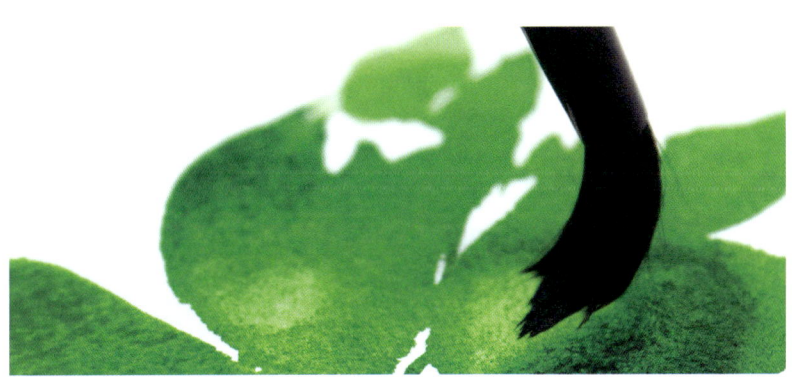

Bleeds

Bleeds occur when wet paint flows into another wet area, creating soft, organic edges, perfect for blended backgrounds and creating depth. Wet your paper first, then add pigment and watch the magic happen as paint bleeds onto it. The key is controlling the water content on your brush and paper.

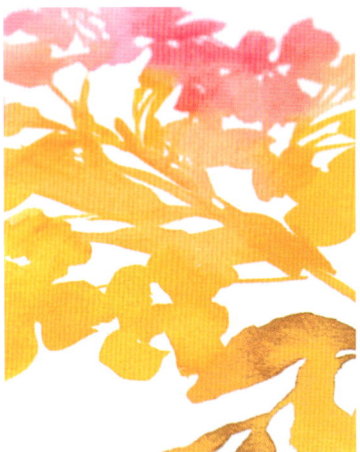

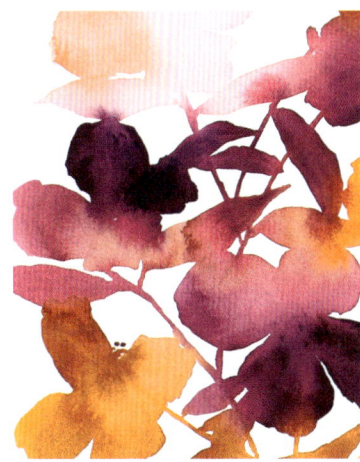

Controlled bleed: apply two colors side by side while the paint is wet. Controlled bleeds suggest delicacy: think of fading flower edges or the gentle blur of overlapping leaves.

Bloom: drop water or a lighter color into a wet wash to create a soft-edged shape. This produces an irregular burst or spreading effect with soft, feathery edges—much like a spreading flower.

Finding Your Creative Flow

Developing your style in botanical watercolor starts with finding your creative flow—that magical state where technique and artistic vision merge seamlessly.

Remember that finding your flow is personal, so be patient as you discover what works for you. Your unique rhythm will emerge through consistent practice and playful experimentation. Here are some ideas for cultivating this essential element of your practice.

Set the stage
- Create a nurturing environment.
- Organize materials for easy access.
- Display inspiring botanical pieces.
- Ensure proper lighting.
- Consider soft background music..

Daily practice
- Begin each session mindfully.
- Start with warm-up exercises.
- Practice basic brushstrokes.
- Mix colors intentionally.
- Try quick gestural drawings.

Mindful observation
- Connect deeply with your subjects.
- Observe plants in nature.
- Sketch from life.
- Study color variations.
- Notice intricate details.

Exploration techniques
- Work in series to develop themes.
- Paint subjects in various stages.
- Try different color palettes.
- Challenge yourself with time limits.

Creative development
- Embrace imperfection.
- Experiment with limitations.
- Combine different techniques.
- Keep a watercolor journal.

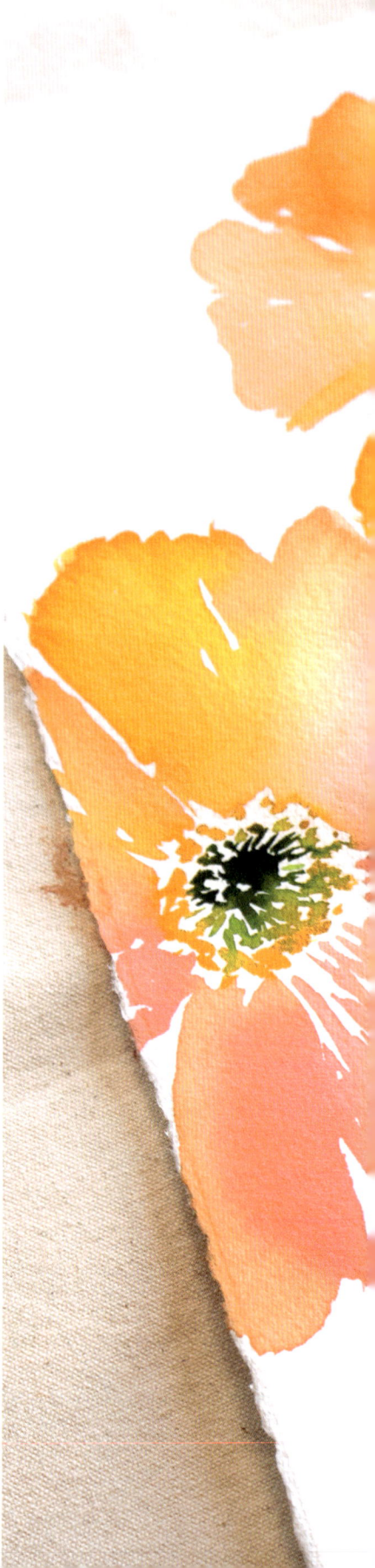

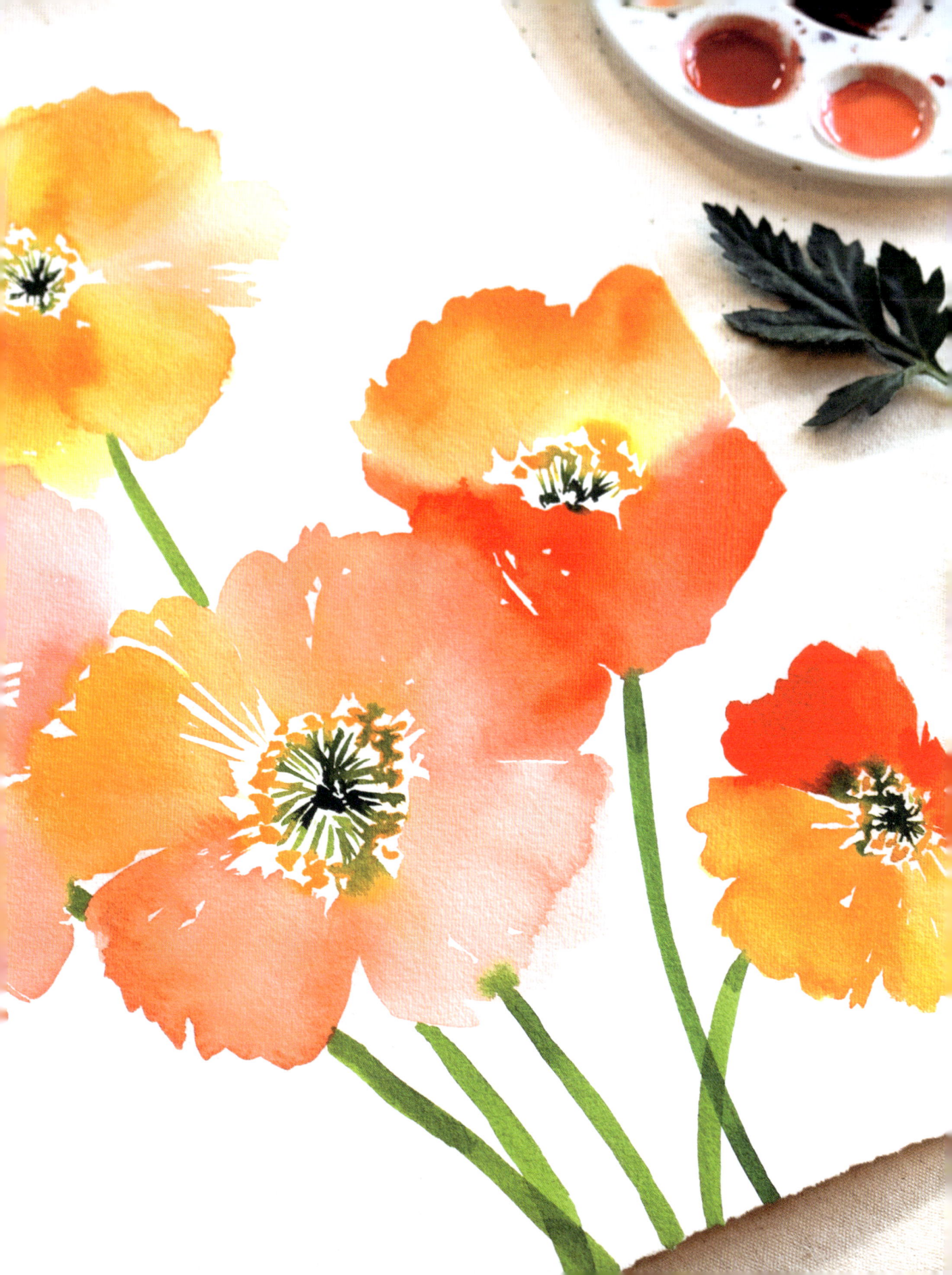

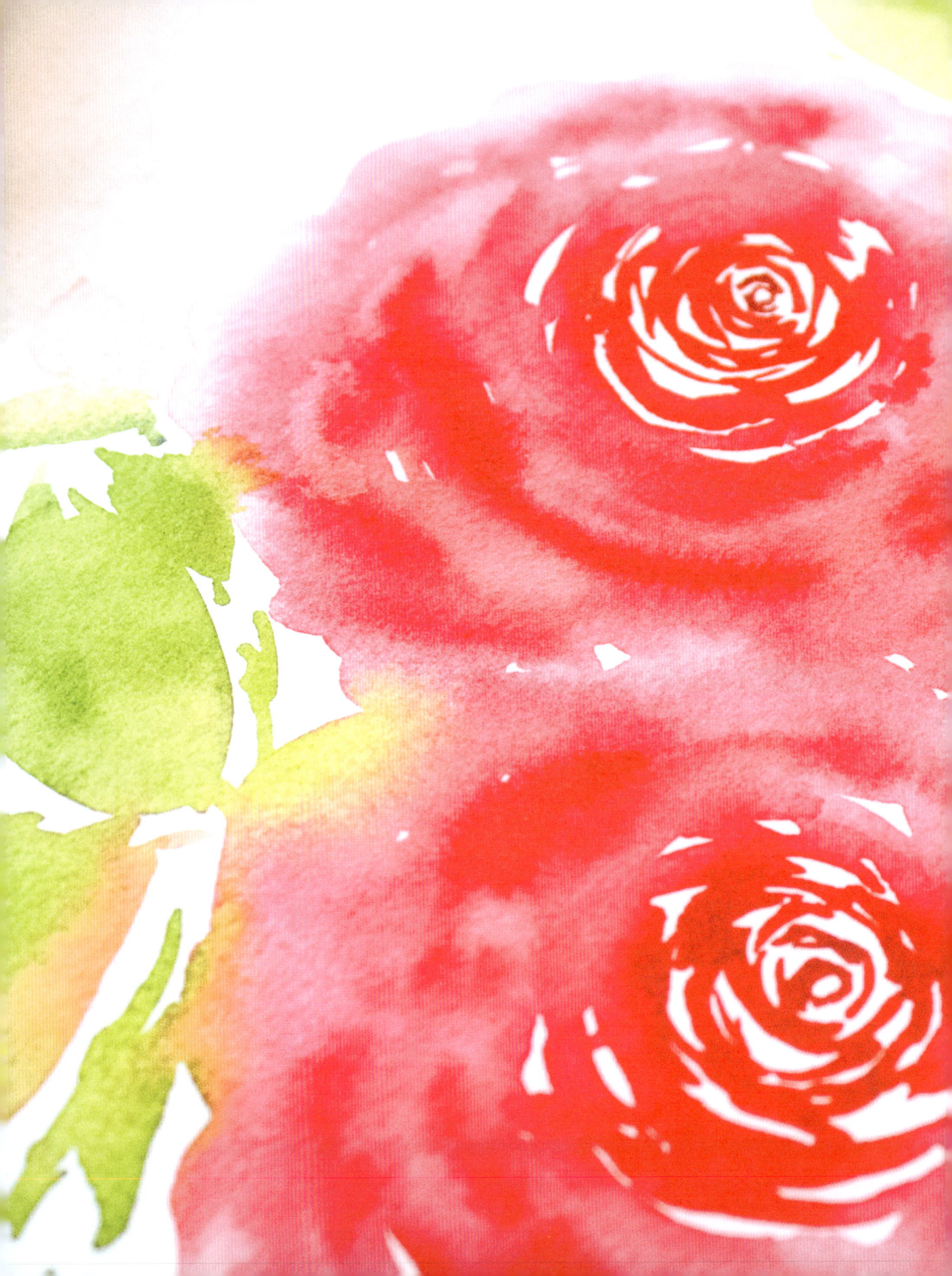

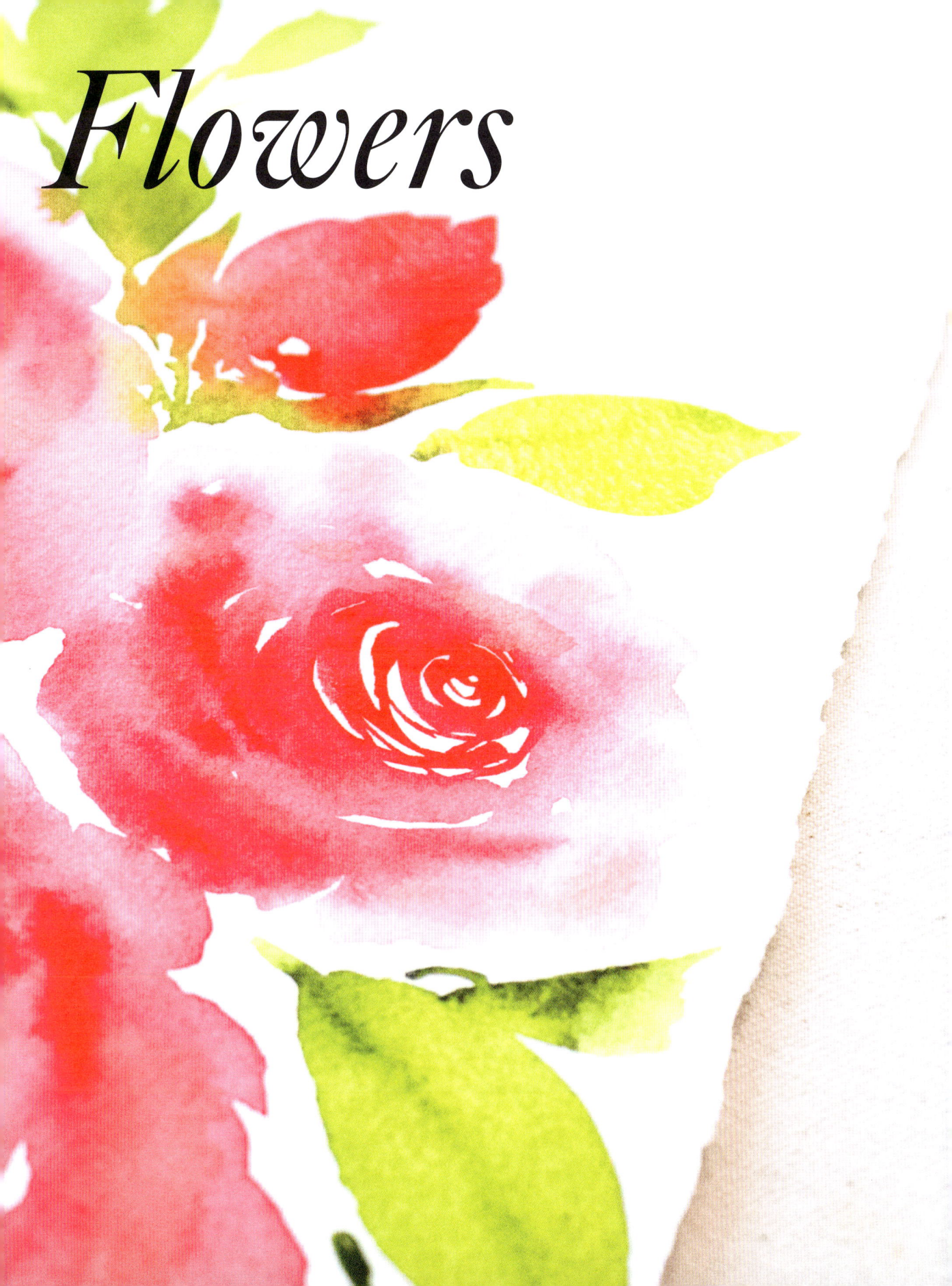

Flowers

Poppies

Capture the poppy's expressive beauty using a wet-on-wet technique to create soft, flowing effects that are ideal for their delicate petals. Poppies dance in the breeze, so let your painting capture this sense of movement.

Materials

- Watercolor paper (140lb cold pressed)
- Brushes: quill 0, quill 3/0, foam craft brush
- Paints: Permanent Red, Vermilion, Orange, Yellow Ochre, Sap Green, Viridian, Permanent Yellow Light, Yellow Ochre
- Pencil, eraser, palette, squirt bottle, water container, paper towels

Wet-on-wet technique

Paint on thoroughly dampened paper, allowing colors to flow and blend naturally. The magic happens when you relinquish precise control and let the water work for you (see p.45).

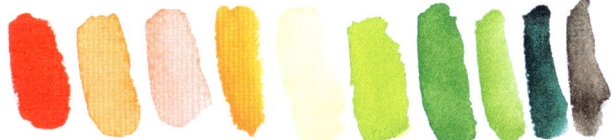

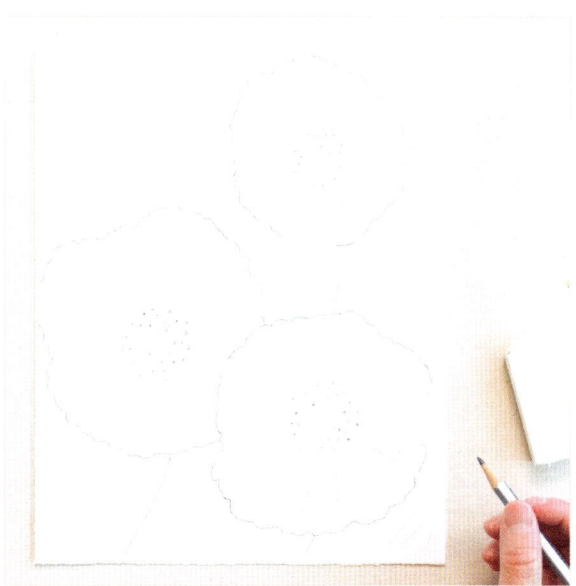

1. Sketch

Create a light pencil sketch using simple circles for blooms and loose lines for stems and leaves. Keep your sketch minimal—circles and directional lines will provide just enough structure while allowing for spontaneous painting.

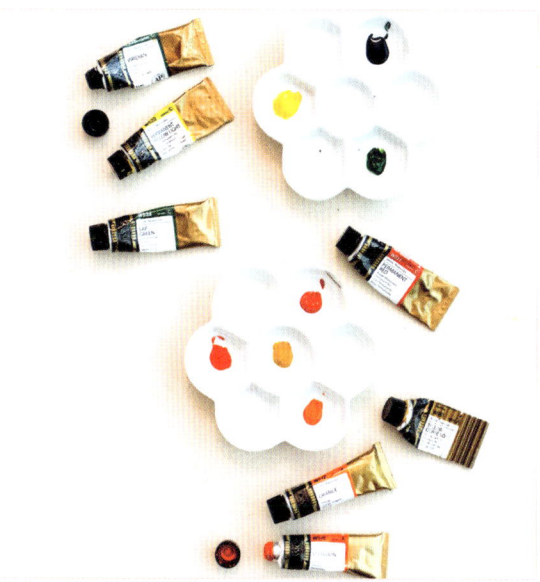

2. Prepare your palette

You will need to use two palettes as you'll be mixing several red and green hues.

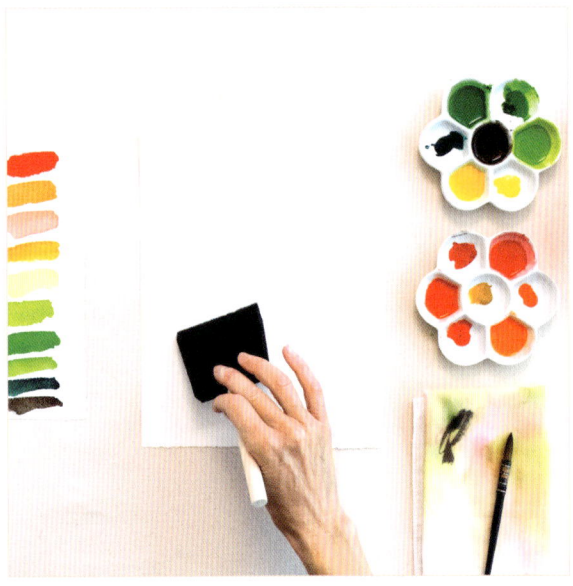

3. Prepare your paper

Use your squirt bottle to saturate the paper with an even layer of water. Distribute it uniformly with your foam craft brush, but don't scrub, as this may damage the paper. You want the paper to be completely wet but without puddles standing on the surface.

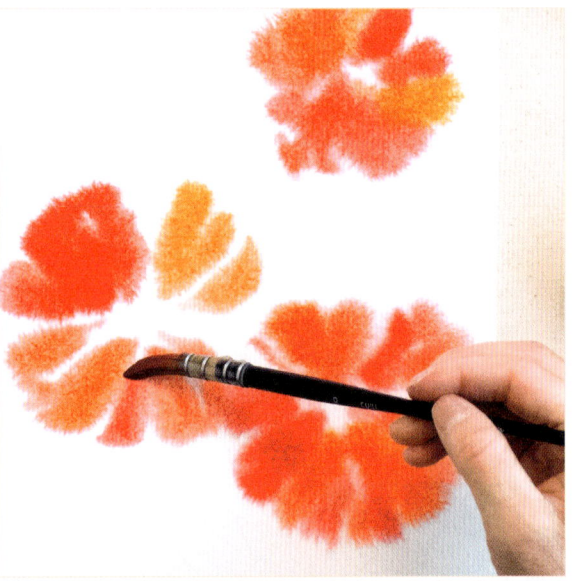

4. Paint the blooms

On the wet paper, using the quill 0 brush, begin with Permanent Red, moving to Vermilion, then Orange in tea and milk consistencies. Work quickly between colors, allowing them to blend where they meet. Bounce between blooms, adding all three colors loosely while leaving white space for highlights.

5. Add centers

Drop Yellow Ochre in cream consistency into the center of each poppy. The thicker paint will create natural blooms as it spreads into the wetter areas, producing those signature soft-edged centers.

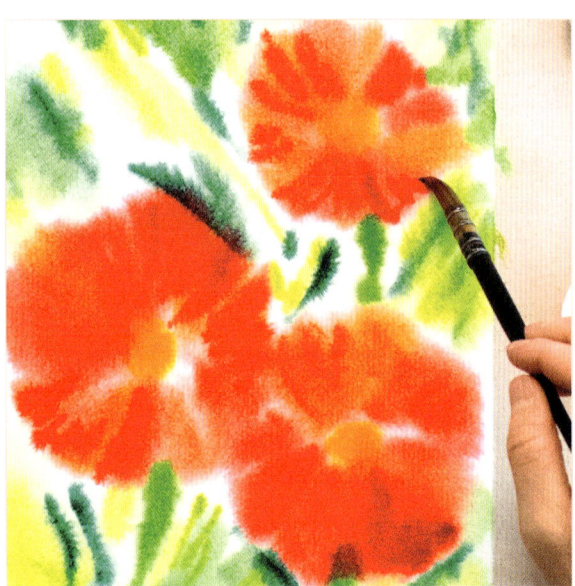

6. Create the background

While the paper is still damp, add foliage using mixtures of Sap Green, Permanent Yellow Light, and Viridian. Use loose, varied brushstrokes, and embrace the blotchy marks that form as the paper gradually dries—these add character to your garden scene.

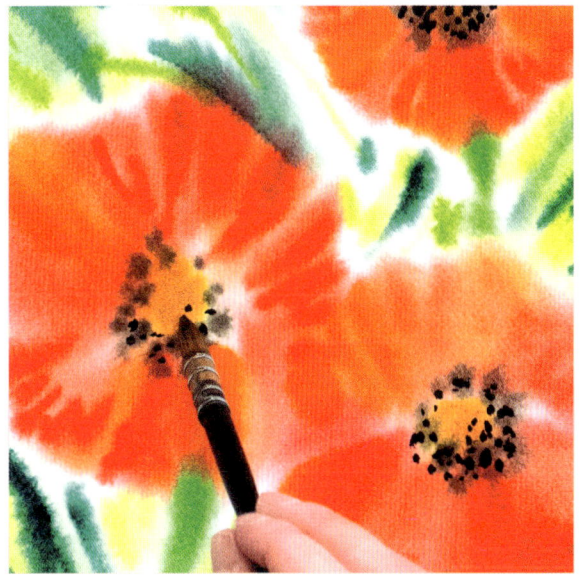

7. Add dark centers

For the trademark dark centers, using the quill 3/0 brush, mix Permanent Red, Viridian, Yellow Ochre, and Sap Green to create a rich dark brown. Build from light to dark.

8. Further definition

Once the initial layers are dry, use thicker consistencies of Permanent Red and Vermilion to add some defining marks to the petals.

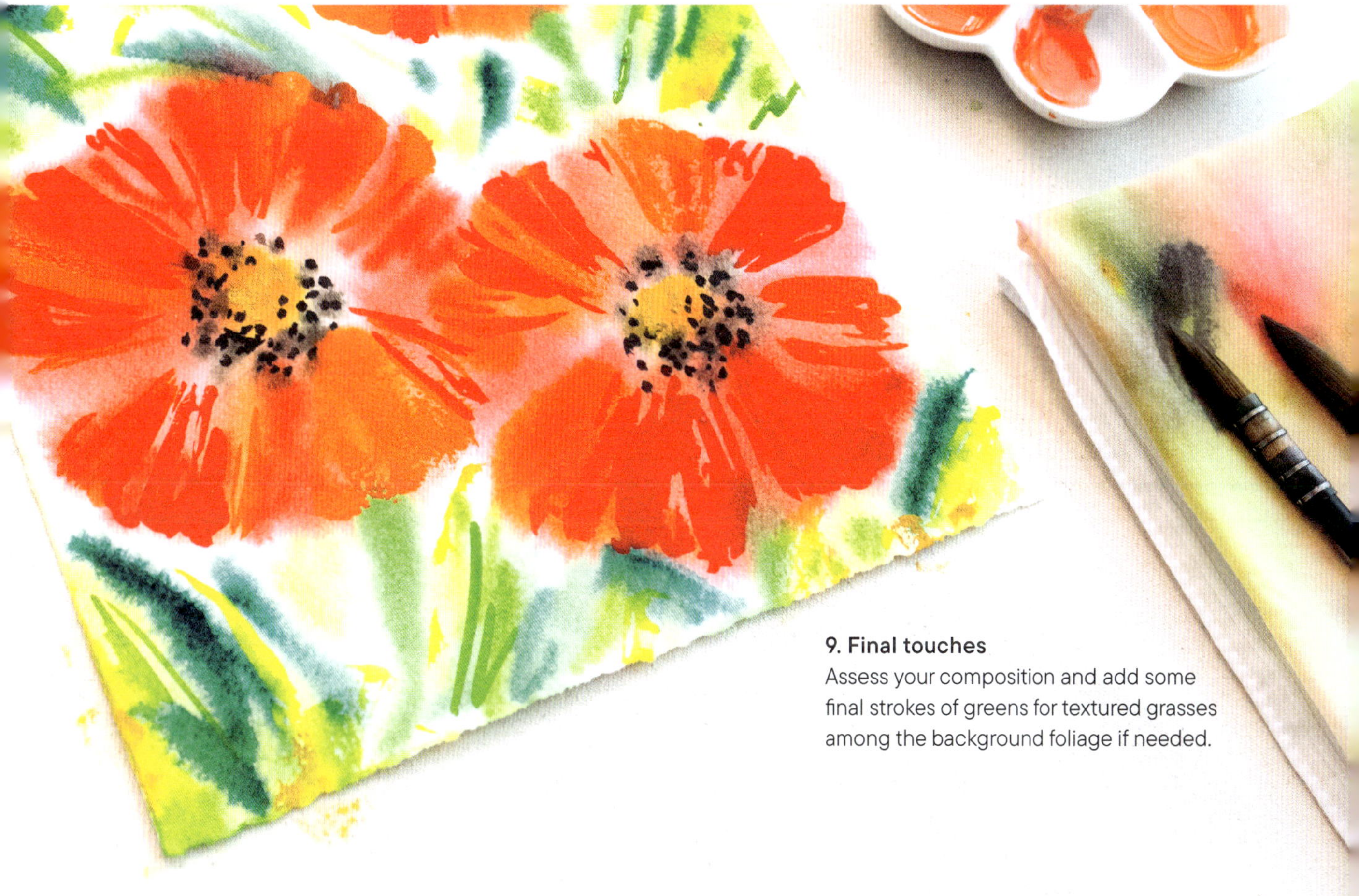

9. Final touches

Assess your composition and add some final strokes of greens for textured grasses among the background foliage if needed.

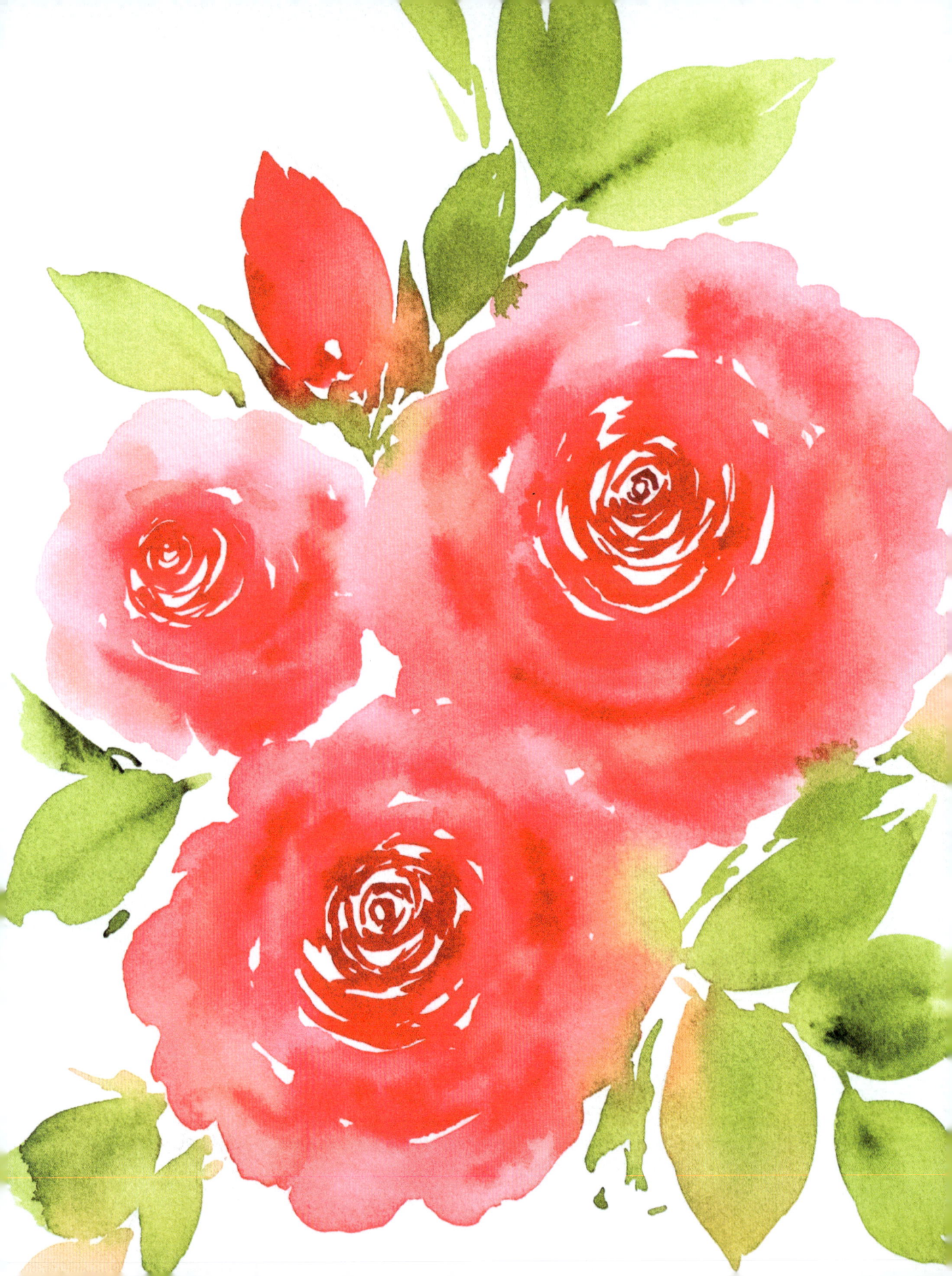

Roses

With their layered petals and subtle color variations, roses have long been a favorite of watercolor artists, from the botanical illustrations of the 16th century to their present-day popularity. Capture their romantic essence with loose, expressive brushwork instead of tight precision.

Materials

- Watercolor paper (140lb cold pressed)
- Brush: quill 0
- Paints: Quinacridone Permanent Rose, Shell Pink, Olive Green
- Pencil, eraser, palette, water container, paper towels

Color bleeds technique

Keep your hand relaxed and movements confident, allowing the colors to mingle and blend naturally. Embrace "happy accidents" as part of the process. See p.45 for more info.

1. Sketch

Focus on simple circles for the roses and directional lines for stems and leaves. Vary the size and fullness for a natural composition. Make your sketch is dark enough to see while working, but light enough to be covered by paint. Perfection isn't the goal—embrace a loose, expressive approach from the start.

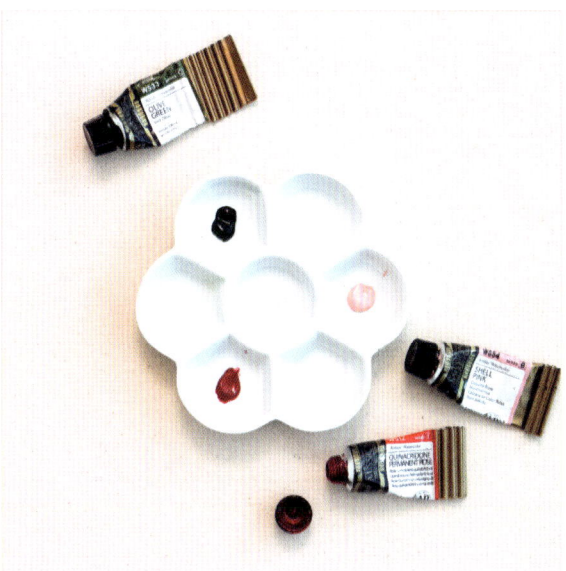

2. Prepare your palette

Mix six hues of pink and green to work with.

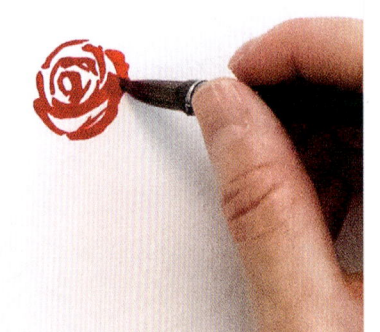

3. Base of rose

Mix Quinacridone Permanent Rose to a milk consistency. Using your quill 0 brush, work from the center outward to paint gentle C-curves in a circular pattern to form the first layer. Keep your movements fluid and confident.

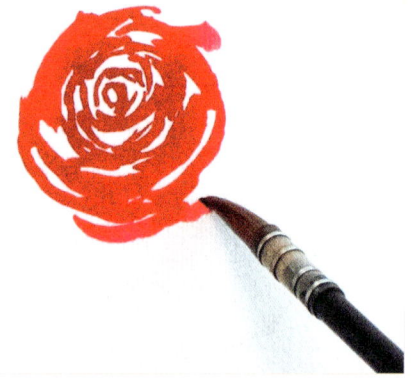

4. Build petals

While the base is still wet, add more concentrated Quinacridone Permanent Rose to suggest inner petals. Continue working from the center outward, allowing colors to naturally blend and create depth.

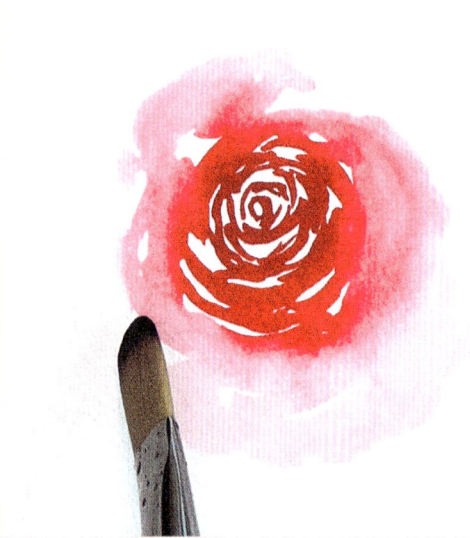

5. Create soft edges

Use a your damp quill 0 brush to gently soften the edges of the outer petals. This creates the fluffy appearance of rose petals. Think of the rose as a complete silhouette as you work around the outer edges. The white of your paper provides highlights so don't cover every area.

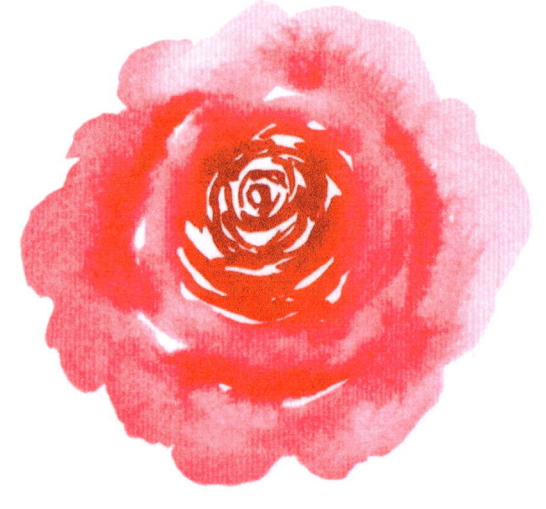

6. Add definition

While the base is still slightly damp, use a thicker consistency of Quinacridone Permanent Rose to add defining marks. These will create natural bleeds as they meet the wet areas, suggesting the delicate folds of petals.

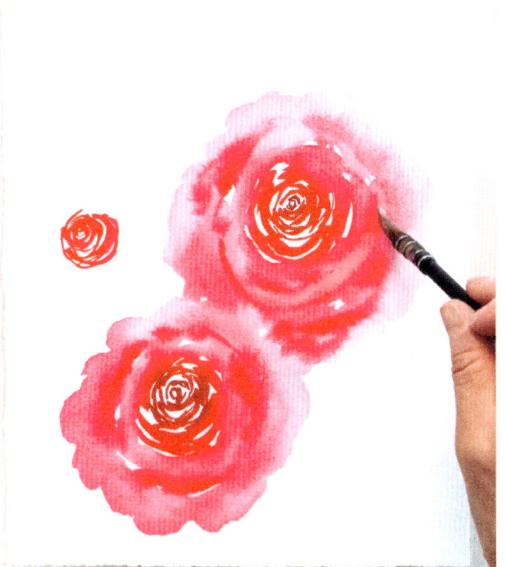

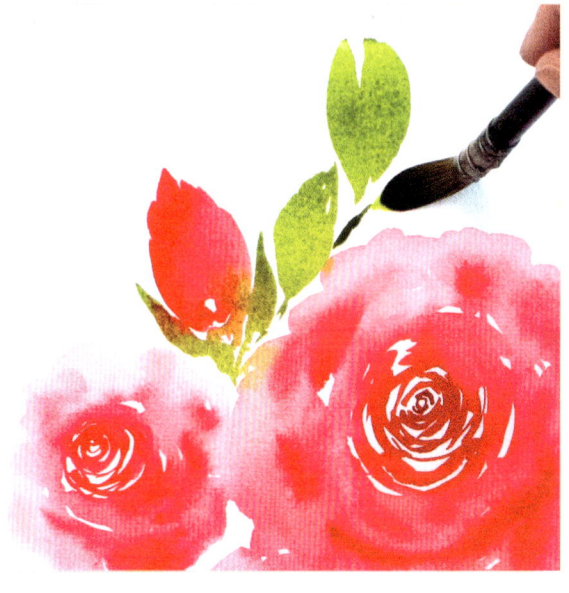

7. Add more blooms

Add the next rose, beginning with your creamy Quinacridone Permanent Rose as in step 3 and building it outward, as shown in steps 4 and 5. Complete the process again for your third rose. Using your quill 0, add defining marks to the center of the roses and touches to the edges for depth and interest.

8. Stems and leaves

Add stems in varying directions to create movement and flow. For the leaves, first add a medium tone wash with your quill 0 brush. Add darker green veins while the leaves are still wet. Allow some green to bleed into the edges of your roses where they meet the stems. Add paler leaves using your lightest Olive Green wash.

9. Final touches

While the leaves are still slightly damp, add touches of light Shell Pink and Quinacridone Permanent Rose to some of their edges and allow them to blend into the green.

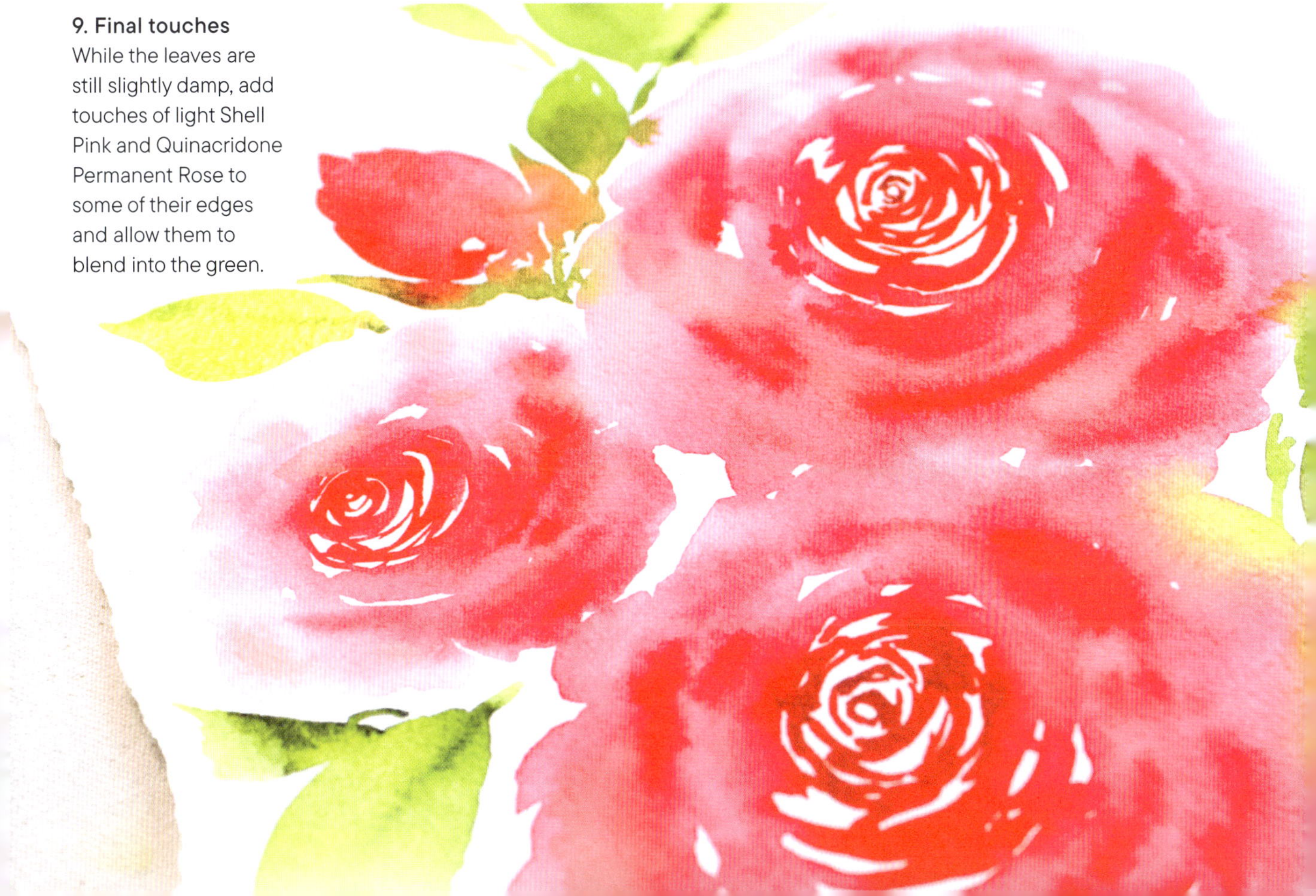

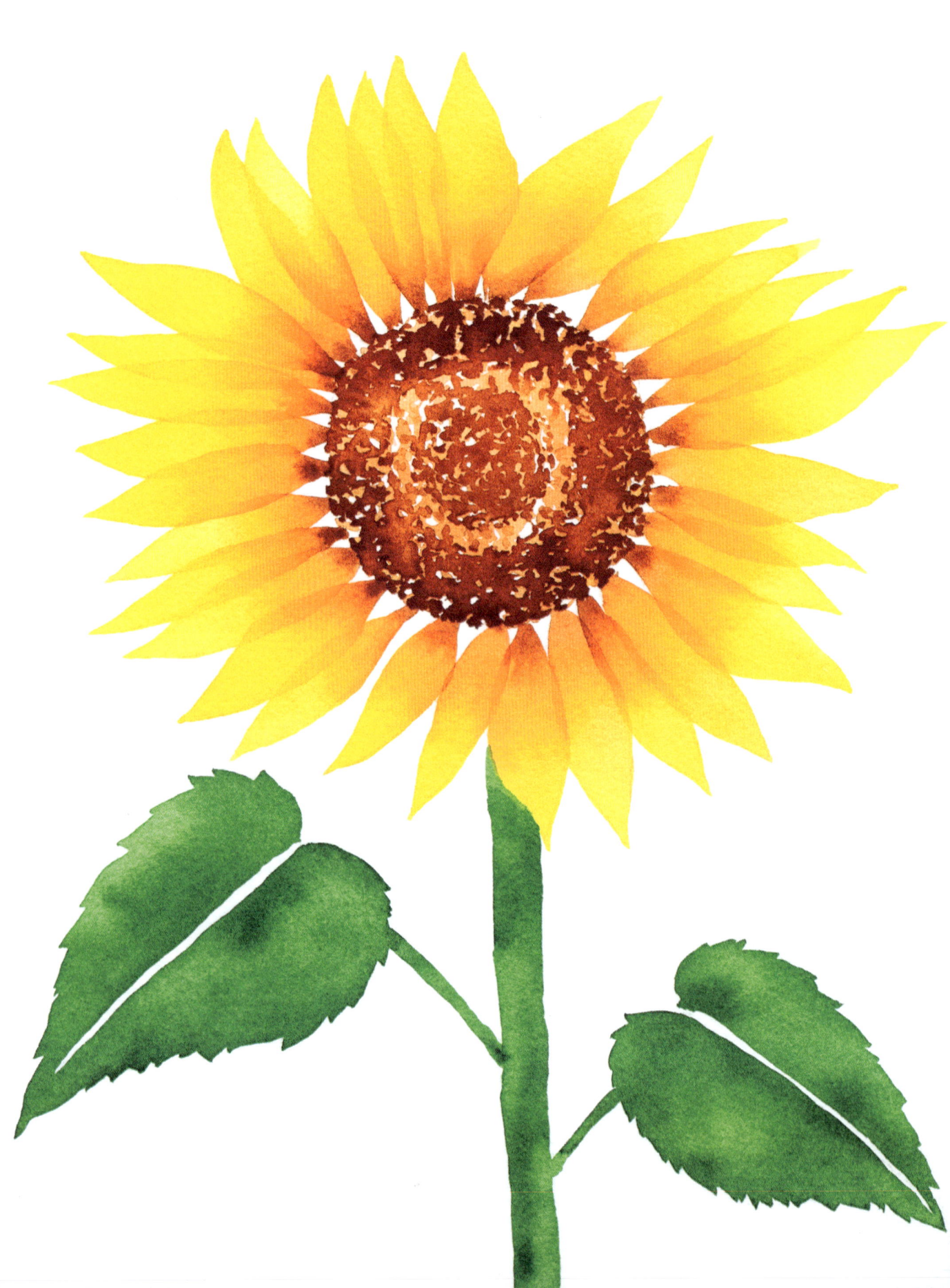

Sunflower

The sunflower, with its radiant petals and textured center, creates a happy focal point. Capture its cheerful, optimistic character using layered gradient techniques.

Gradient layering technique

Create depth and dimension through subtle color transitions within individual elements (see p.44). This produces realistic form by focusing on color shifts rather than excessive detail.

(see p.44)

Materials

- Watercolor paper (140lb cold pressed)
- Brushes: quill 3/0, round #6
- Paints: Hooker's Green, Burnt Sienna, Permanent Yellow Deep, Permanent Yellow Light, Naples Yellow
- Pencil, eraser, palette, water container, paper towels

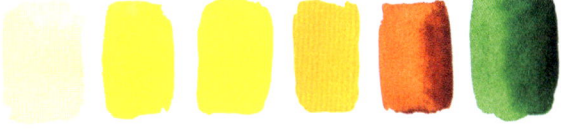

1. Sketch

Create a light outline of your sunflower, marking the circular center disc and the radiating petals. Keep your pencil marks minimal—just enough to guide your hand without restricting your painting.

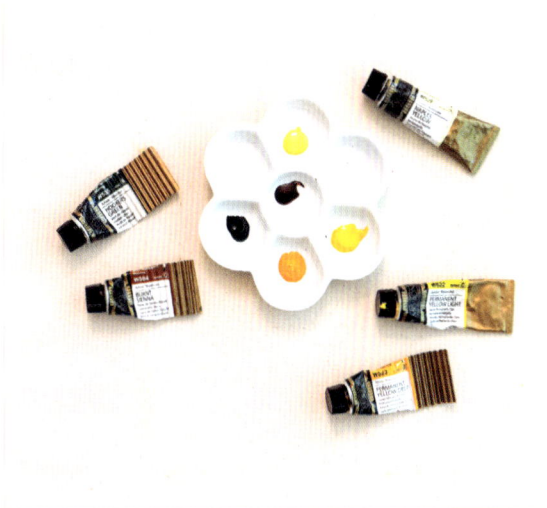

2. Prepare your palette

You need to create four sunny yellow hues plus washes of Burnt Sienna and Hooker's Green. Keep your yellows pure and vibrant for that characteristic sunflower glow.

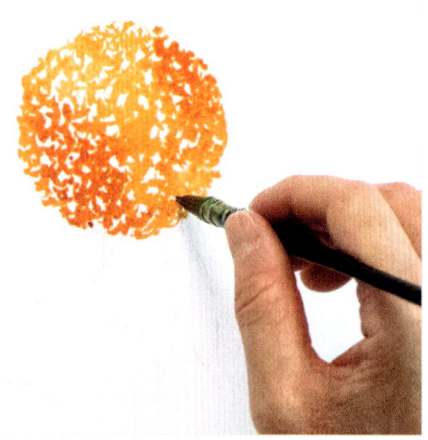

3. Center disc: first layer

Using your 3/0 quill brush with Burnt Sienna in tea consistency, apply small dots in a circular pattern to create the textured center. Allow your brush to dance across the surface, creating an organic, seedlike texture.

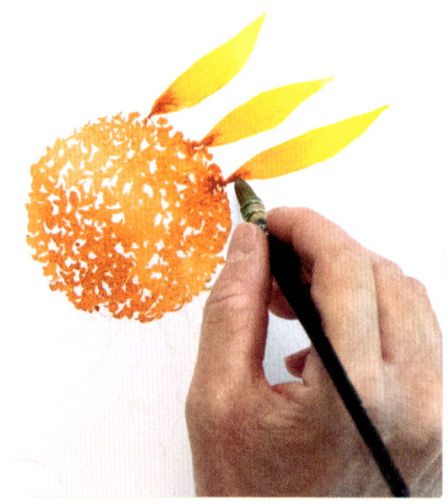

4. First set of petals

Mix a gradient palette ranging from Burnt Sienna to Naples Yellow. Paint alternating petals, working with a heavier concentration of Burnt Sienna near the center that gradually transitions to yellow toward the petal tips.

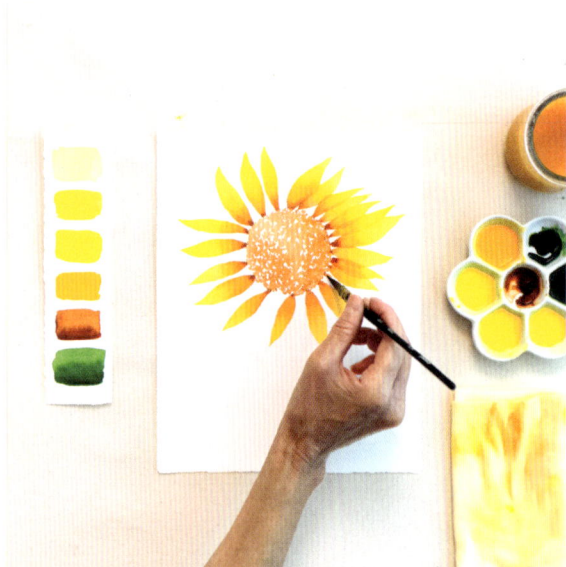

5. Second set of petals

Allow this first layer to dry completely. Paint the second petal layer using the same technique, ensuring the gradient remains consistent throughout.

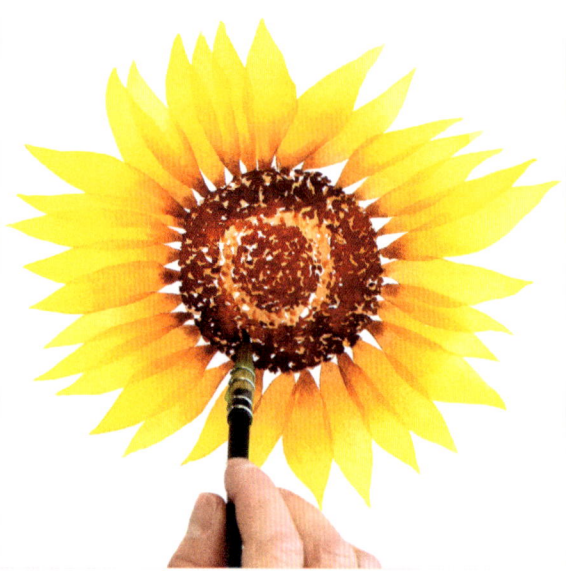

6. Center disc: second layer

Return to the center disc with a milk consistency of Burnt Sienna. Leave a small circular highlight in the very center, then apply darker pigment around it. Add lighter speckles with a more diluted mix to create texture in the seed area.

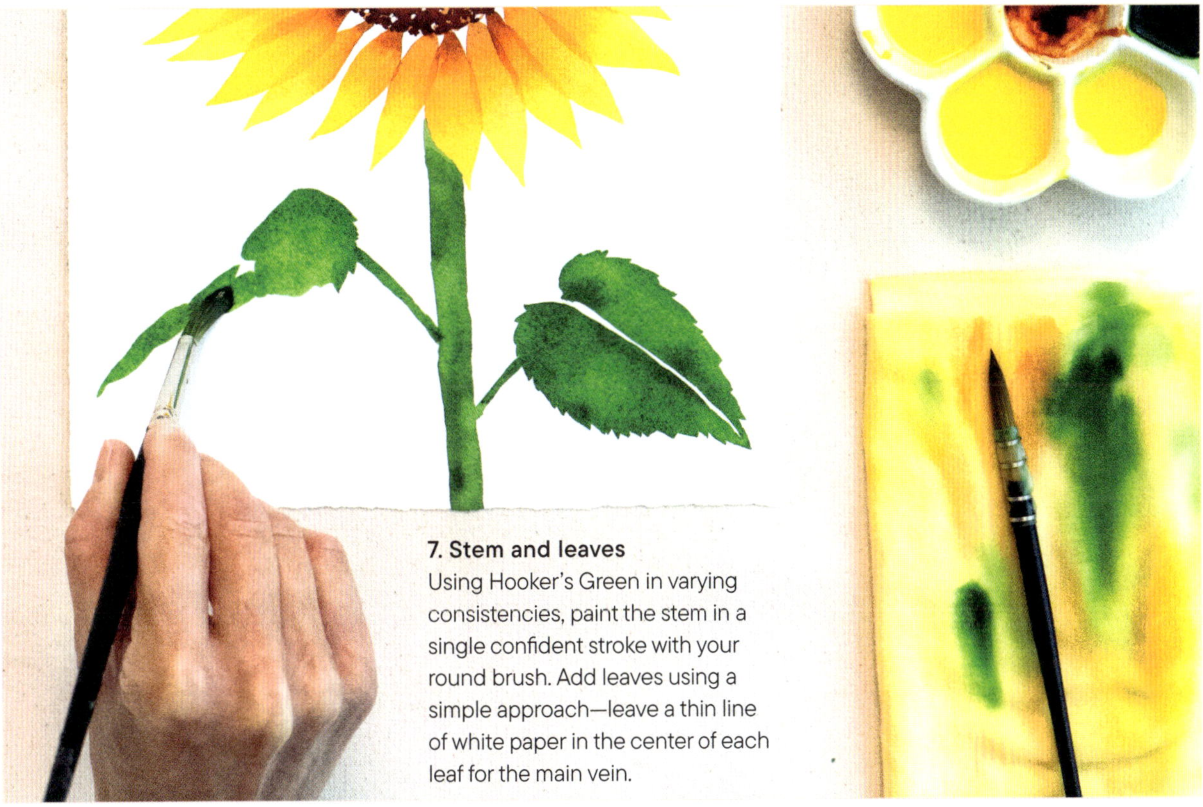

7. Stem and leaves

Using Hooker's Green in varying consistencies, paint the stem in a single confident stroke with your round brush. Add leaves using a simple approach—leave a thin line of white paper in the center of each leaf for the main vein.

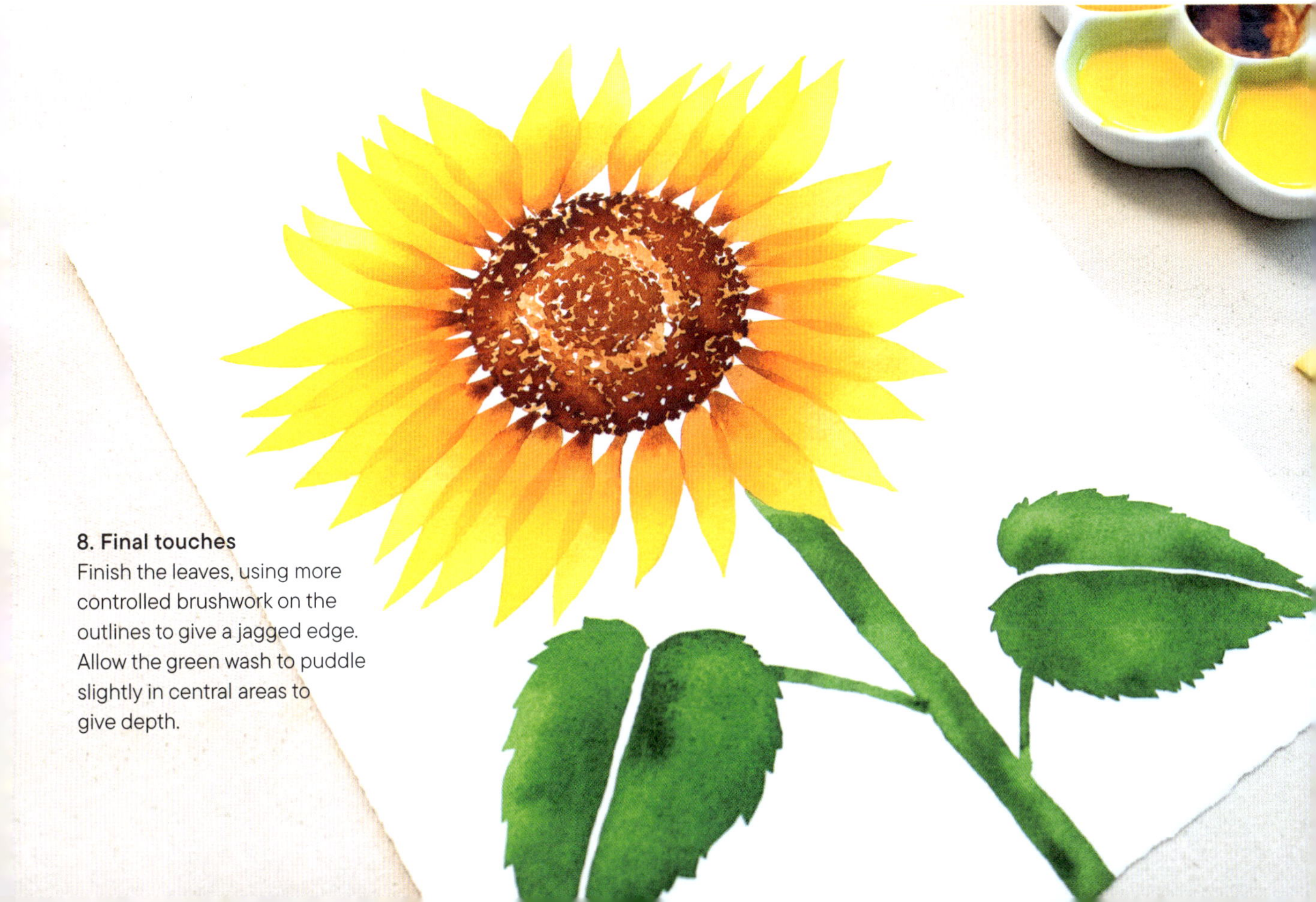

8. Final touches

Finish the leaves, using more controlled brushwork on the outlines to give a jagged edge. Allow the green wash to puddle slightly in central areas to give depth.

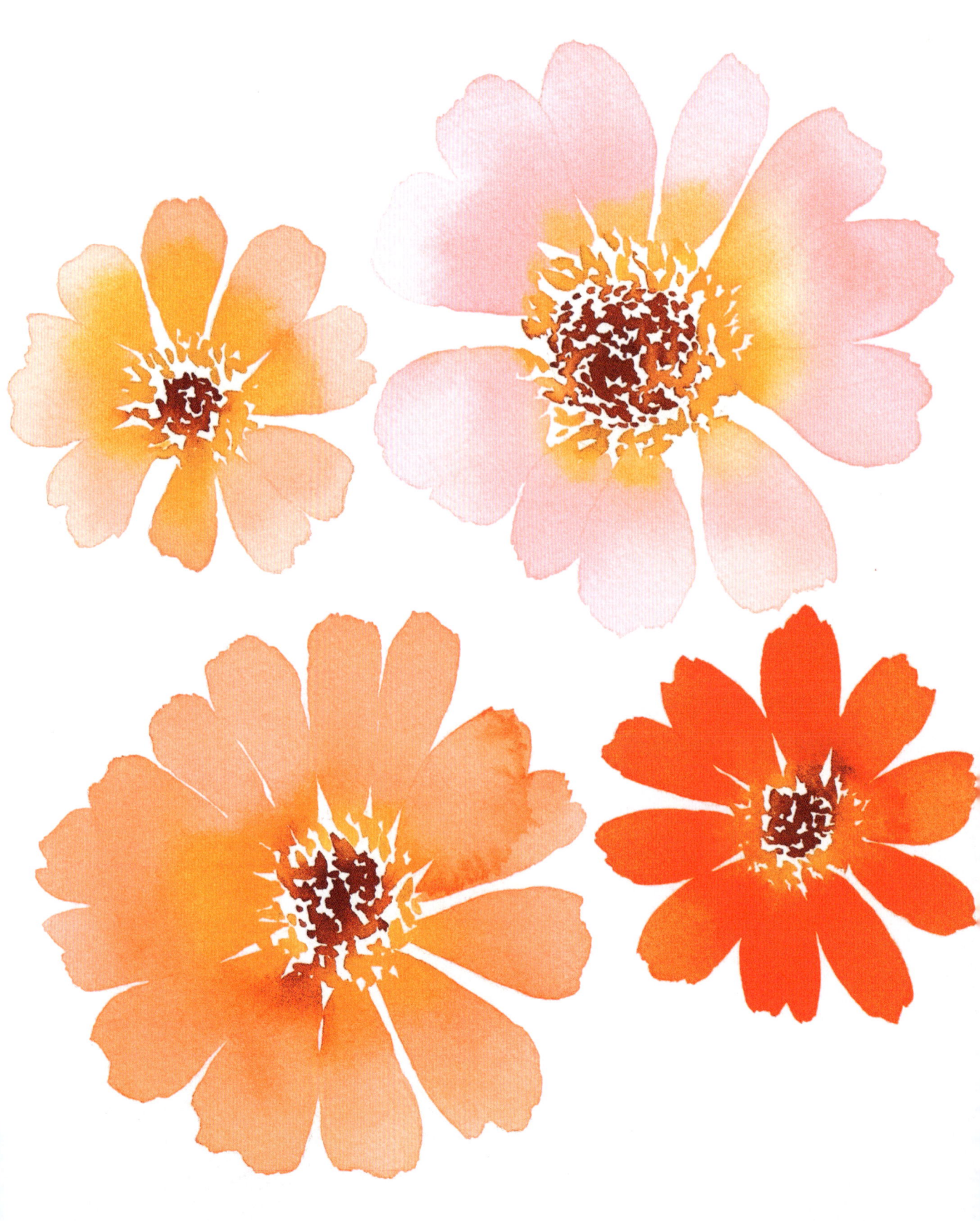

Zinnias

These bright blooms represent endurance and lasting friendship. Let your painting capture their cheerful character through confident brushwork and warm color transitions. The layered petals and vibrant centers offer a perfect study in controlled bleed techniques.

Materials

- Watercolor paper (140lb cold pressed)
- Brushes: quill 3/0, round #4
- Paints: Yellow Ochre, Shell Pink, Brilliant Pink, Vermilion, Burnt Sienna, Burnt Umber
- Pencil, eraser, palette, water container, paper towels

Crisp petal bleeding technique

This combines precise petal painting with controlled bleeds in the centers. The contrast between clean edges and soft transitions creates expressive blooms. See p.45 for more info.

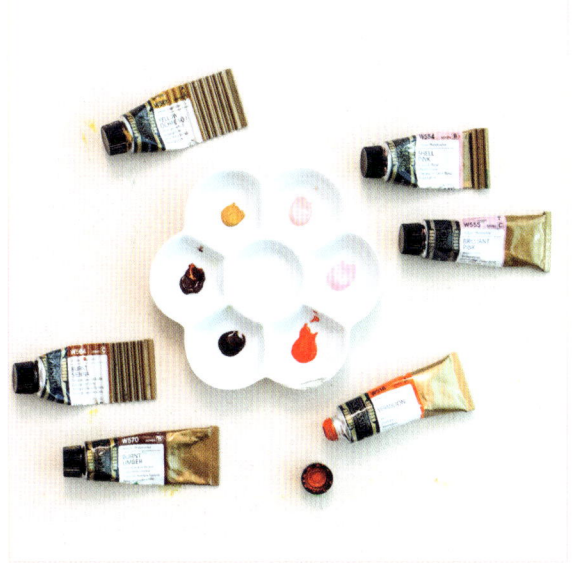

1. Sketch

Create light outlines of four zinnias in different sizes. Plan for each bloom to showcase a different shade within your warm color range, from Shell Pink to vibrant Vermilion.

2. Prepare your palette

Mix your colors to create harmonious gradients, with a range of strong and pale hues.

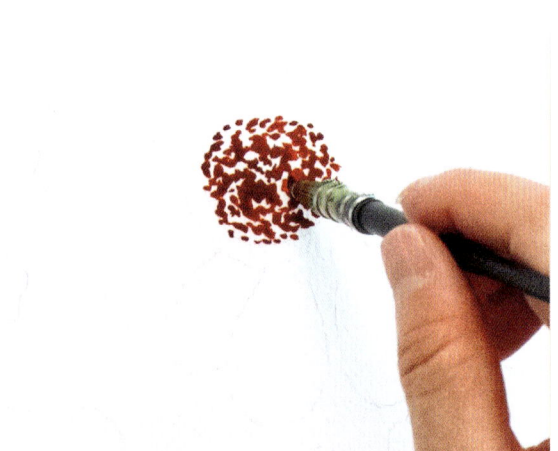

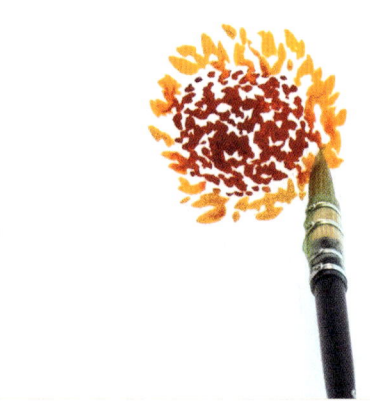

3. Paint the centers

Using your 3/0 quill brush with Burnt Sienna/Burnt Umber, gently tap and dance the brush in the center of each flower to create varied circular marks that resemble the textured seed head.

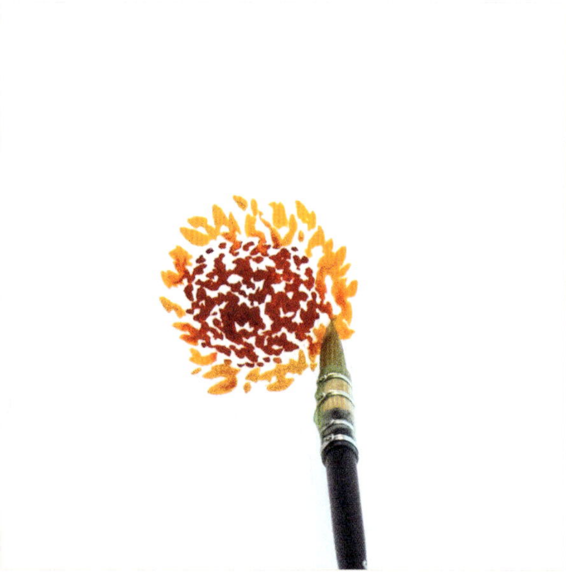

4. Add pollen areas

While it is still slightly damp, work around the outer edge of each center with Yellow Ochre, creating tiny marks that resemble miniature rice grains. Allow the colors to bleed together naturally as you work in a circle.

5. First flower

Begin with your palest flower using Shell Pink. With your round brush, paint each petal with clean, confident strokes. Keep the petal edges clean and confident as hesitation shows in watercolor. Allow the Yellow Ochre from the center to bleed naturally into the pink petals, creating a soft, warm transition. Let the centers set slightly before adding any petals for optimal bleed control.

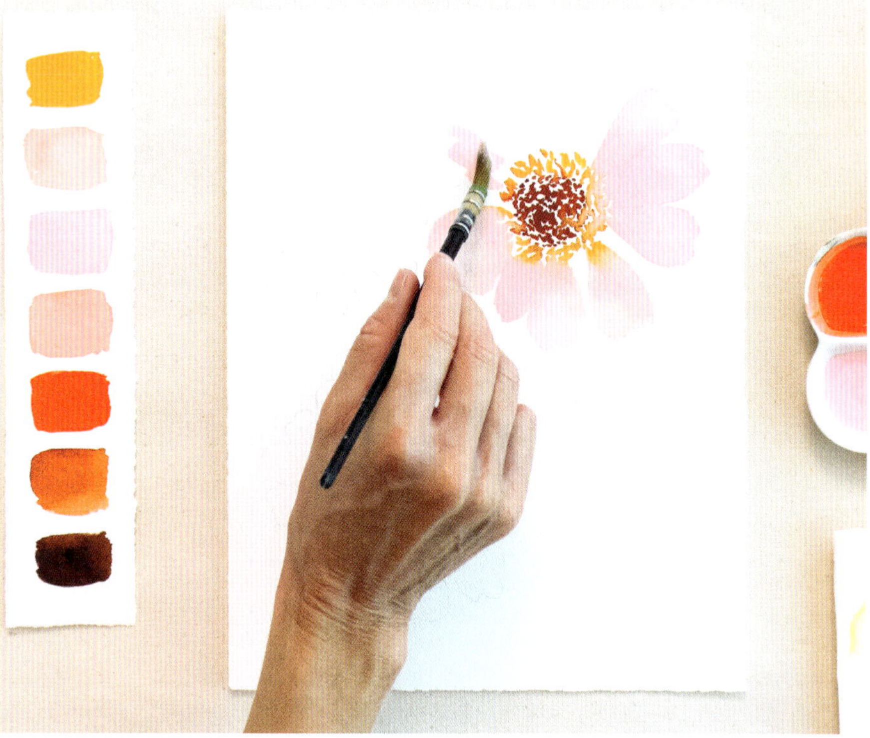

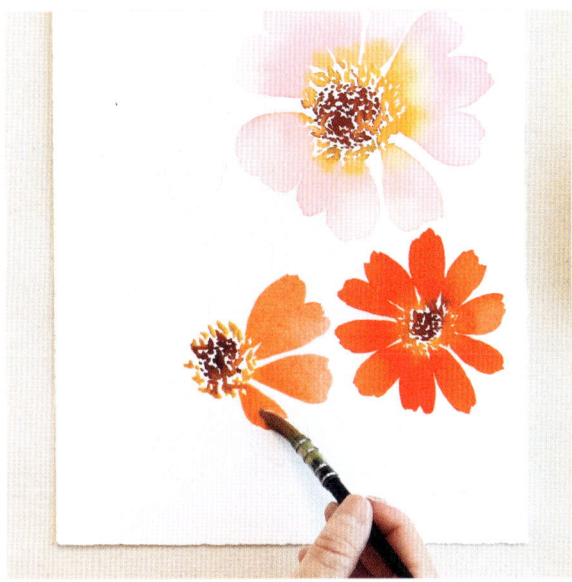

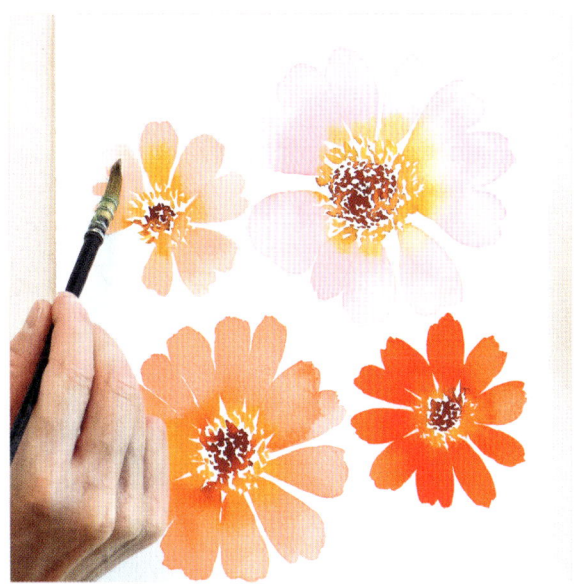

6. Build color intensity

Progress through your color range with Brilliant Pink and Vermilion flowers, following the same process.

7. Create a natural look

Mix colors to create intermediate shades for extra flowers, maintaining harmony throughout your composition. Vary the intensity of the colors, flower sizes, and orientations for natural garden appeal.

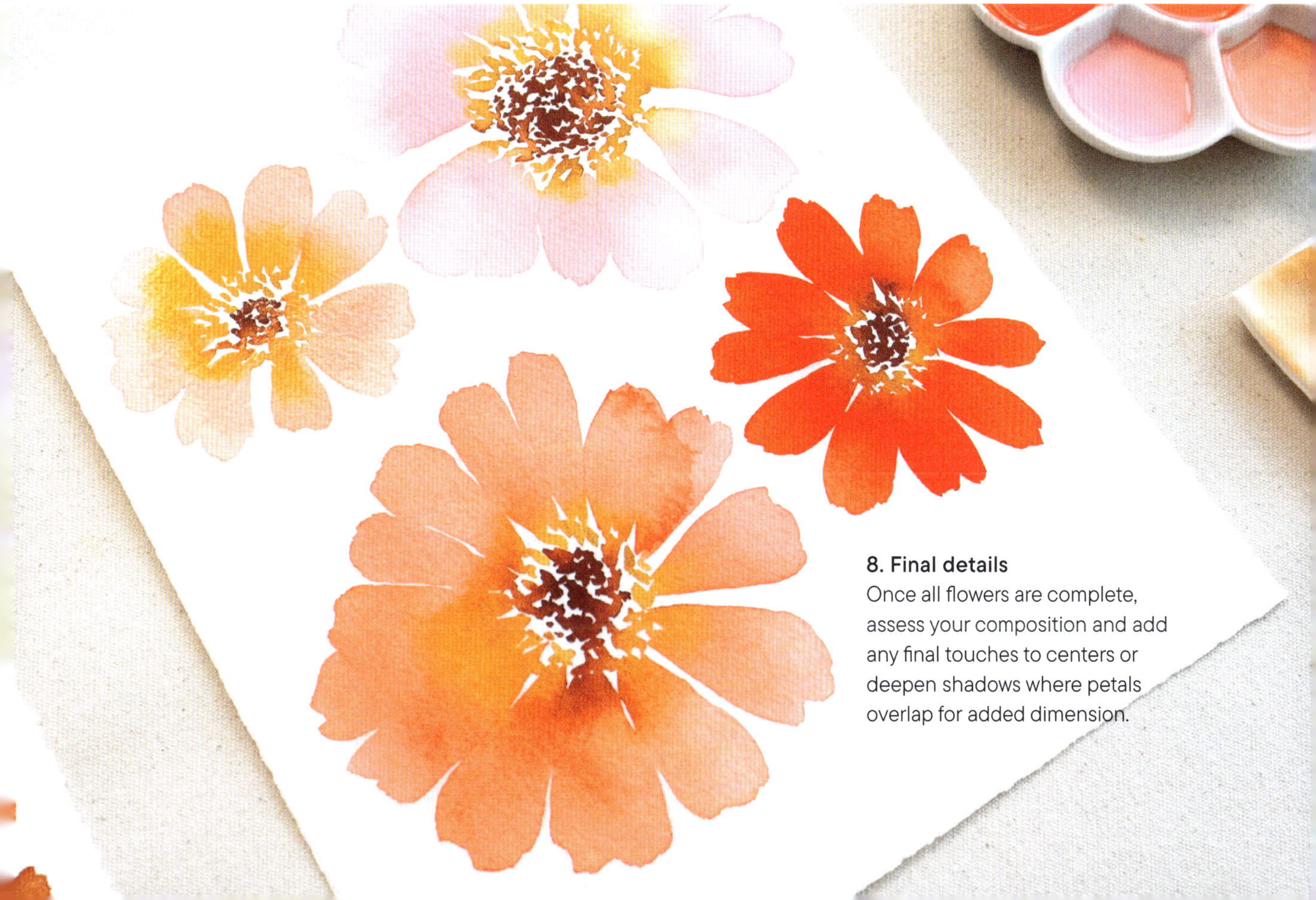

8. Final details

Once all flowers are complete, assess your composition and add any final touches to centers or deepen shadows where petals overlap for added dimension.

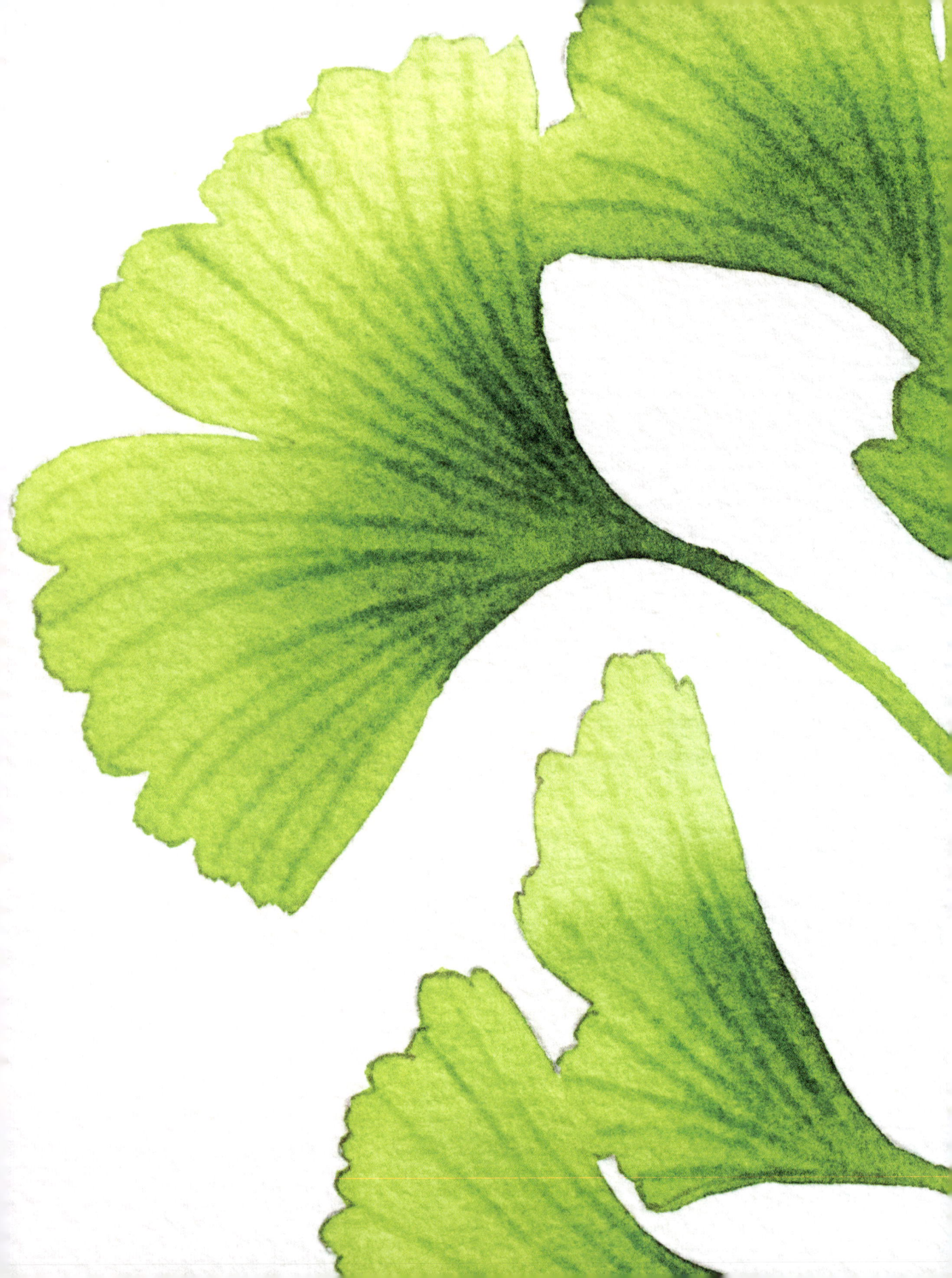

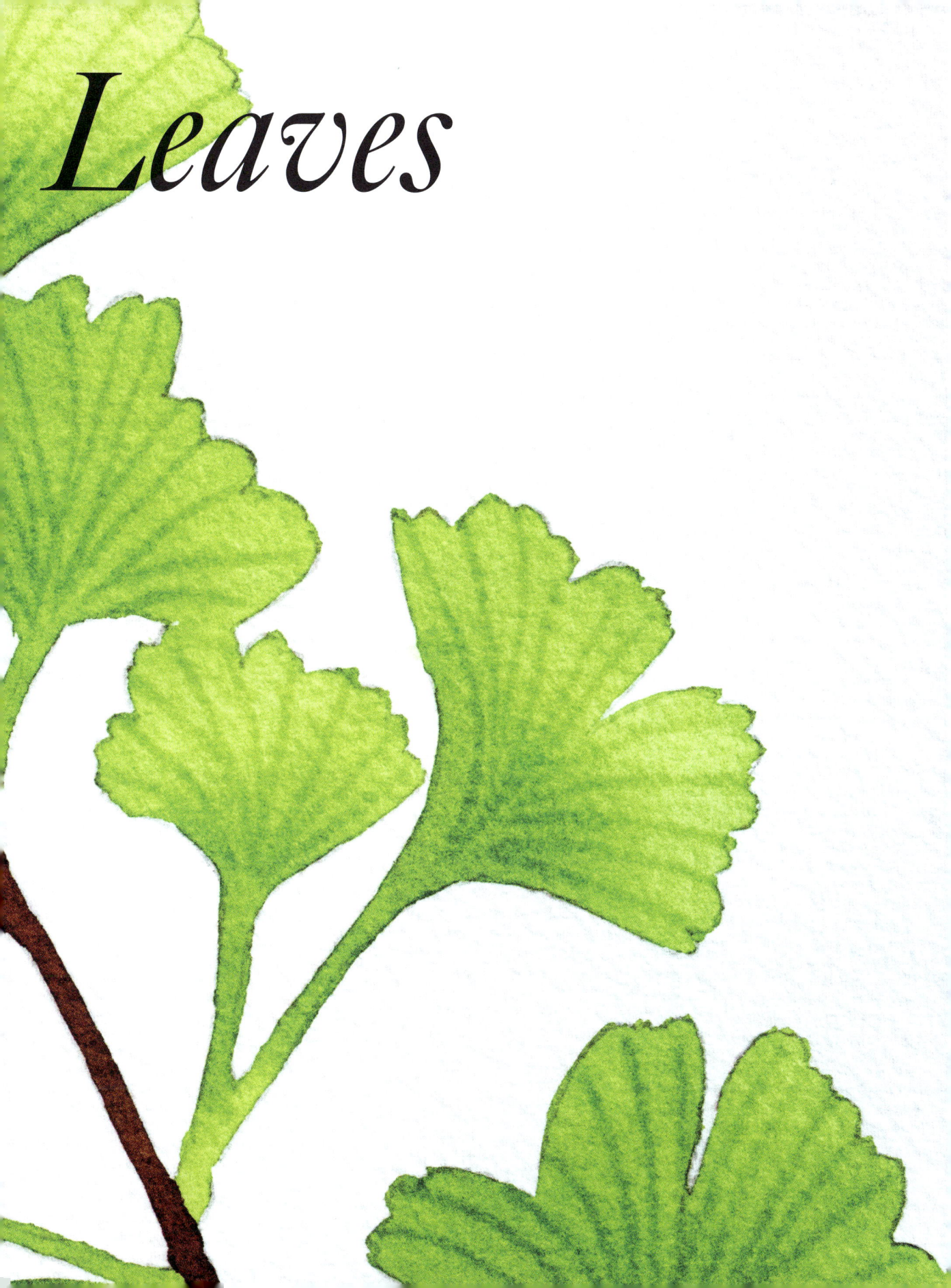

Leaves

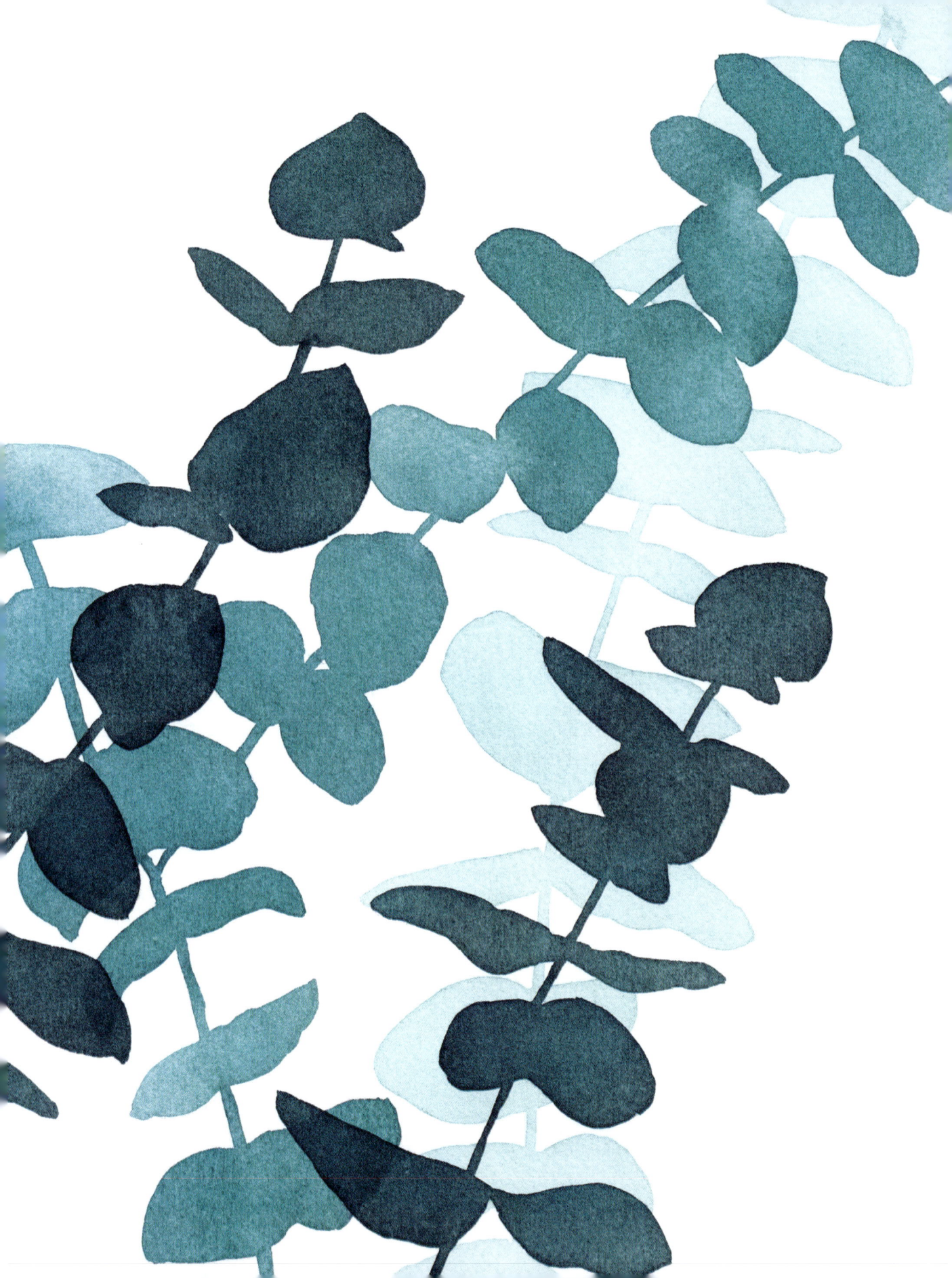

Eucalyptus

The eucalyptus, with its silvery-blue leaves and graceful form, allows us to explore strong silhouettes and color gradation using a wet-on-dry approach. Eucalyptus has a natural architectural quality, so let your painting celebrate this with strong, simplified forms.

Materials

- Watercolor paper (140lb cold pressed)
- Brush: round #8
- Paints: Shadow Green, Hooker's Green, Peacock Blue, Titanium White
- Pencil, eraser, palette, water container, paper towels

Layered silhouettes technique

Create distinct layers by allowing each element to dry completely before adding the next. This produces depth and atmosphere by layering translucent washes of color and darker silhouettes for a graphic, screen-printed effect.

1. Sketch

Create a balanced composition of eucalyptus stems with varied positions and slight overlaps. Keep your lines clean and minimal, focusing on the overall silhouette rather than interior details.

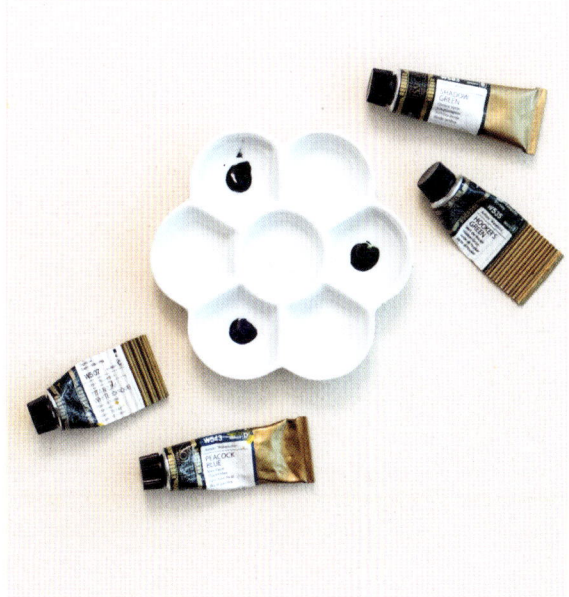

2. Prepare your palette

Prepare three distinct shades of blue green, from light to dark. These will create an ombre effect when layering the stems. Mix Shadow Green, Hooker's Green, and Peacock Blue in varying proportions, adding touches of Titanium White to lighten as needed.

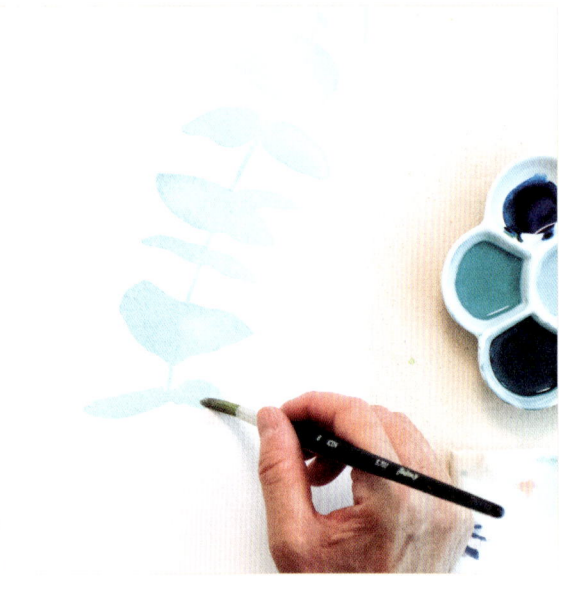

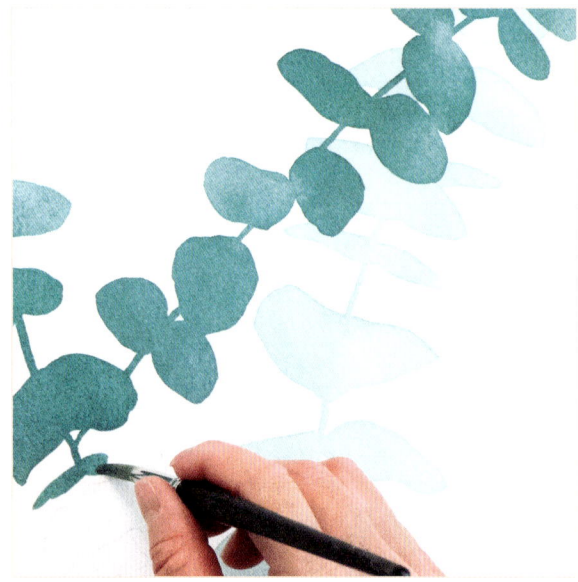

3. First layer

Using your lightest shade, paint the complete first stem with a solid, even color. Work with confident strokes to maintain clean edges. This stem will appear furthest back in your composition. Allow this layer to dry completely.

4. Second layer

Once the first stem is thoroughly dry, paint the second stem using your medium shade. Again, apply even color, paying careful attention to maintaining the silhouette shape.

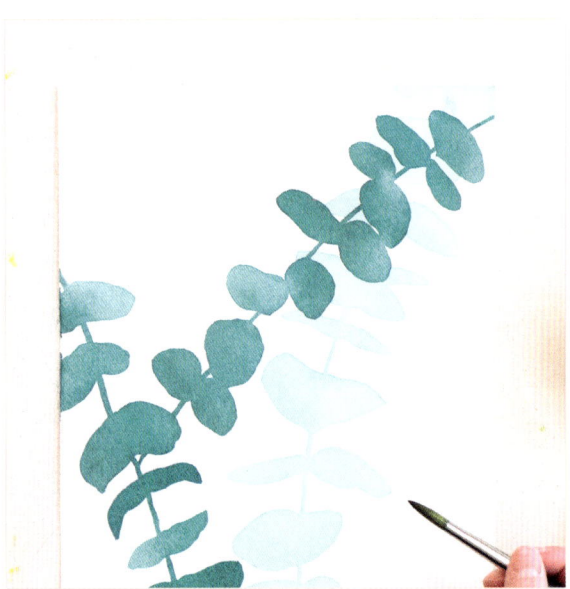

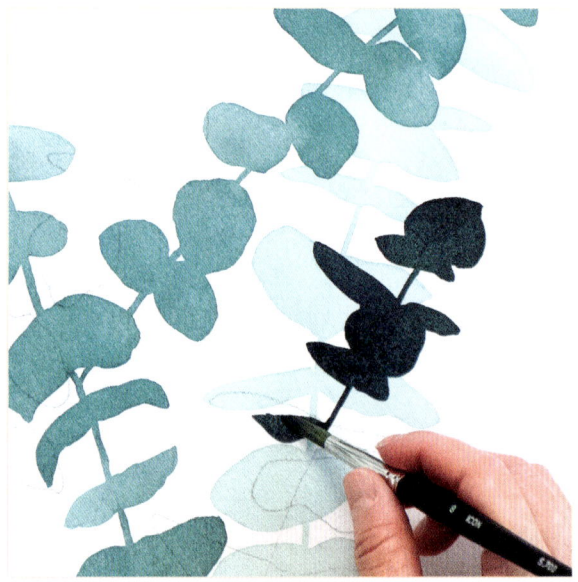

5. Embrace tonal differences

Don't try to make every leaf the same: work with the natural gradation effects of the paint on the paper and embrace the slight differences to produce a natural, tonal result. Allow this layer to dry completely.

6. Third layer

With your darkest blue-green mixture, paint the remaining stems. This foremost layer will create the strongest visual impact. Take care around edges where stems overlap to maintain crisp definition.

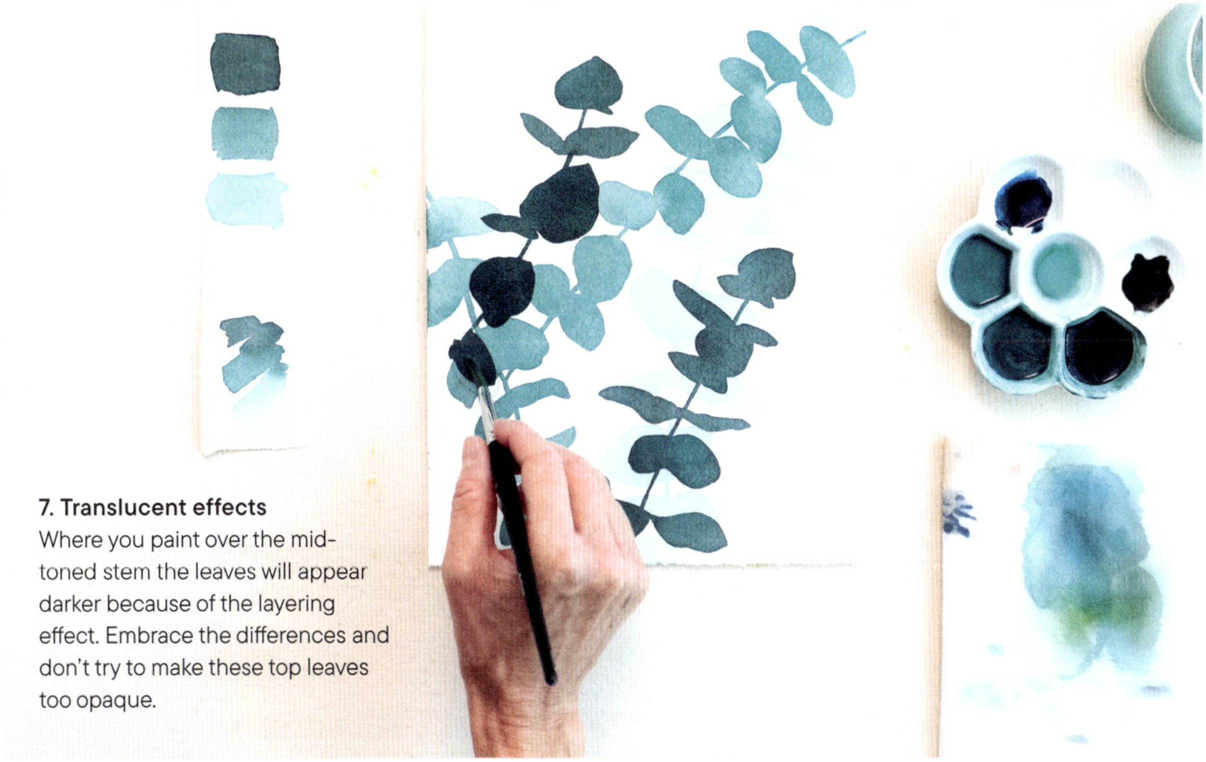

7. Translucent effects

Where you paint over the mid-toned stem the leaves will appear darker because of the layering effect. Embrace the differences and don't try to make these top leaves too opaque.

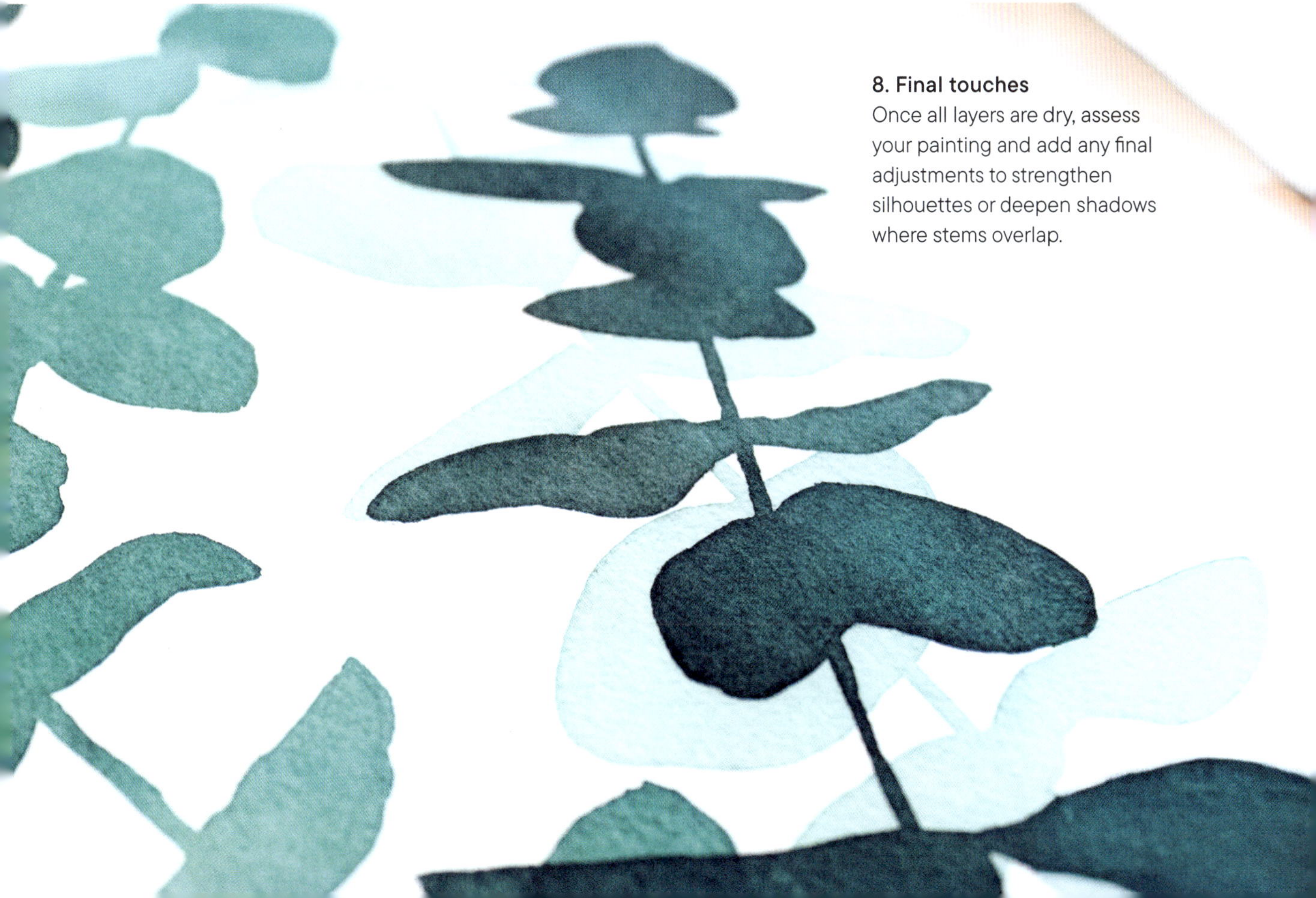

8. Final touches

Once all layers are dry, assess your painting and add any final adjustments to strengthen silhouettes or deepen shadows where stems overlap.

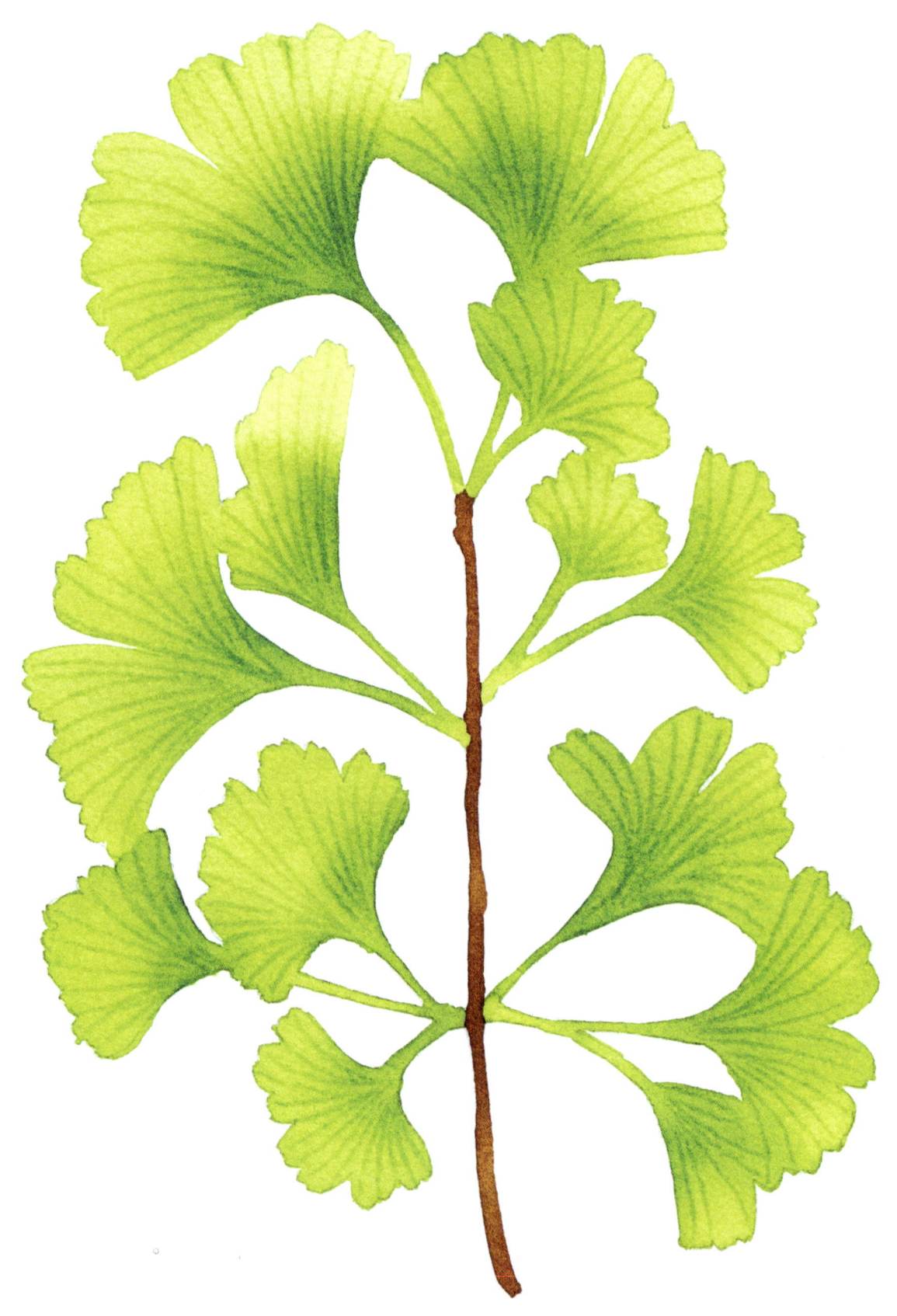

Ginkgo Shoot

Ginkgo is one of the oldest tree species on earth. Let your painting capture its ancient beauty and elegance using a special line-texturing technique. The fan-shaped leaves and distinctive petioles (stalks) are the perfect subject for exploring subtle textures and color gradients.

Materials
- Watercolor paper (140lb cold pressed)
- Brush: quill 3/0
- Paints: Sap Green, Greenish Yellow, Olive Green, Burnt Sienna
- Pencil, eraser, palette, water container, paper towels

Brush-end texturing technique
Create delicate patterns by using the pointed end of your brush handle to score lines into wet paint. This leaves a texture that's perfect for capturing natural veining patterns.

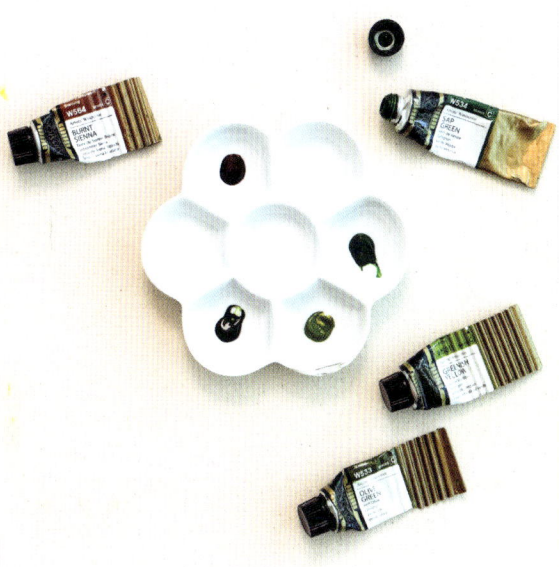

1. Sketch
Create a light sketch of your ginkgo shoot, including 10–15 leaves arranged in a pleasing composition. Keep your pencil marks minimal and light, focusing on the overall structure of the shoot.

2. Prepare your palette
Prepare one green using multiple greens (Sap Green, Greenish Yellow, Olive Green) in a graduated range. Also mix a bit of your green mixture into the Burnt Sienna to create a harmonious stem color.

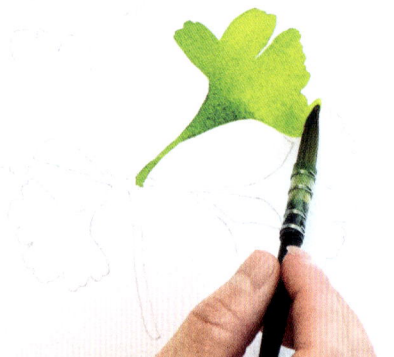

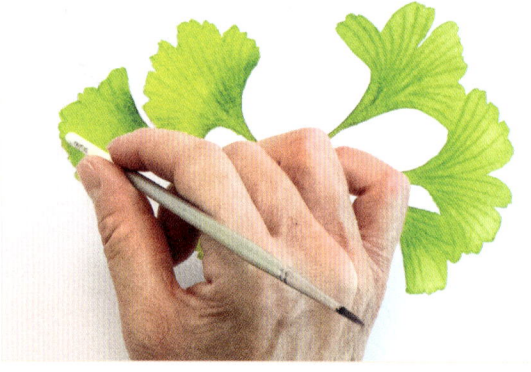

3. Paint the leaves

Working one leaf at a time, apply your lightest green wash to the outer portion of each leaf. Gradually introduce darker green toward the base where it connects to the petiole, creating a natural gradient. Be careful to paint only the leaves and petioles, leaving space for the main stem.

4. Create vein texture

While each leaf is still wet, turn your brush around and use the pointed end of the handle to score delicate lines, maintaining consistent pressure. Work from the outer edge inward, creating radiating lines toward the petiole. This technique only works while the paint is still wet.

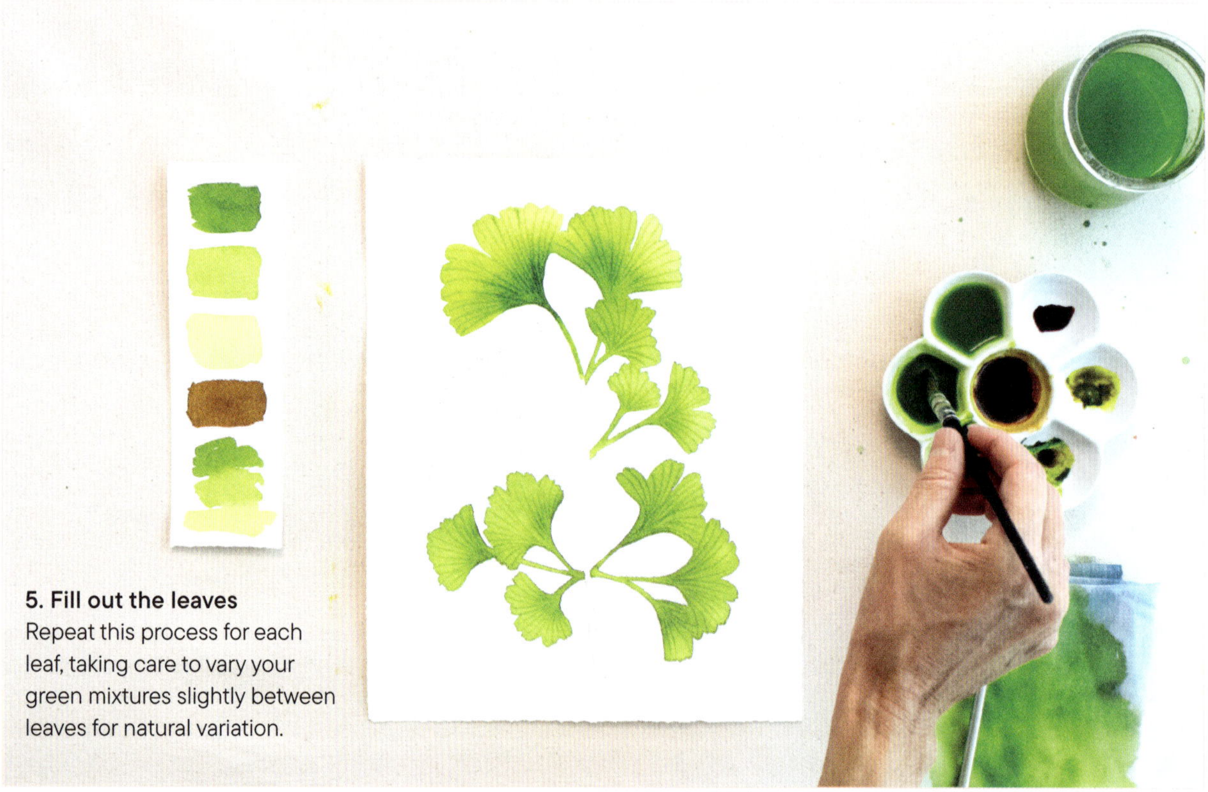

5. Fill out the leaves

Repeat this process for each leaf, taking care to vary your green mixtures slightly between leaves for natural variation.

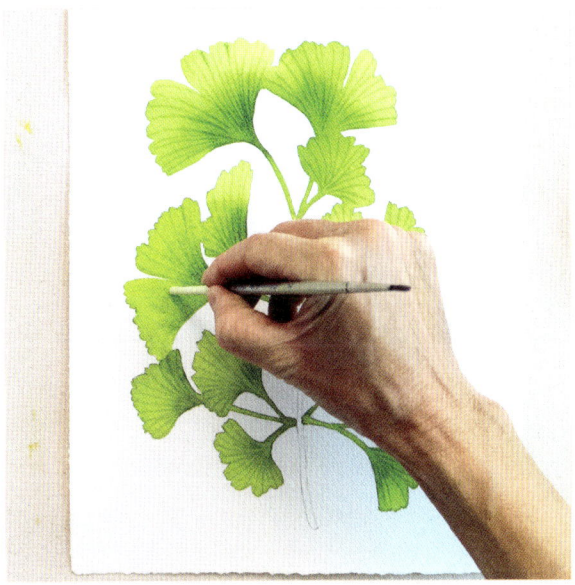

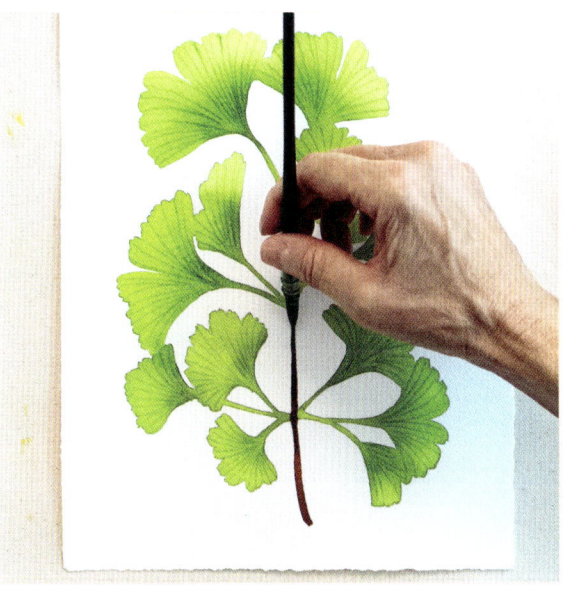

6. Focus on one leaf at a time

This methodical approach allows you to give each leaf individual attention. Timing is crucial—the paint must be wet enough for the lines to form.

7. Add the main stem

Once all leaves and petioles are completely dry, add the main stem using Burnt Sienna in a milk consistency. Hold your brush vertically for precise control and a fine, clean line that connects all the petioles.

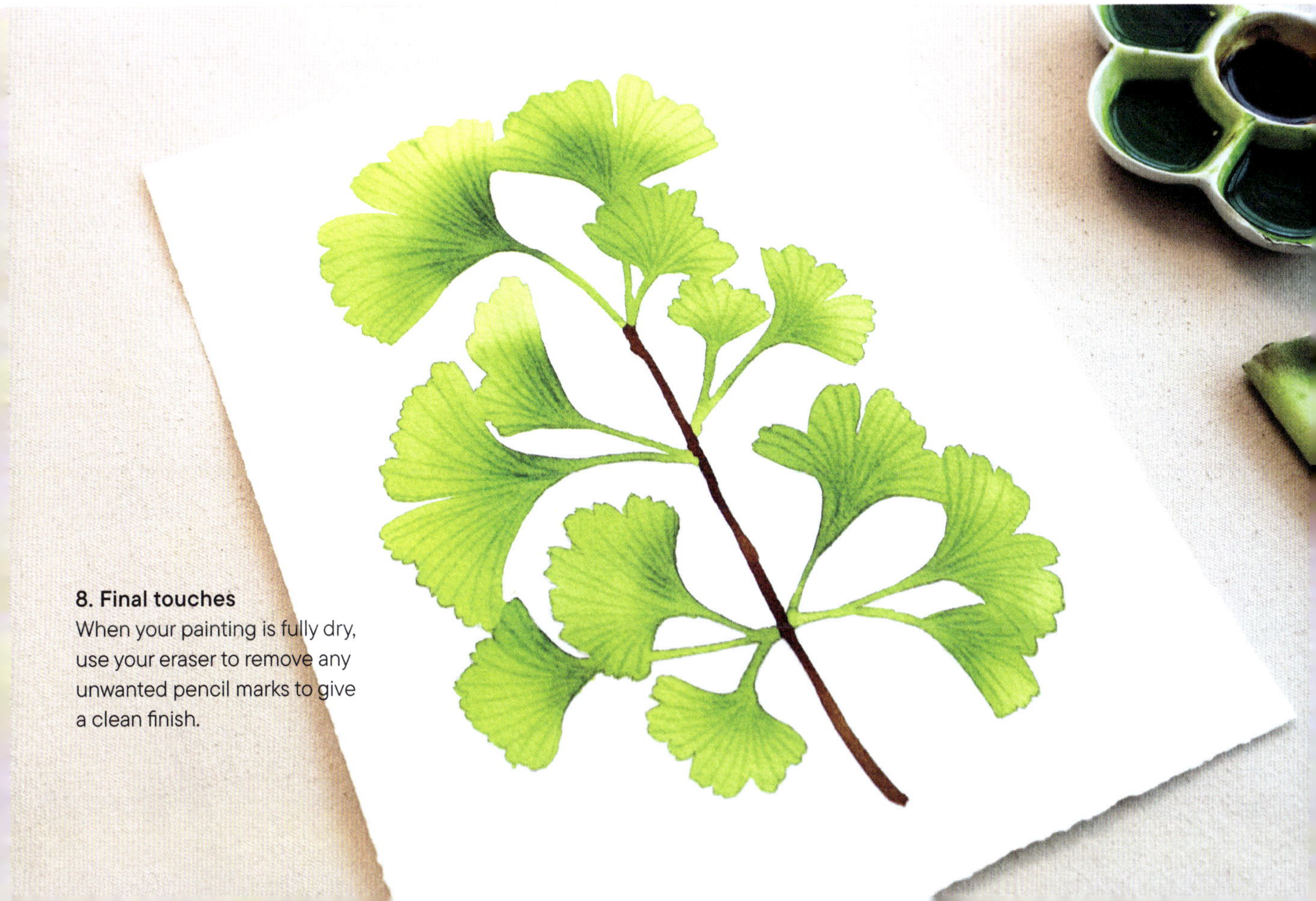

8. Final touches

When your painting is fully dry, use your eraser to remove any unwanted pencil marks to give a clean finish.

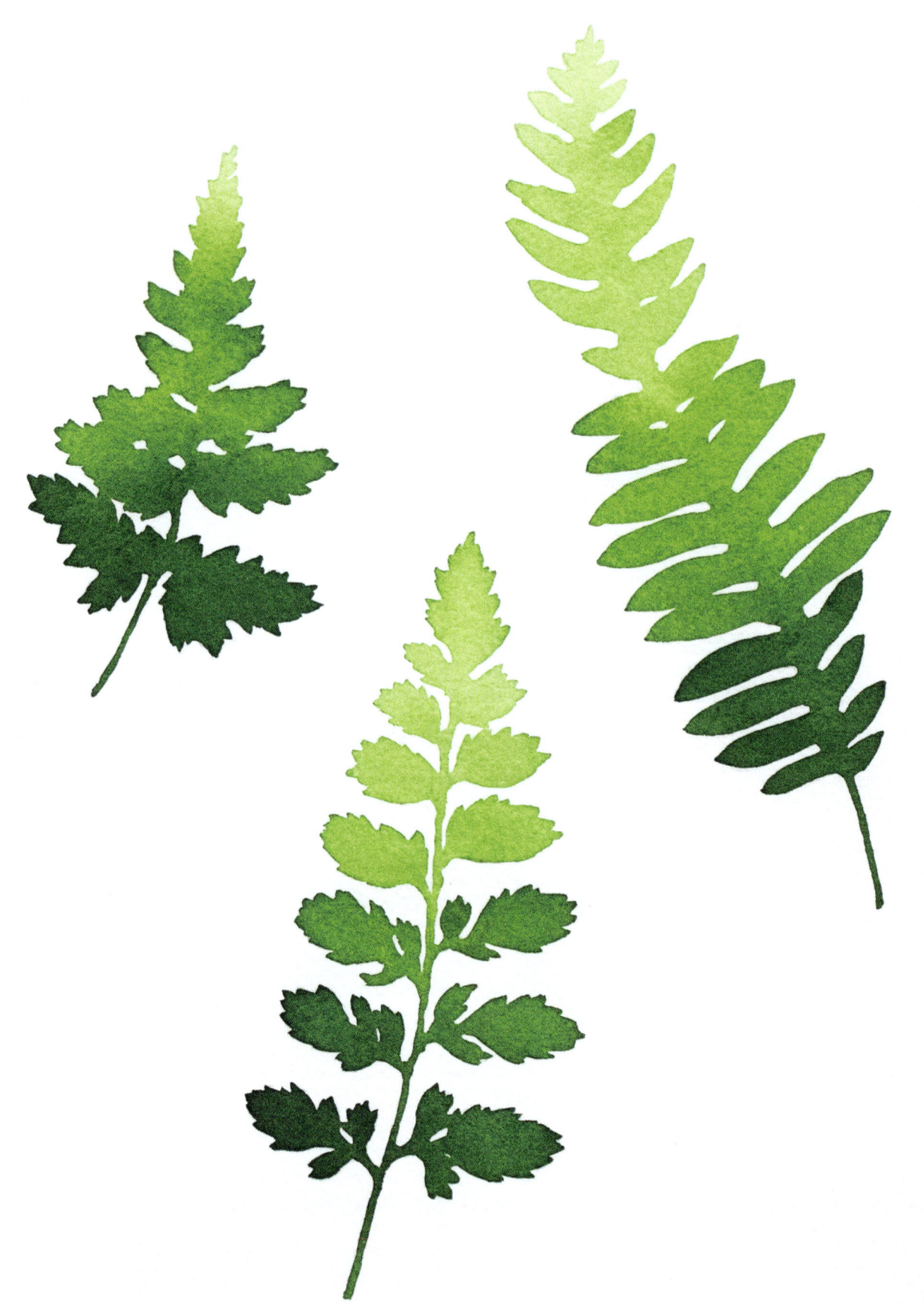

Fern Fronds

The delicate complexity of fern fronds offers a perfect study in subtle gradient techniques and fine detail work. Ferns unfurl with grace: capture their gentle nature through observation and careful brushwork.

Materials
- Watercolor paper (140lb cold pressed)
- Brush: round #8
- Paints: Sap Green, Hooker's Green, Olive Green
- Pencil, eraser, palette, water container, paper towels

Delicate gradients technique
Combines precise brush control with subtle transitions to create realistic yet simple-to-achieve detail. Work systematically through tonal sections.

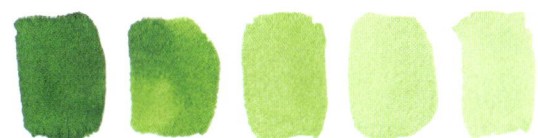

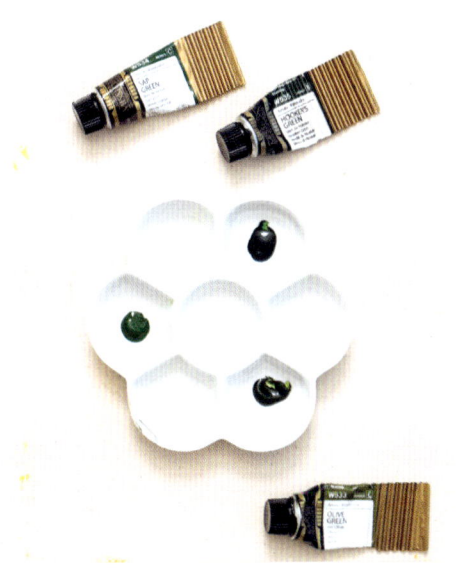

1. Sketch
Create light outlines of three different fern varieties. I've used a woodland fern, a sword fern, and a rabbit's foot fern. Keep your pencil marks minimal, focusing on the main stems and general frond shapes.

2. Mix your palette
Prepare three different concentrations of yellow-toned greens using Sap Green, Hooker's Green, and Olive Green. Create light, medium, and dark values that will form your gradient from top to bottom.

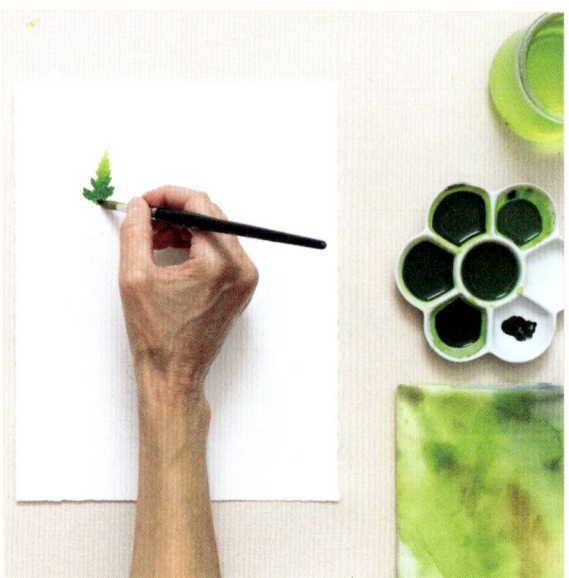

3. Start with the lightest wash

Begin at the very tip of each fern with your lightest green mixture. Work from top to bottom, dividing each frond into three sections: top (light), middle (medium), and bottom (dark).

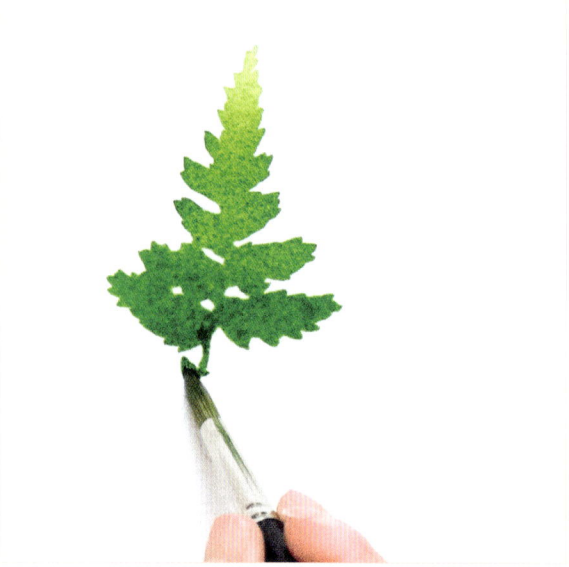

4. Create textured edges

Use the tip of your round brush to carefully paint the characteristic serrated edges of the first fern. Let the brush glide and don't press too hard, or you'll splay the tip. Don't overwork the edges—natural irregularity looks more realistic.

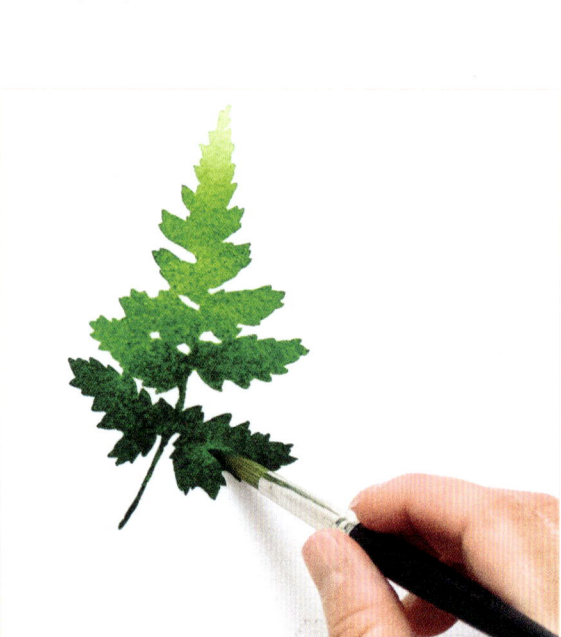

5. Build the gradient

As you work down each frond, gradually increase the pigment concentration. Add clean water to your brush as needed to help blend transitions smoothly between the three tonal sections. With the damp brush, gently pull the edge of the paint outward, softening it.

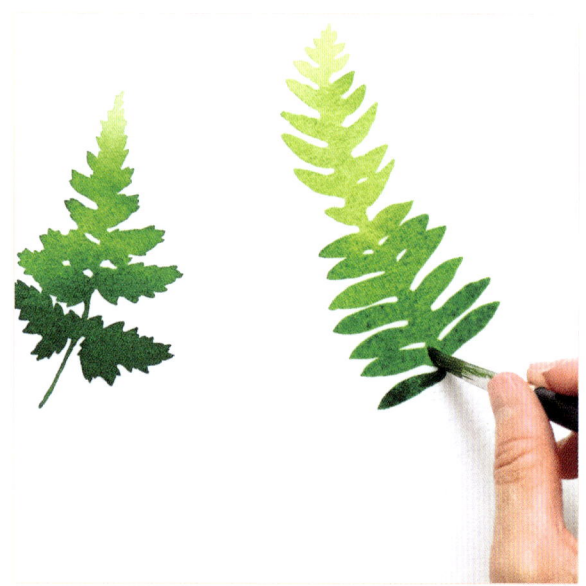

6. Vary the fern textures

Create the second frond. Vary the texture slightly between the three ferns—keep edges natural and irregular rather than perfectly uniform. Again, gradually increase the concentration to create a smooth gradient. Work quickly within each section to maintain smooth color blending.

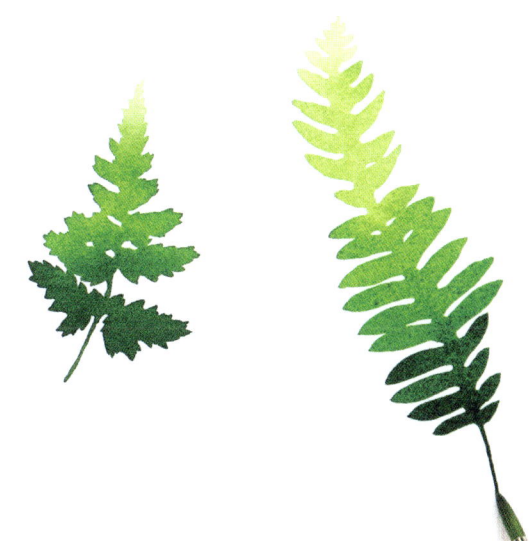

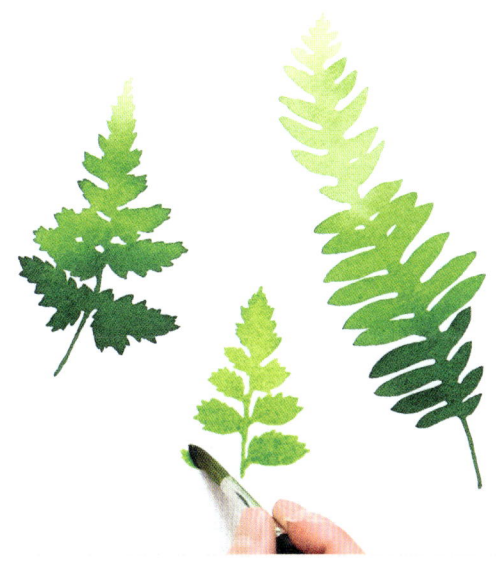

7. Paint delicate stems

Create each fern with thin, precise stem lines using your darkest green mixture. Keep these lines fine—the slender stems are essential to maintaining the characteristic delicacy of ferns.

8. Create the third fern

Move on to the third fern, again beginning with your lightest green mixture and varying leaf textures and gradients as before, allowing each section to flow naturally into the next. Maintain a consistent light source direction across all three ferns so they work as a group.

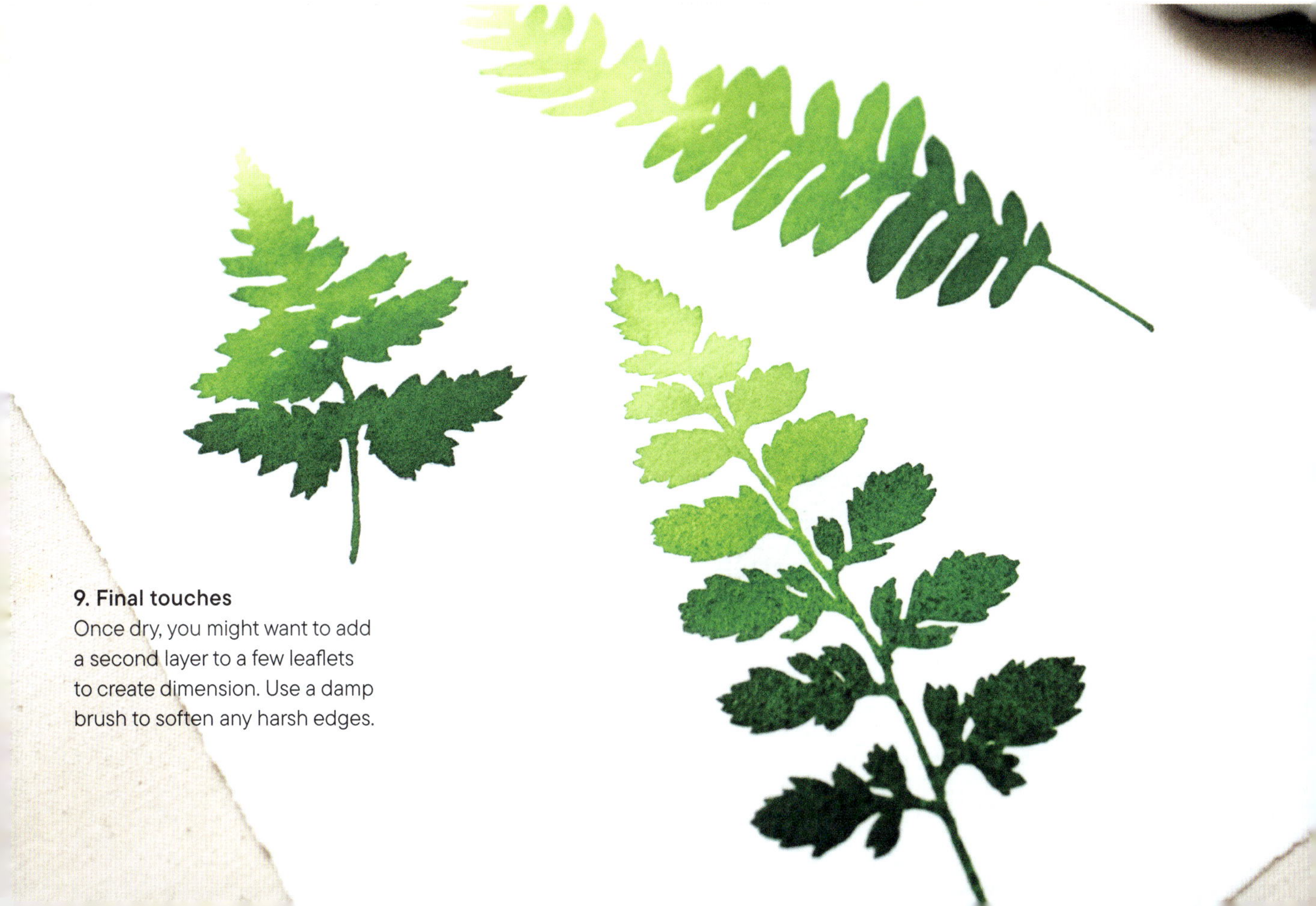

9. Final touches

Once dry, you might want to add a second layer to a few leaflets to create dimension. Use a damp brush to soften any harsh edges.

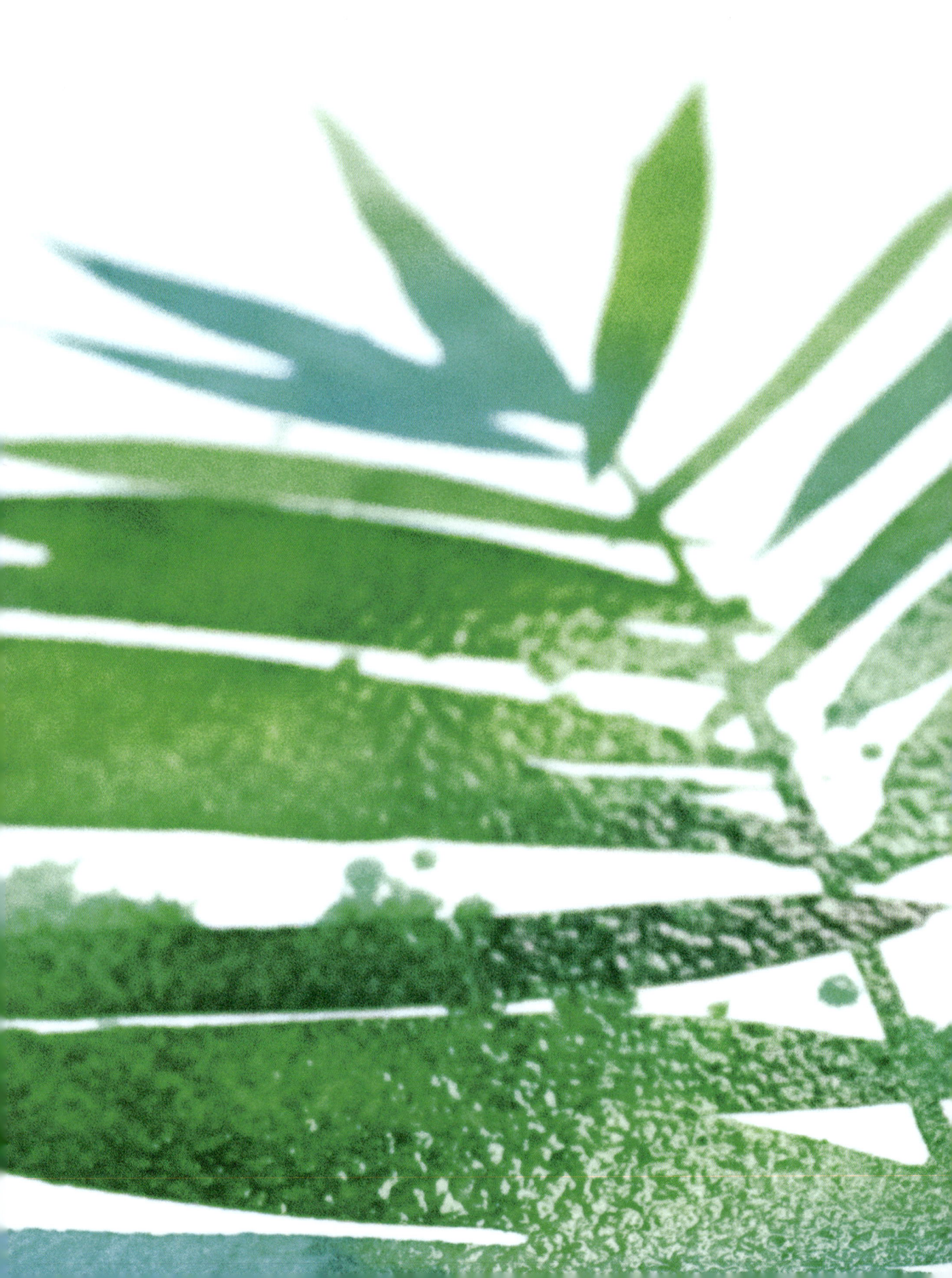

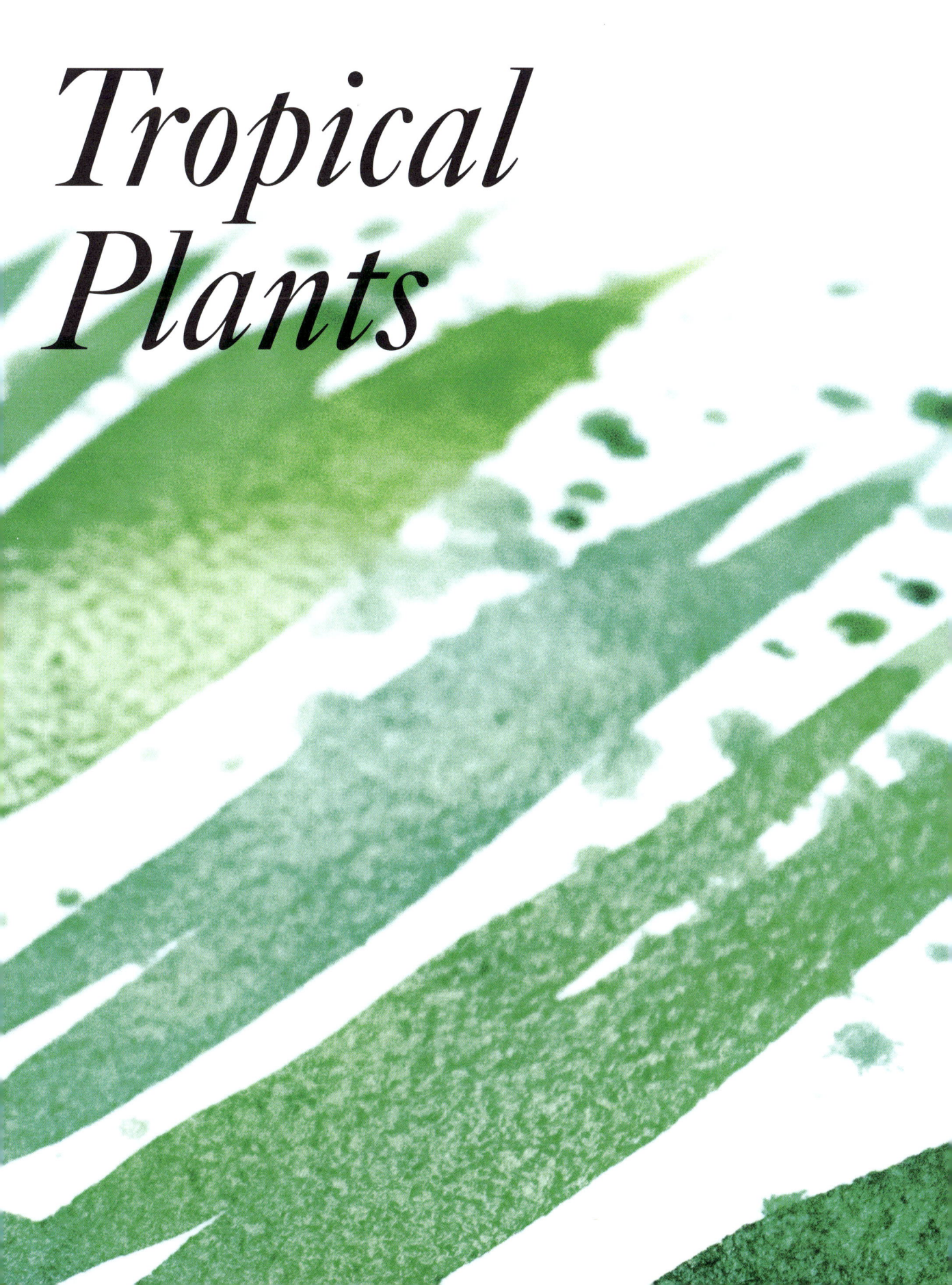

Tropical Plants

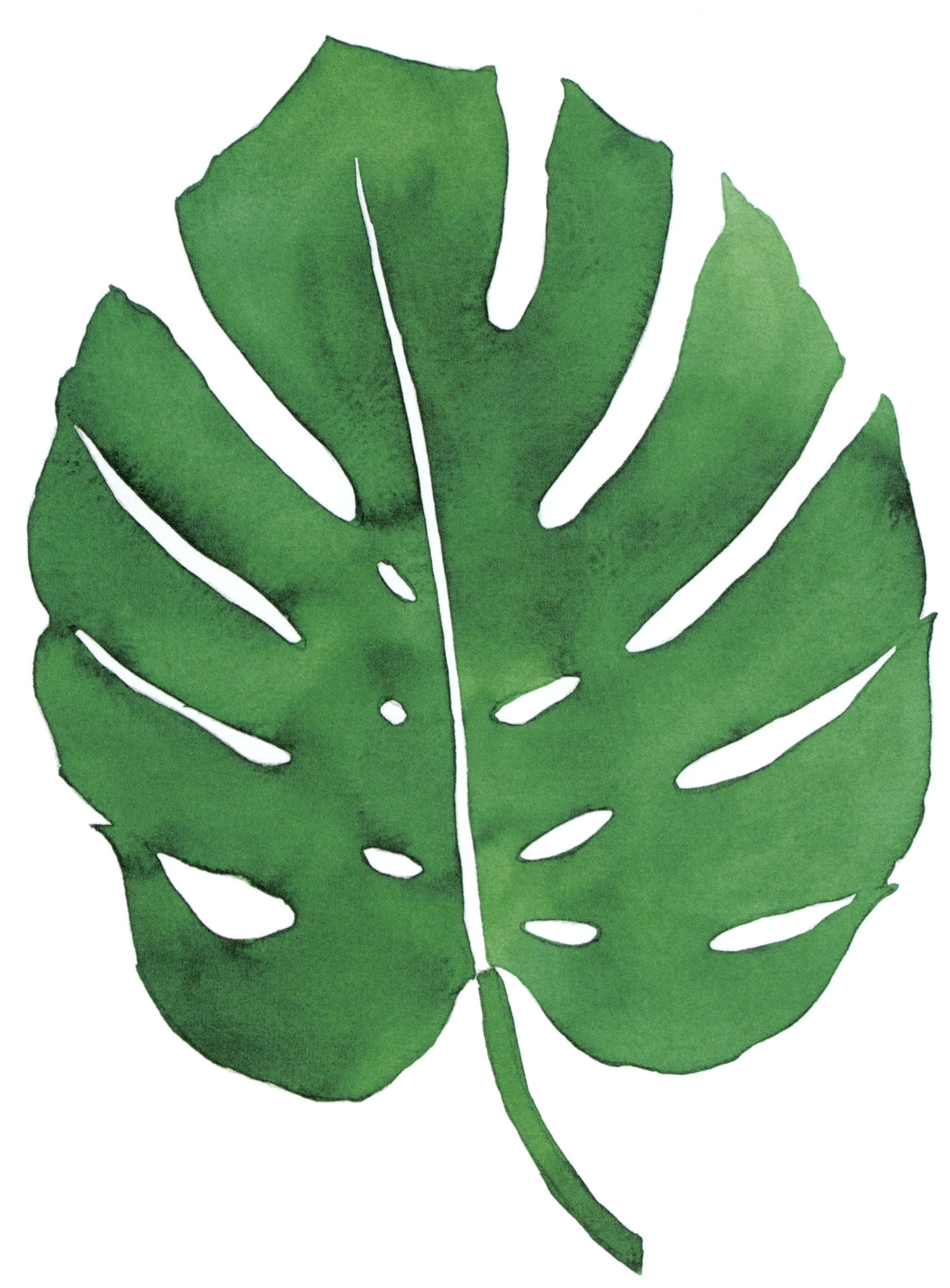

Swiss Cheese Plant

With its iconic perforated leaves, this plant is ideal for showcasing gradient washes and organic textures. Every leaf is unique, so feel free to personalize the shape, perforations, or colors to create your own tropical masterpiece.

Materials

- Watercolor paper (140lb cold pressed)
- Brushes: round #8, old brush for masking fluid (if using)
- Paints: Sap Green, Hooker's Green, Viridian, Yellow Ochre
- Pencil, eraser, palette, water container, squirt bottle, masking fluid (optional), paper towels

Continuous wash navigation technique

This maintains wet, flowing washes while carefully working around reserved white spaces. The challenge is keeping paint edges wet and workable while navigating the complex positive and negative shapes.

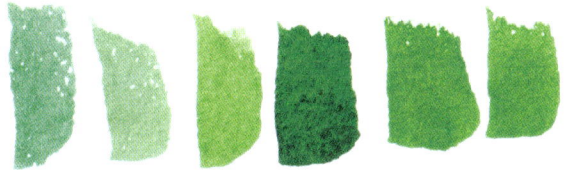

1. Sketch

Lightly outline the leaf, capturing its distinctive holes, splits, and veins. Keep your lines fluid and natural.

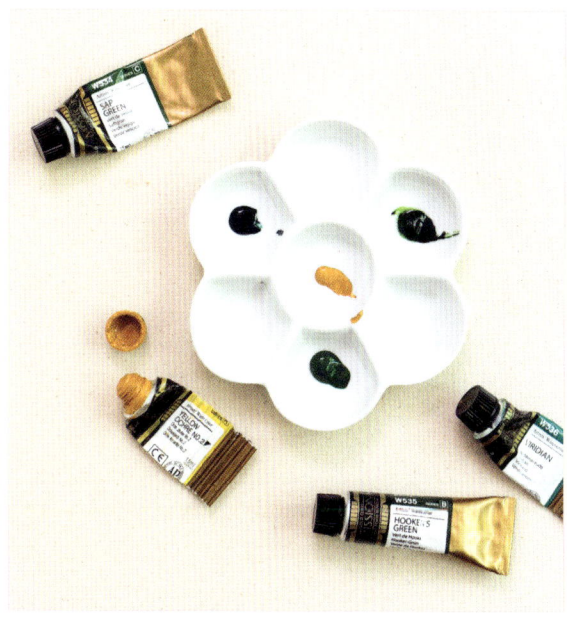

2. Prepare your palette

Mix six hues of green, ranging from green to blue-green and yellow-green.

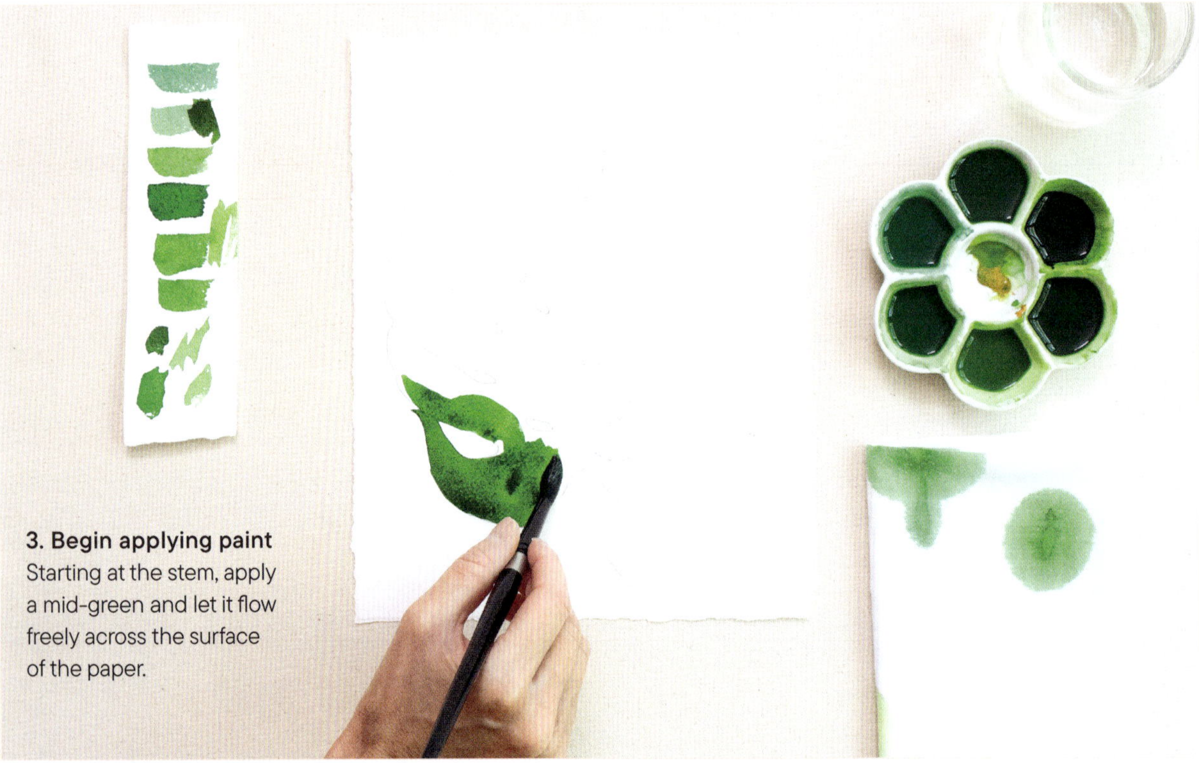

3. Begin applying paint

Starting at the stem, apply a mid-green and let it flow freely across the surface of the paper.

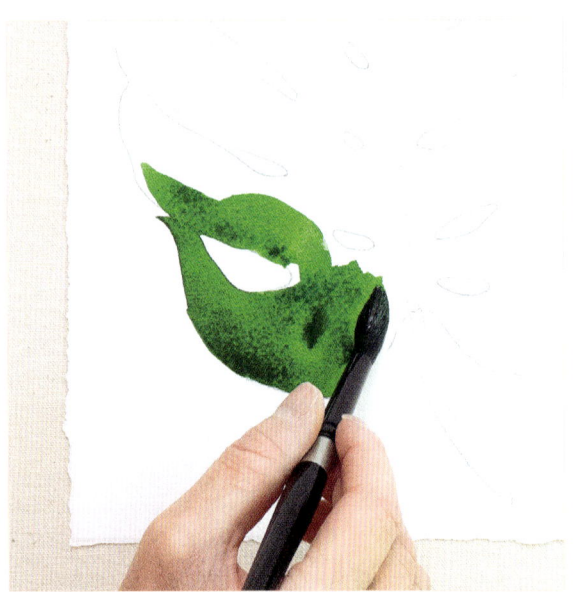

4. Continuous washes

Work outward in a mazelike pattern, using a continuous wash while alternating green shades. Try to maintain a steady pace, working swiftly but precisely within the pencil outlines.

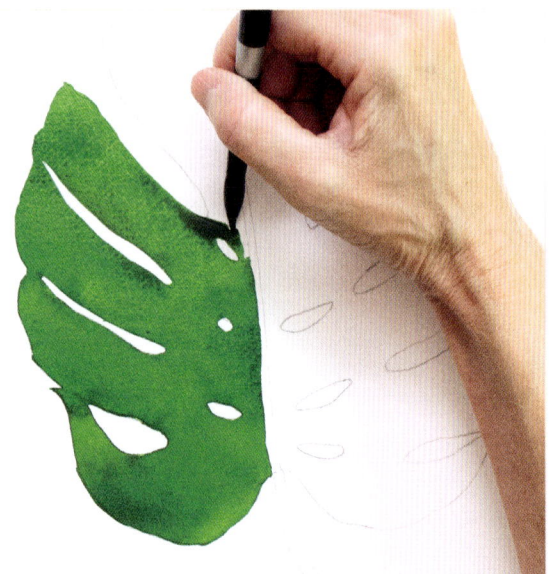

5. Veins and holes

Reserve white spaces for veins and holes. Try to carefully work around these, but if you're not confident, use a fine brush to apply masking fluid over the veins and holes and let it fully dry before painting.

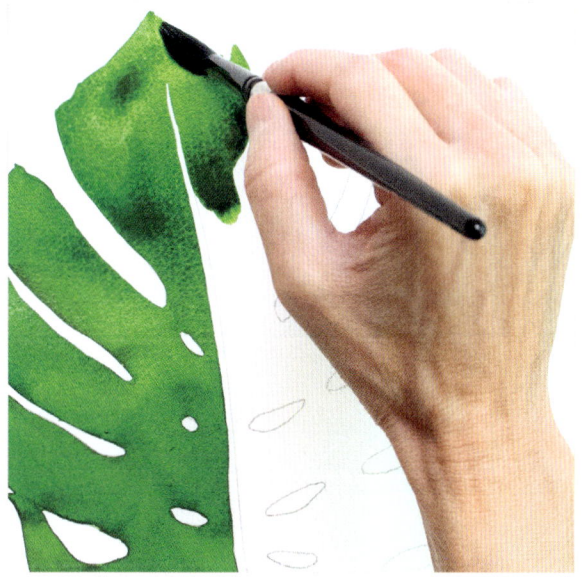

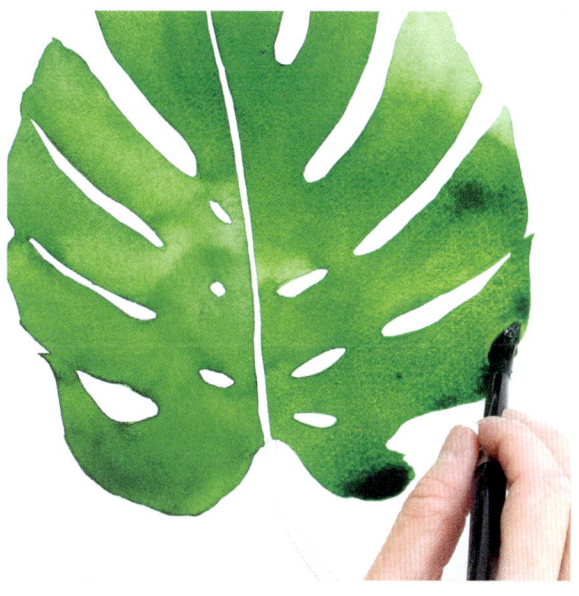

6. Build form

Define form by deepening areas with more concentrated pigment while still keeping edges soft. While still wet, drop in Sap Green around leaf veins and centers.

7. Refine

Add Viridian toward outer edges or shadowed splits. Let the pigments merge softly, tilting the paper slightly for natural blending. Use a fine spray or soft brush to re-wet the paper if you need more time to blend.

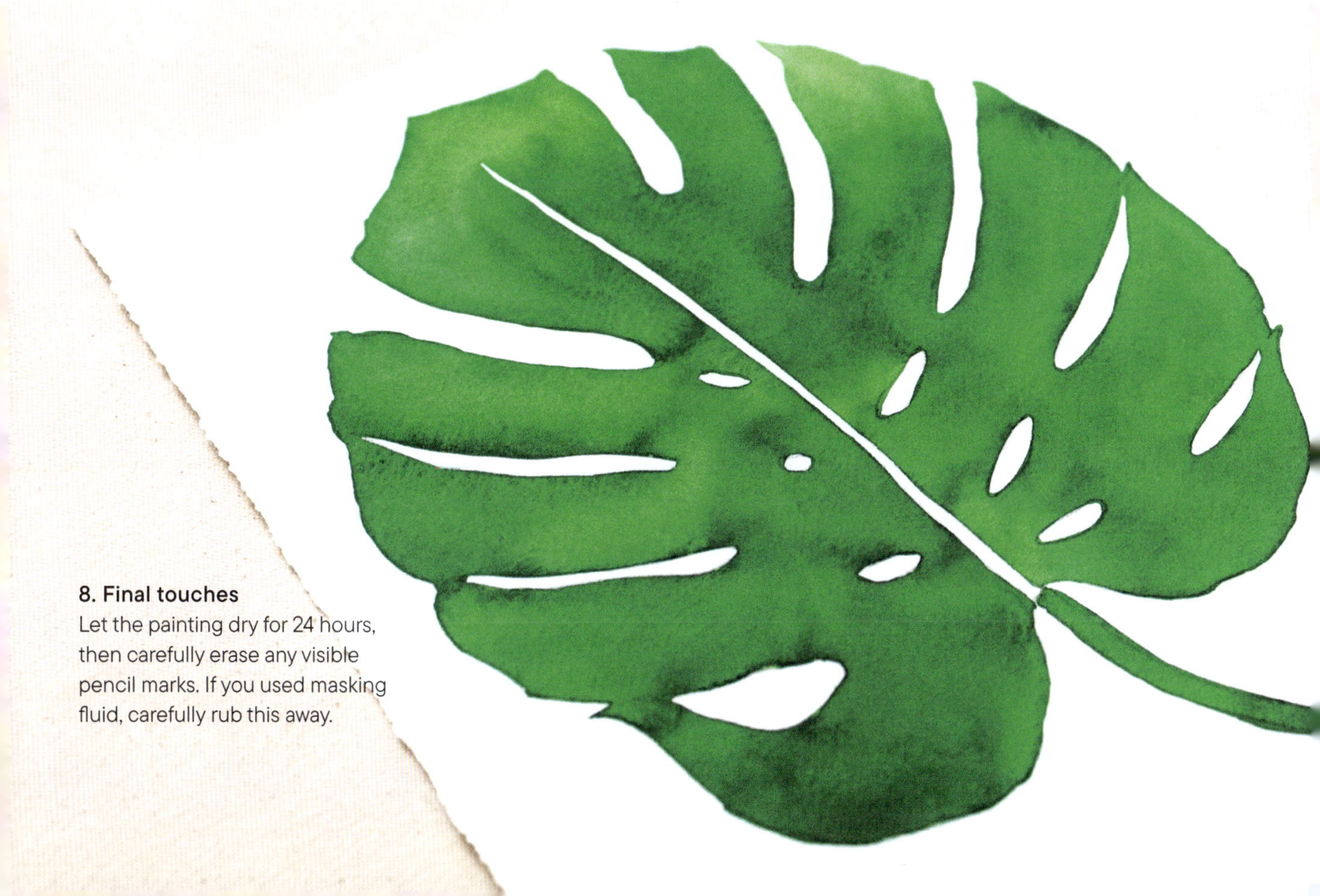

8. Final touches

Let the painting dry for 24 hours, then carefully erase any visible pencil marks. If you used masking fluid, carefully rub this away.

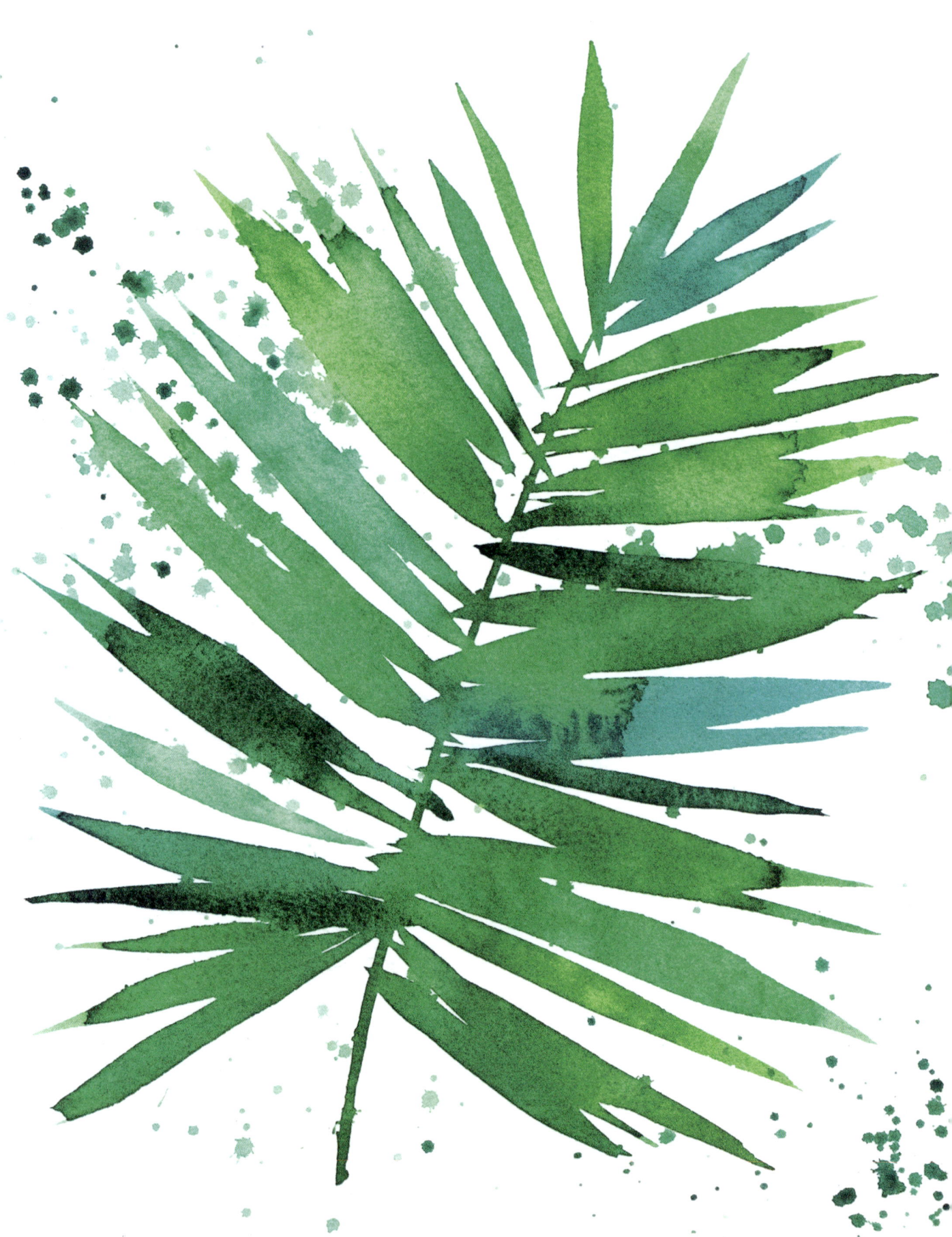

Areca Palm

With its feathery fronds and graceful movement, this is great for exploring expressive brushwork. These palms have a natural rhythm, so let your painting capture this energy using a specialized bamboo brush and spontaneous techniques.

Materials
- Watercolor paper (140lb cold pressed)
- Brushes: bamboo calligraphy brush, quill 3/0, fan #6
- Paints: Sap Green, Olive Green, Emerald Green, Viridian, Manganese Blue
- Pencil, eraser, palette, water container, paper towels

Expressive brushwork & splatter technique

This combines the mark-making capabilities of nontraditional brushes with energetic splatter effects (see p.43). The bamboo brush creates distinctive strokes that can't be achieved with conventional brushes.

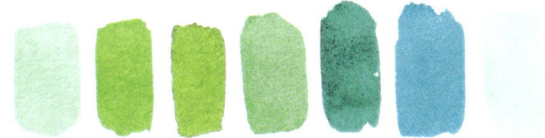

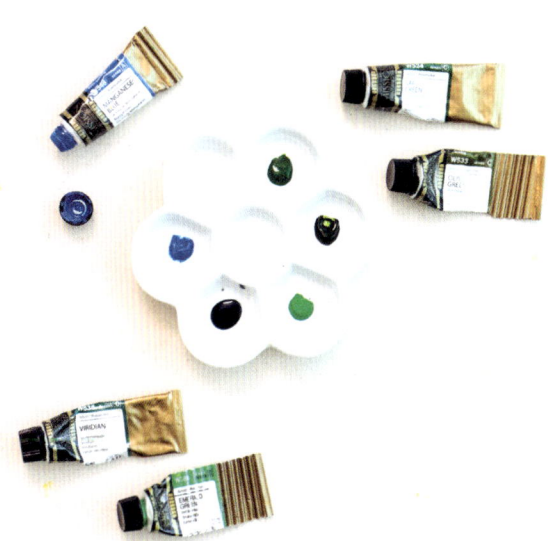

1. Sketch

Create a light, minimal sketch of your palm frond, focusing on the central stem and general placement of leaflets. Render your sketch as a suggestive guide rather than a strict outline.

2. Prepare your palette

Mix several greens (Sap, Olive, Emerald, and Viridian) and blue (Manganese) in milk consistency. Having multiple shades ready will allow you to work quickly and create natural variation.

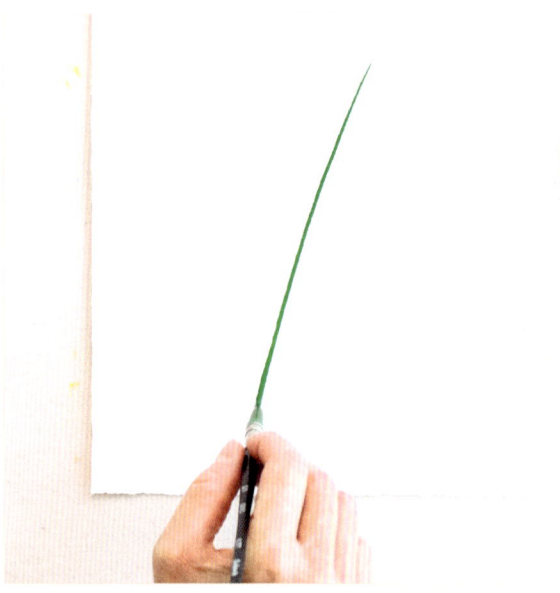

3. Central structure

Using your quill brush, paint the stem with a confident, flowing line. This provides the backbone for your composition and guides the placement of your leaflets.

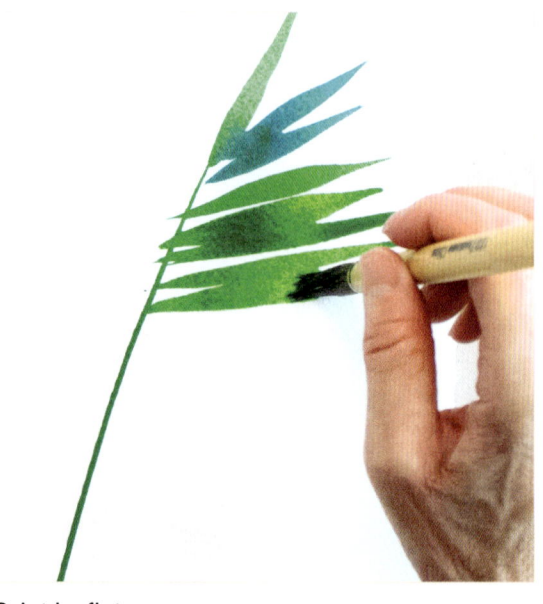

4. Paint leaflets

Switch to your bamboo calligraphy brush and begin adding individual leaflets, working from the top downward on one side. The soft bristles create distinctive edges.

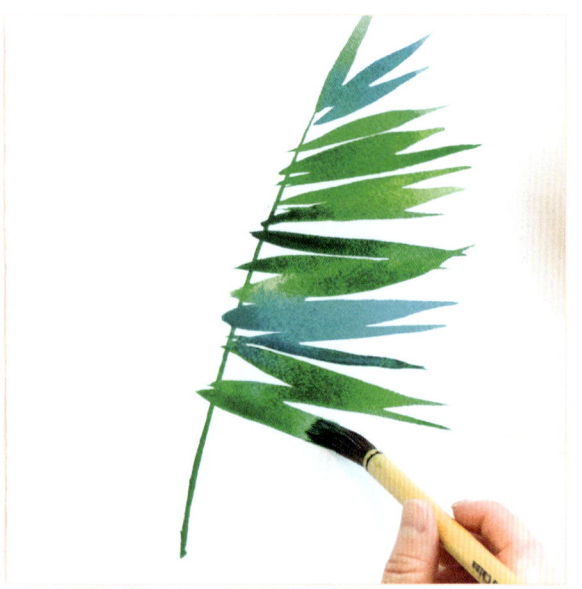

5. Build variation

Work quickly with your bamboo brush, alternating between different green mixtures for each leaflet. This faster pace, combined with the unique properties of the bamboo brush, creates interesting dry-brush effects.

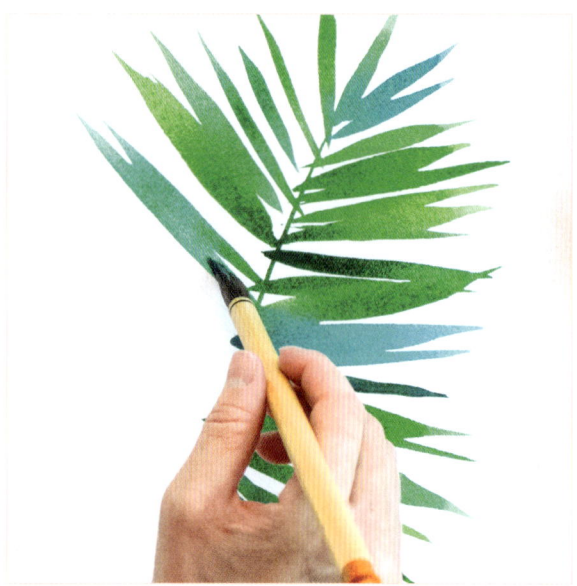

6. Repeat on the other side

When one side is complete, move on to the other, maintaining a loose symmetry. Don't worry about creating "perfect" leaflets—the irregular marks are what give the painting character. Work at a slightly faster pace than usual to maintain spontaneity.

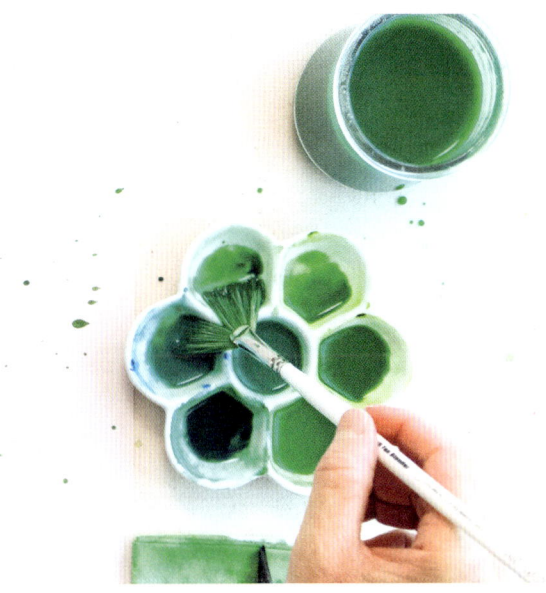

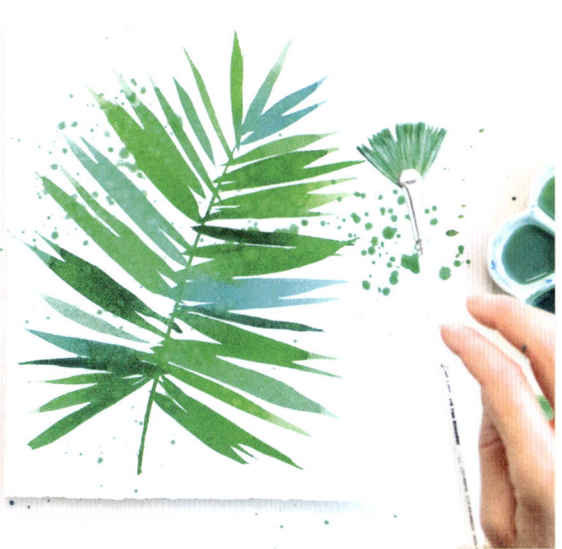

7. Add splatter

While your painting is still damp, use your fan brush to create energetic splatter effects. First dip the brush into multiple colors simultaneously.

8. Create a balanced composition

Gently tap the metal ferrule, moving the brush around to distribute splatters across your composition.

9. Final touches

Allow some final splatters to interact with wet areas for an integrated effect.

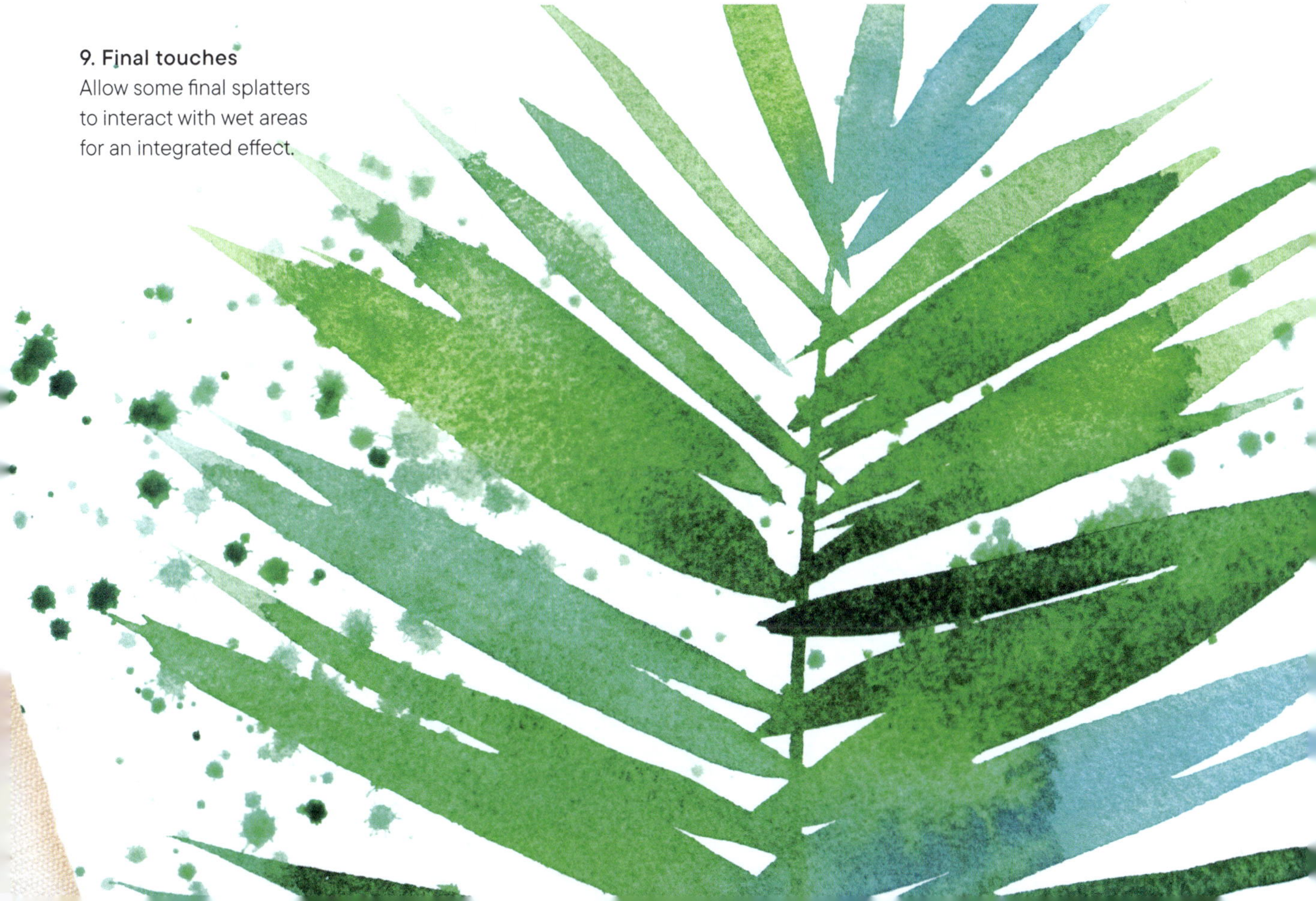

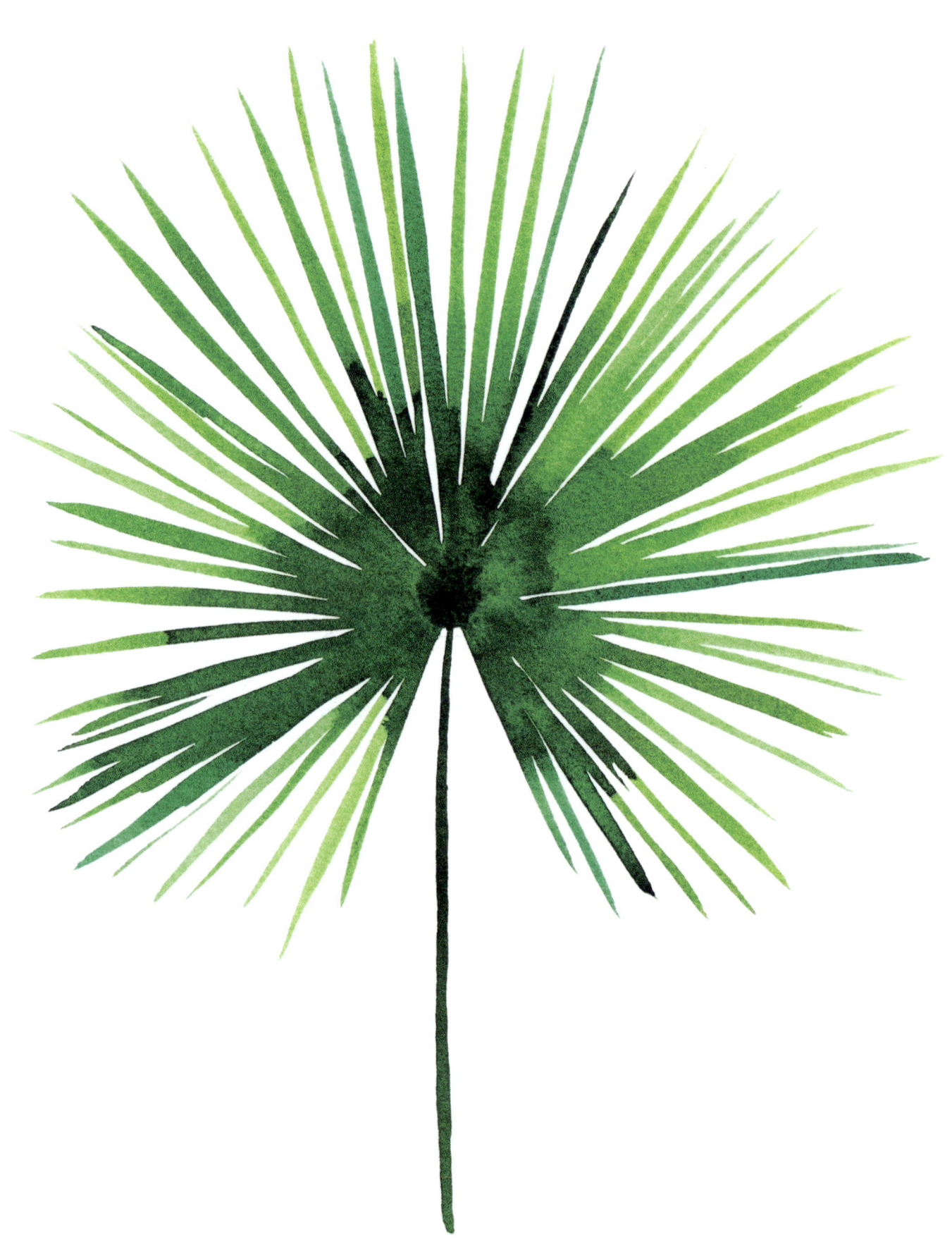

Fan Palm

This dramatic palm, with its radiating fronds, is perfect for exploring loose, expressive brushwork. Fan palms are nature's fireworks, so let your painting explode with tropical colors and energy through quick, confident brushstrokes and spontaneous color-blending techniques.

Materials

- Watercolor paper (140lb cold pressed)
- Brush: quill 3/0
- Paints: Olive Green, Sap Green, Hooker's Green, Viridian
- Pencil, eraser, palette, water container, paper towels

Radiating color bleed technique

This combines spontaneous brushwork with natural color bleeding, working outward from a central point to create an organic, flowing composition. Multiple colors blend naturally as they meet in the central reservoir.

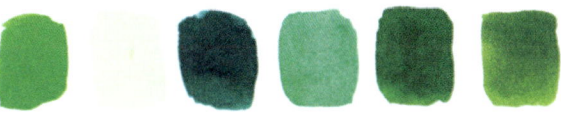

1. Sketch

Create a light sketch showing the basic stem placement and fan shape. Keep your marks minimal and loose—this technique thrives on spontaneity rather than precision.

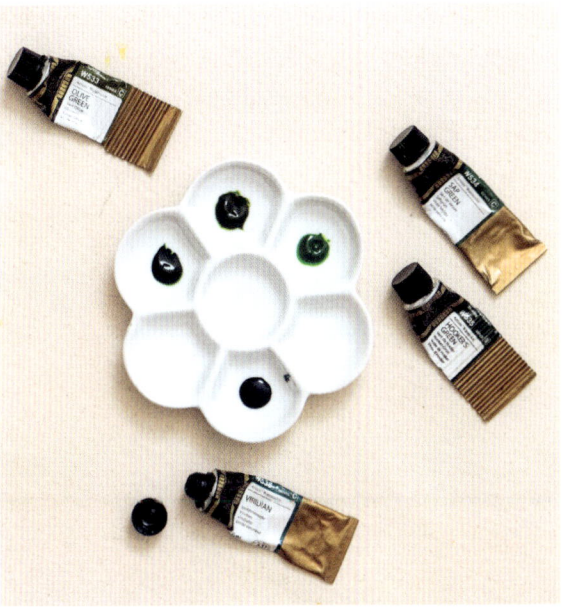

2. Mix your palette

Prepare six different washes using your four green pigments in milk consistency. These should be rich enough to appear vibrant while still allowing for natural bleeding and blending.

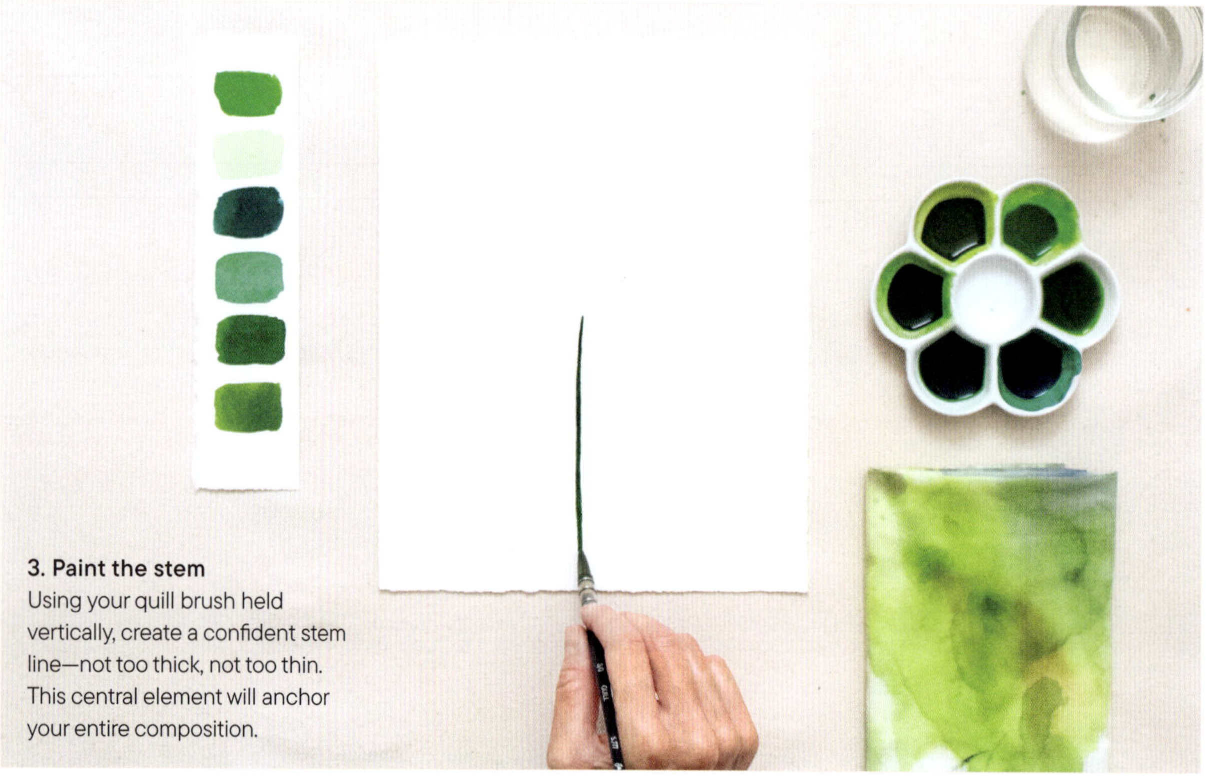

3. Paint the stem

Using your quill brush held vertically, create a confident stem line—not too thick, not too thin. This central element will anchor your entire composition.

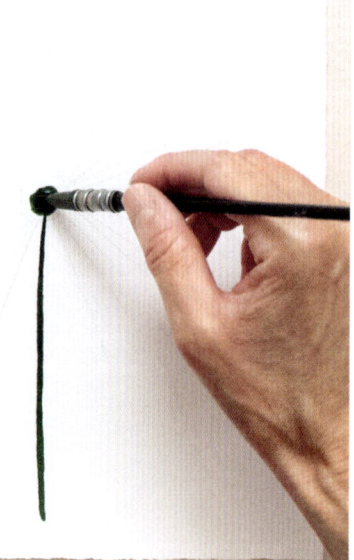

4. Create the central puddle

Load your brush with one of your darker greens and place a generous puddle of paint at the center point. This will be your color reservoir for the radiating fronds.

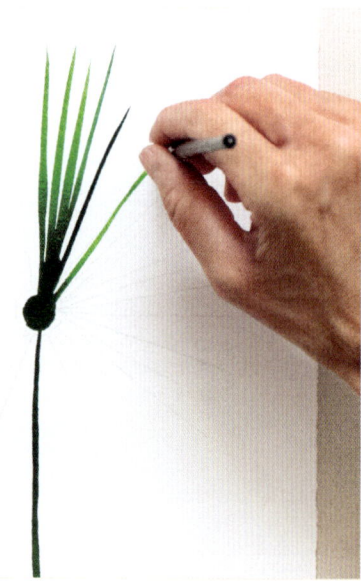

5. Paint radiating fronds

Working from the center puddle outward, draw your brush toward the edges of the paper to create individual leaflets. For every 1–3 leaflets, reload your brush with a different color, allowing natural variation and bleeding.

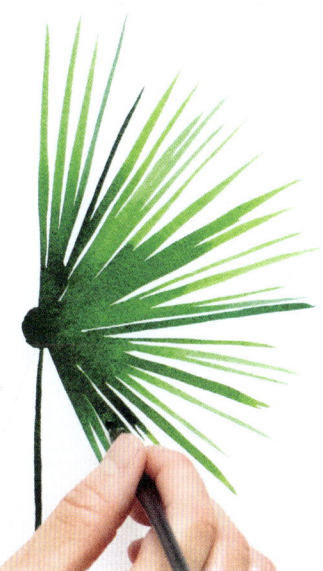

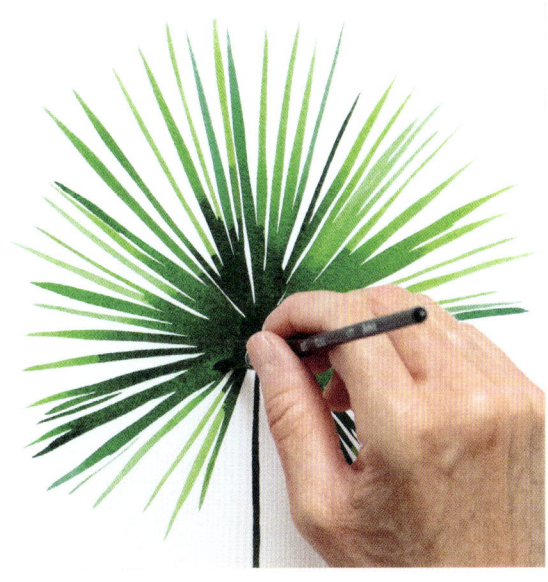

6. Build natural rhythm

Work systematically from the center top around to both sides, varying the length of your strokes for a natural, organic appearance. Allow different greens to surprise you as they appear throughout the piece.

7. Work quickly

Move your hand quickly to maintain a loose, expressive quality—slower movements create more technical-looking results. Trust the process, letting the colors flow naturally.

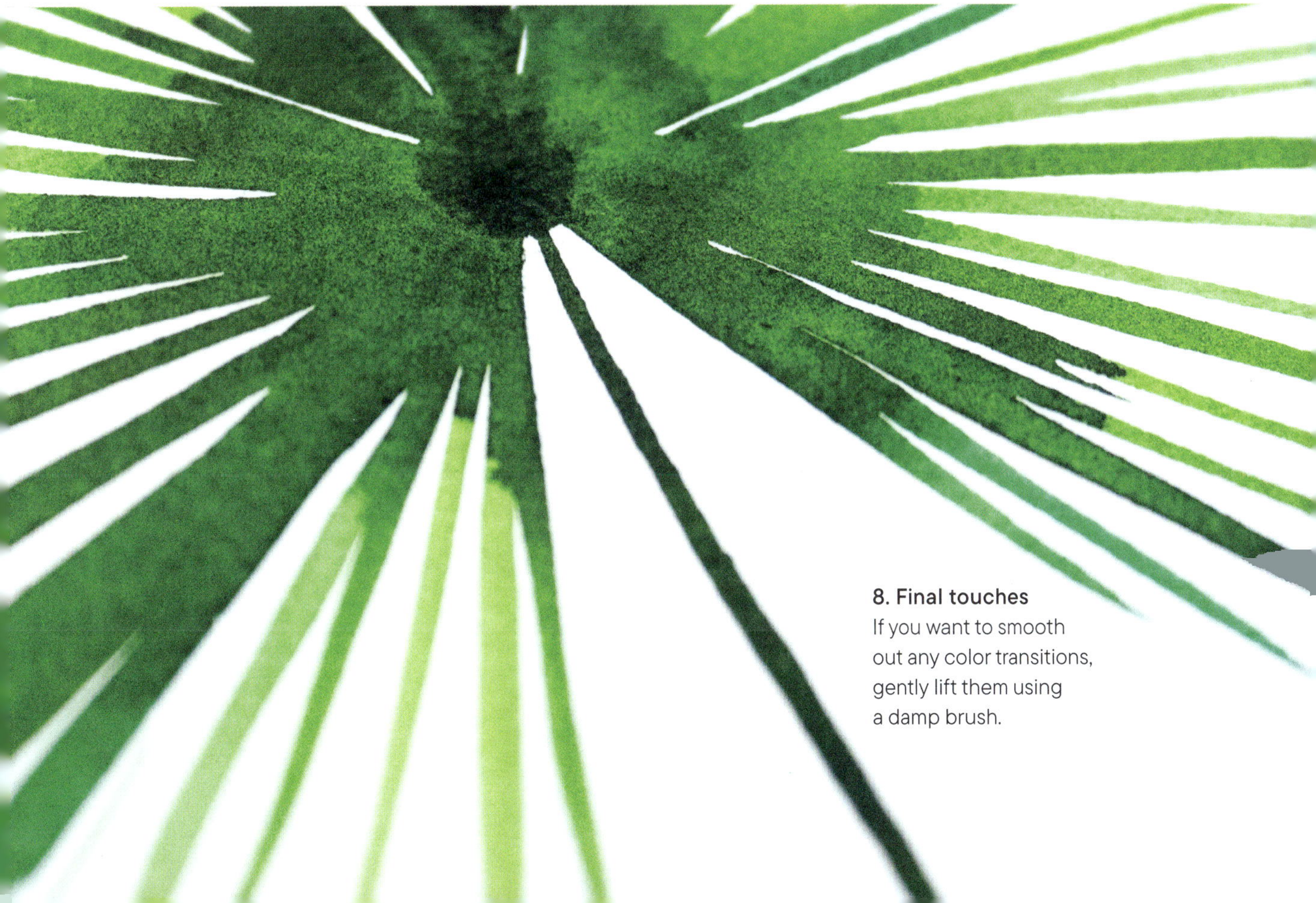

8. Final touches

If you want to smooth out any color transitions, gently lift them using a damp brush.

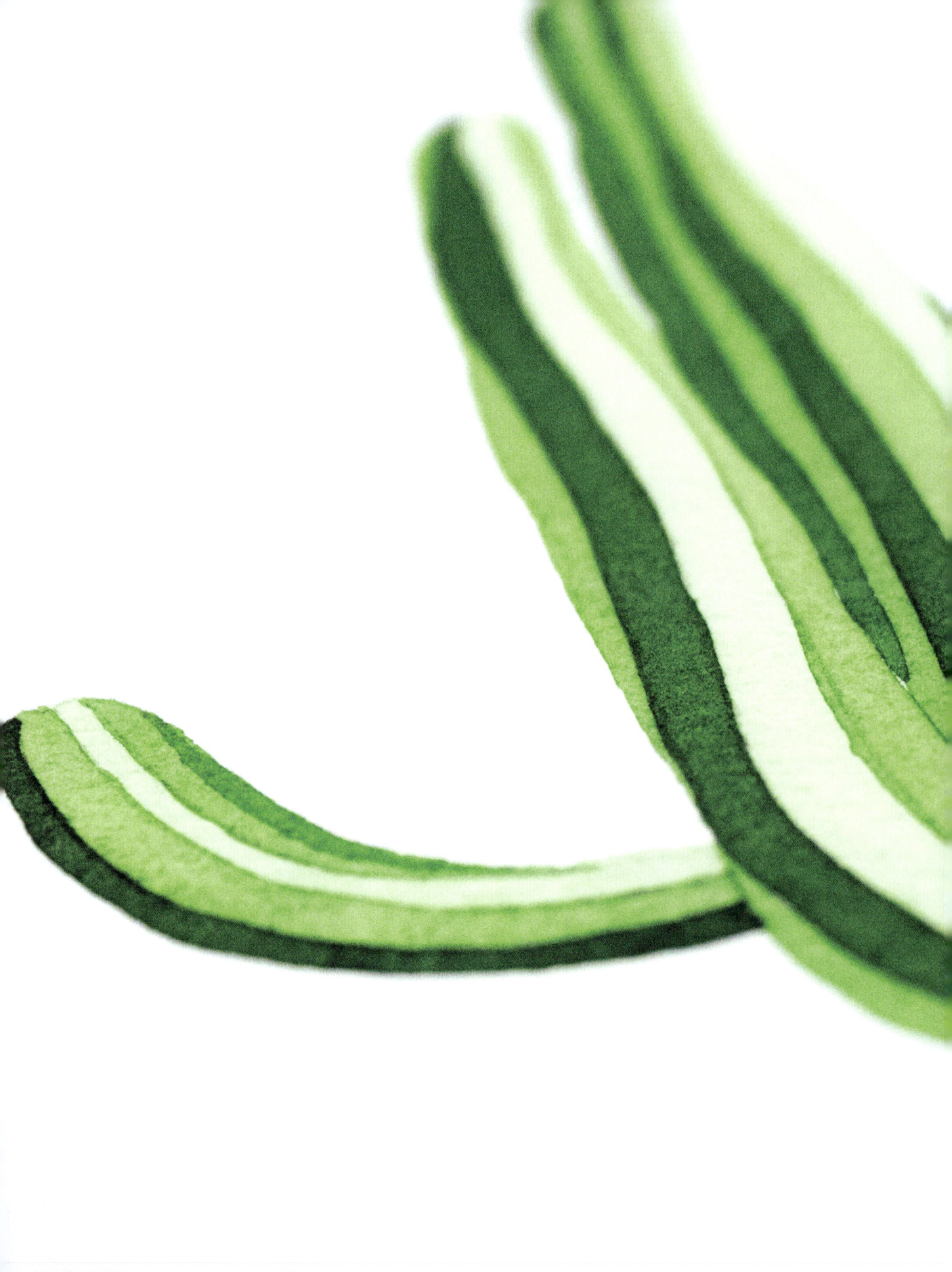

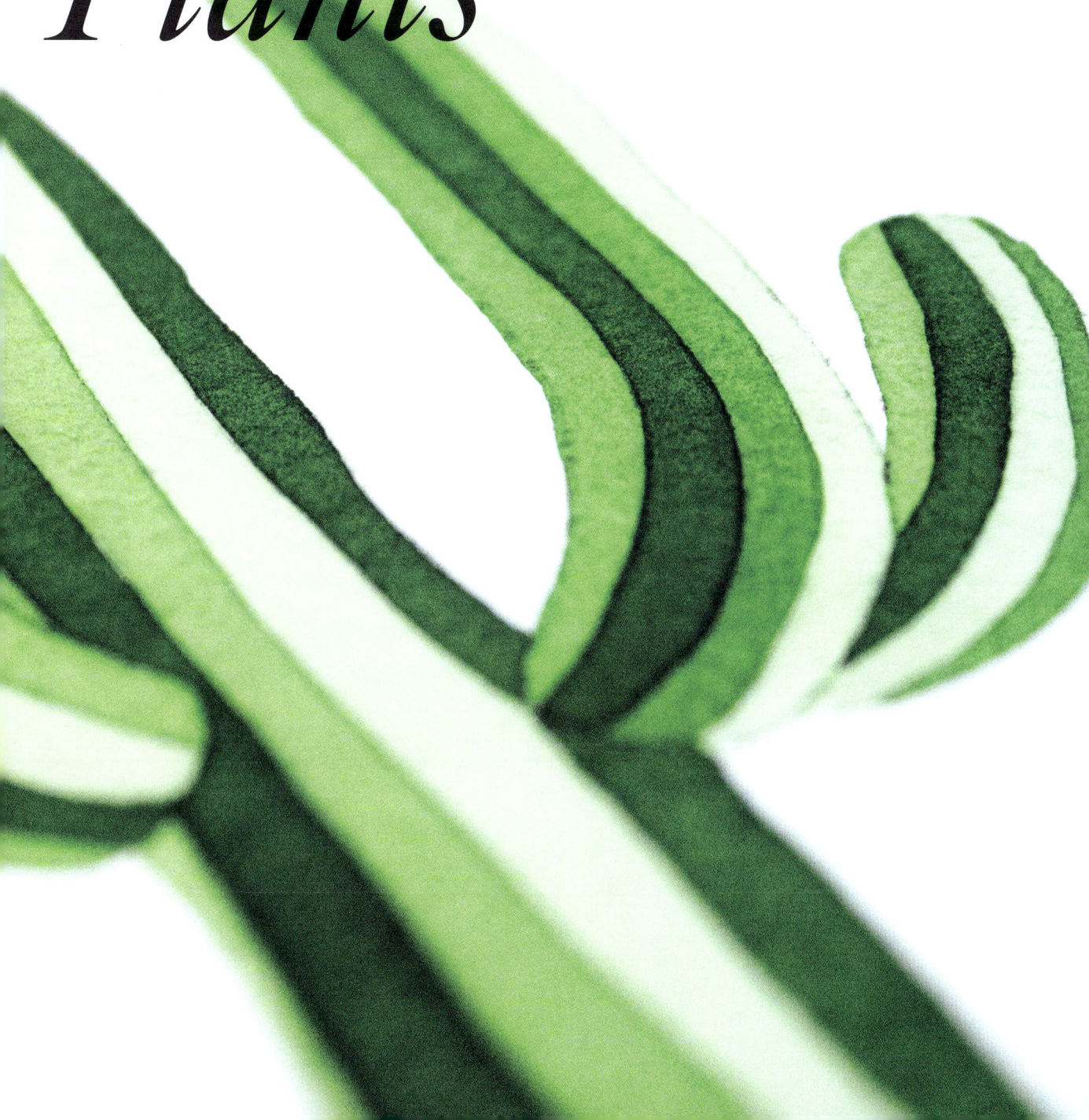

Desert
Plants

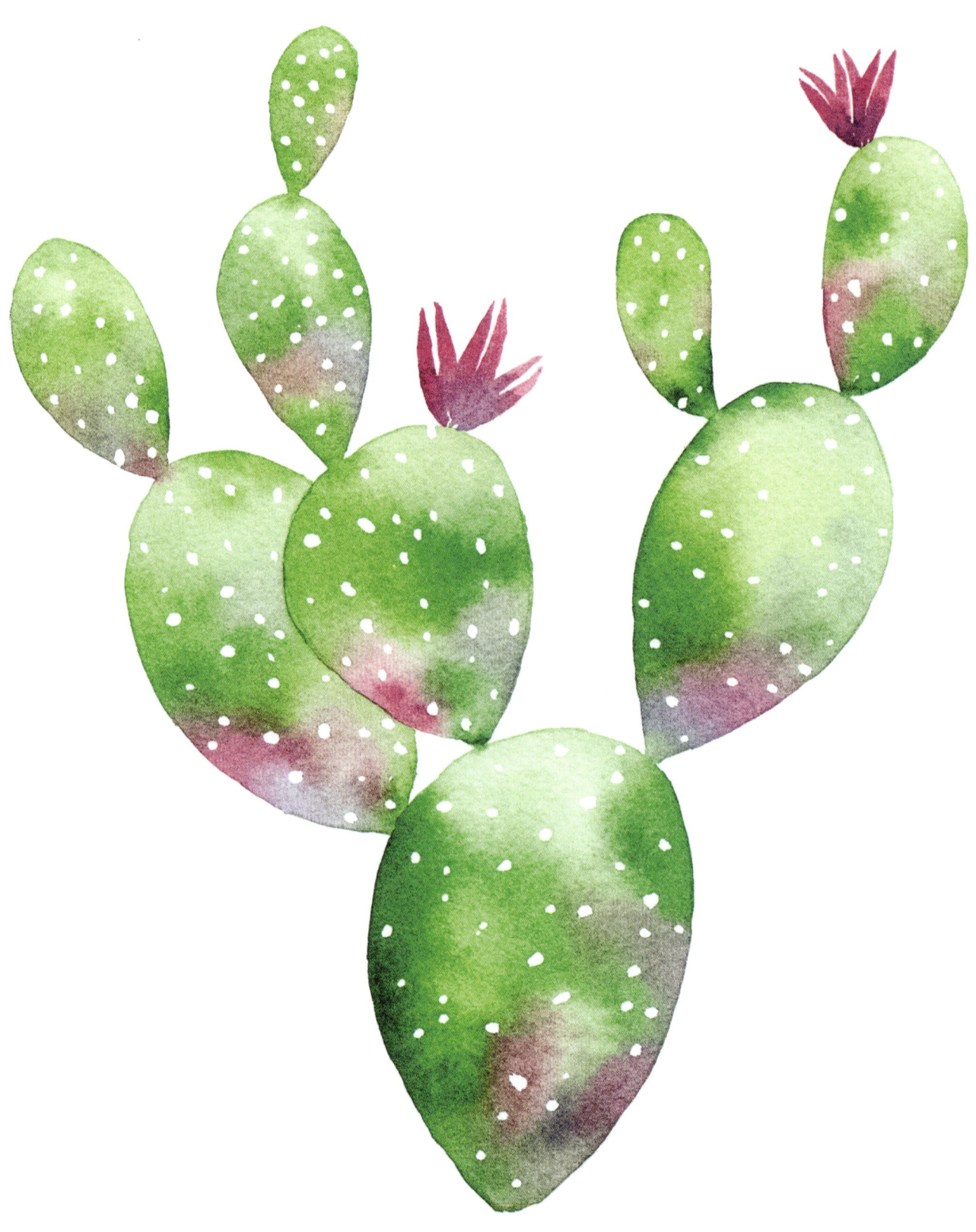

Prickly Pear

With its distinctive paddle shapes and variable colors, this cactus is great for exploring masking techniques combined with organic blending. Prickly pears survive harsh conditions, so capture their resilient beauty through natural color variations and crisp, preserved details.

Materials

- Watercolor paper (140lb cold pressed)
- Brushes: round #6, round #2, old brush for masking fluid
- Paints: Van Dyke Green, Red Violet, Sap Green, Viridian
- Masking fluid, pencil, eraser, palette, water container, paper towels, clean cloth

Masking & color variation technique

This combines masking fluid to preserve patterning alongside natural color variation painting. The masking creates crisp white details while the colors capture the authentic desert cactus.

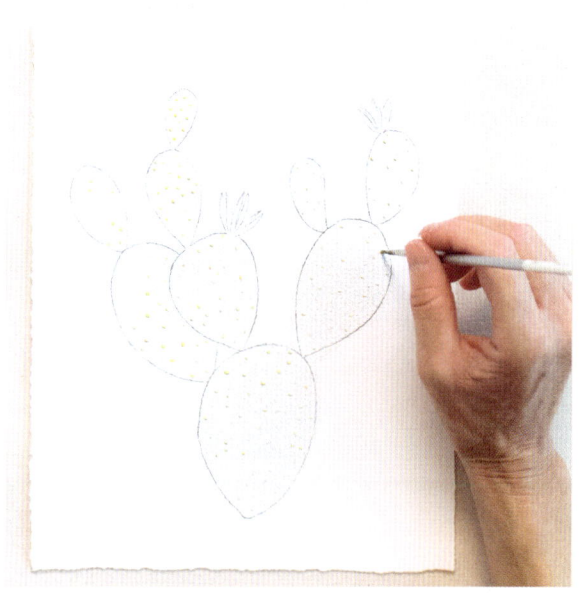

1. Sketch and mask

Create a light outline of overlapping paddle shapes with dots marking the areoles (spine clusters). Using an old brush, apply masking fluid to preserve these white dots, allowing it to dry completely before proceeding.

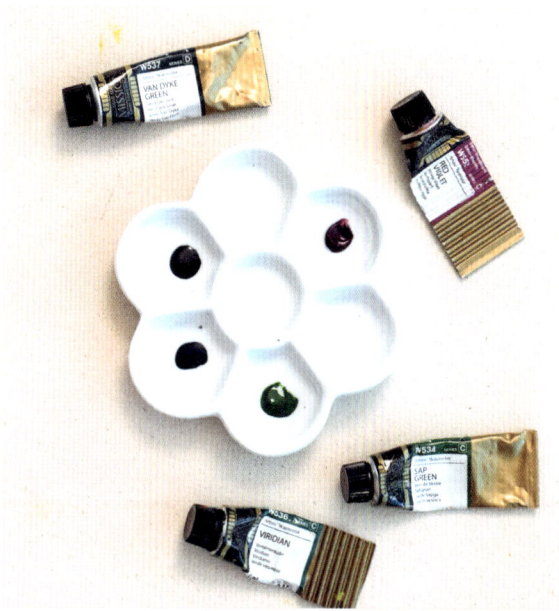

2. Mix your palette

Prepare several green washes ranging from bright Sap Green to darker Van Dyke Green. Also prepare a Red Violet, and mix a darker purple by combining Van Dyke Green with Red Violet.

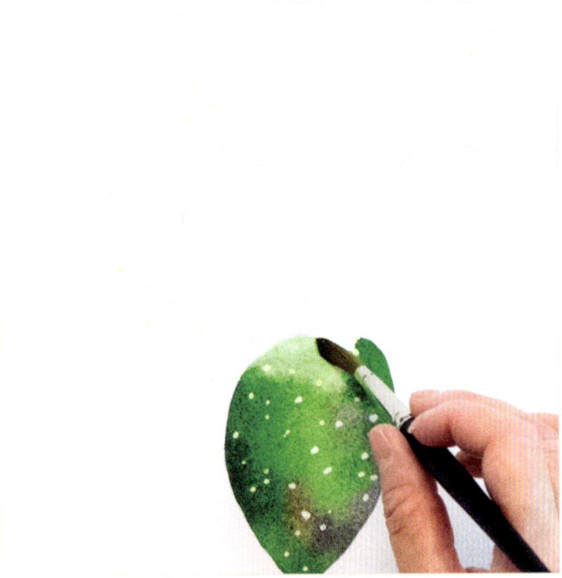

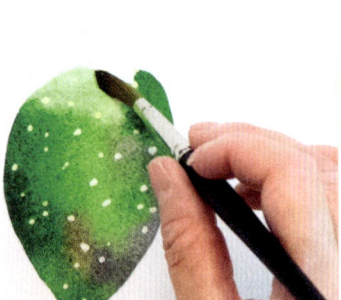

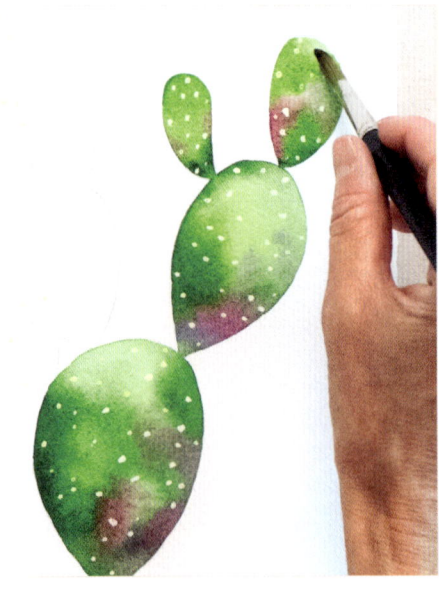

3. Paint base paddles

Start with the bottom paddles, working from Sap Green to Van Dyke Green using your #6 brush. Add highlights with clean water, and touches of Red Violet and purple mix.

4. Build overlapping forms

Continue working upward, ensuring underlying paddles are completely dry before adding overlapping sections.

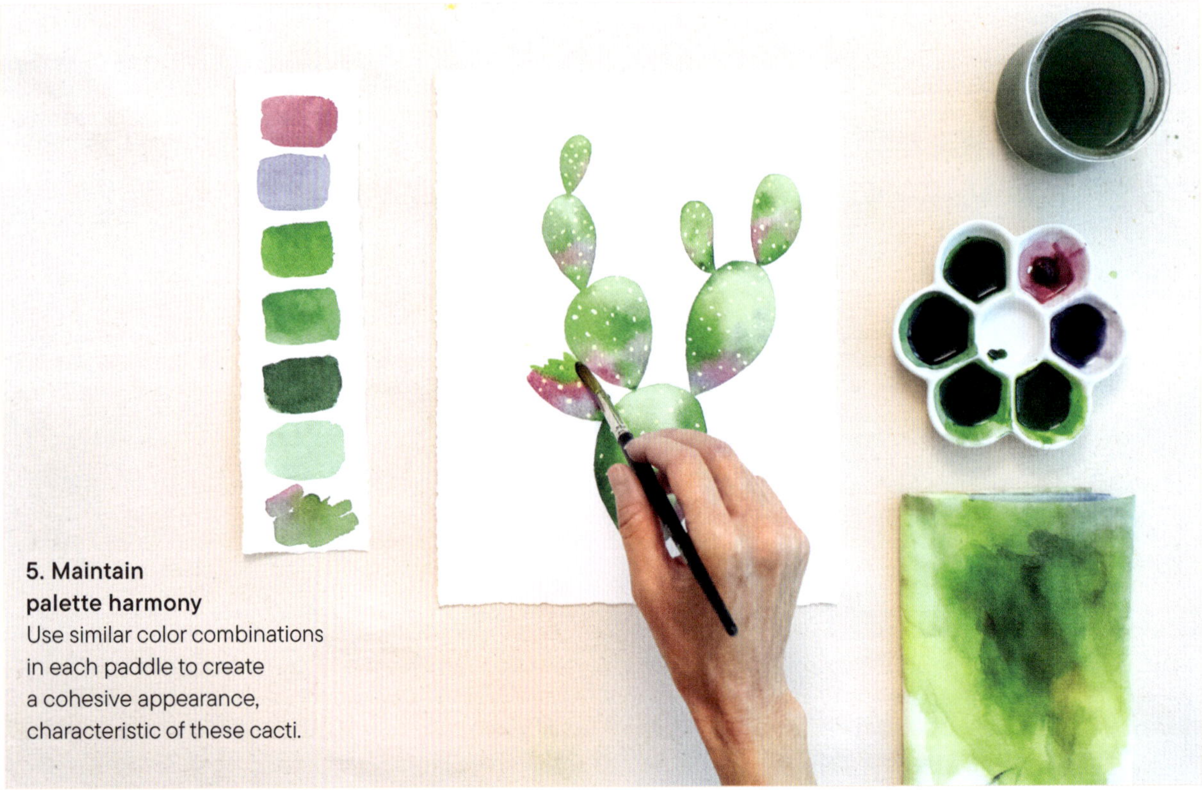

5. Maintain palette harmony

Use similar color combinations in each paddle to create a cohesive appearance, characteristic of these cacti.

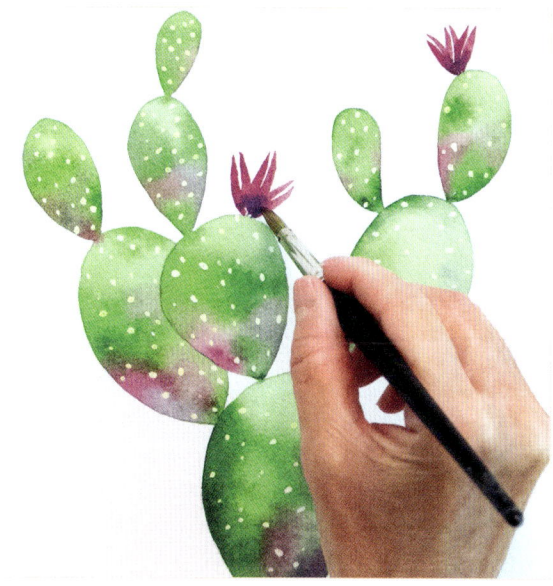

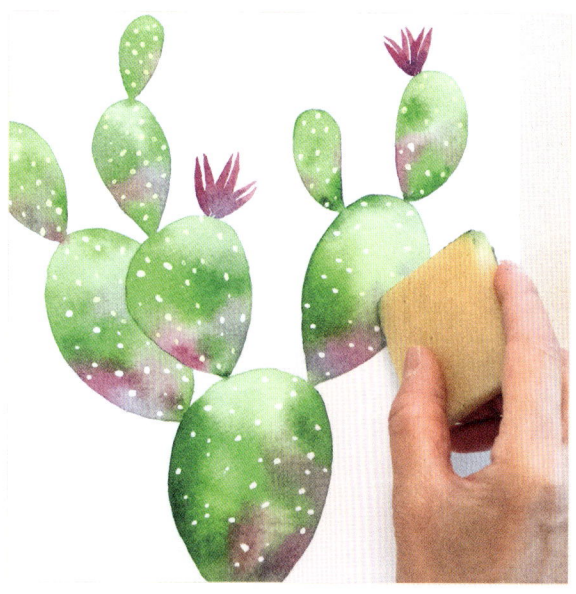

6. Add blooms

With your #2 bush, paint simplified cactus flowers using Red Violet, working from petal tips inward. Add darker purple to flower bases for depth, echoing the purple in the paddle segments.

7. Remove masking fluid

Once the painting is completely dry, carefully remove masking fluid by pressing gently with your finger or eraser. Work slowly to avoid disturbing the surrounding pigment.

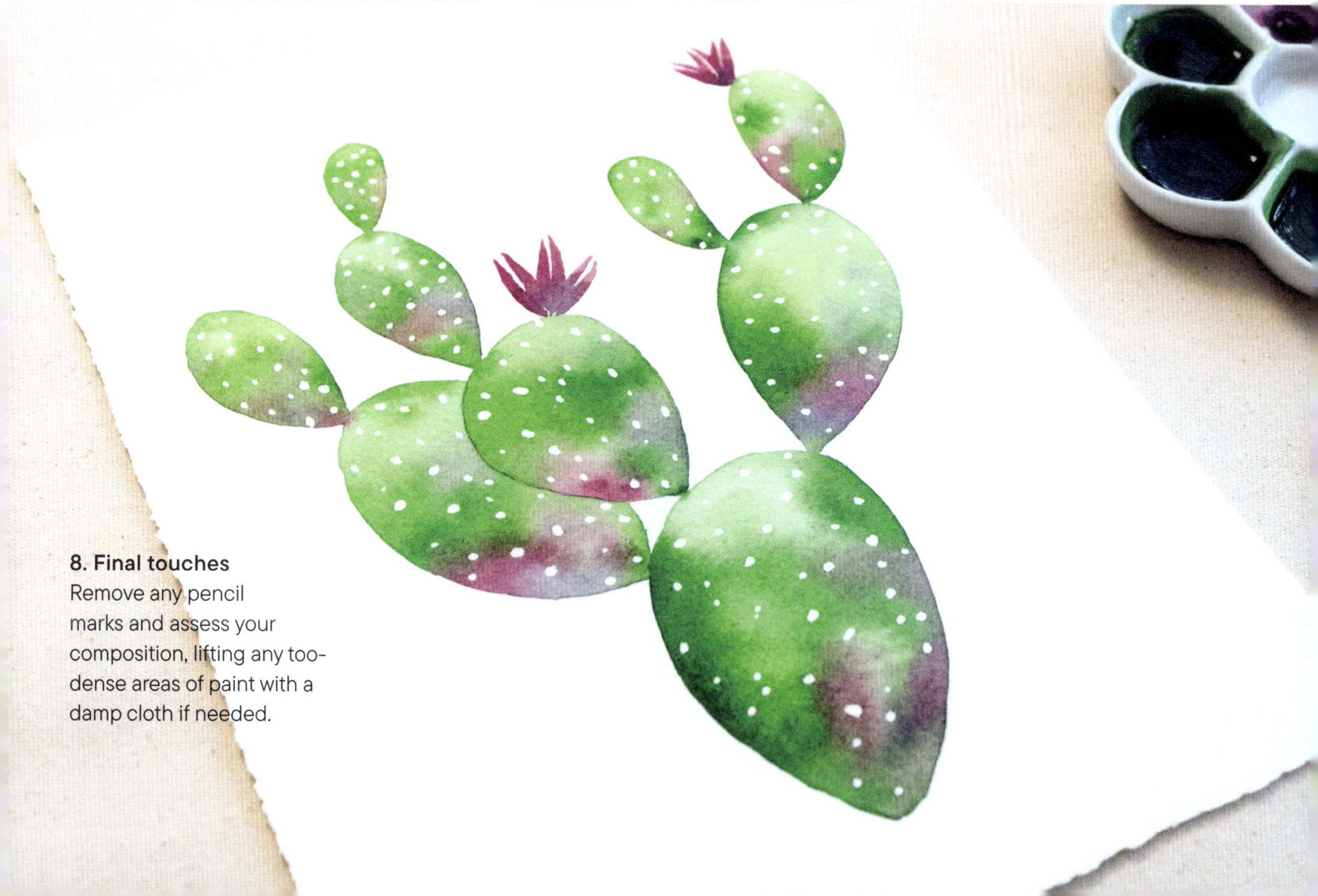

8. Final touches

Remove any pencil marks and assess your composition, lifting any too-dense areas of paint with a damp cloth if needed.

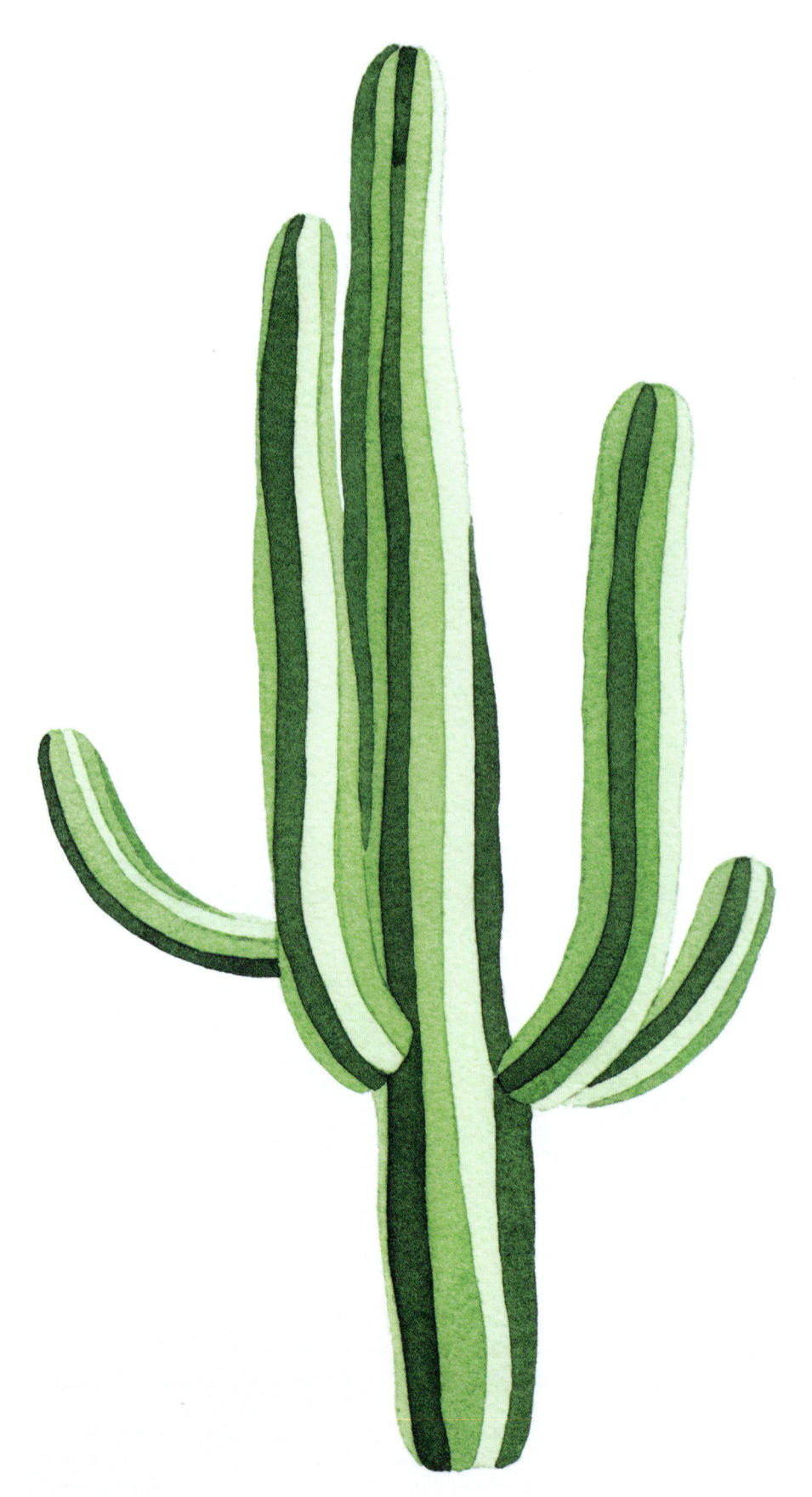

Saguaro Cactus

With its towering presence and distinctive arms, this iconic cactus is good for exploring graphic, linear techniques. Focus on its natural architectural quality and celebrate this structural elegance with clean, segmented strokes.

Materials

- Watercolor paper (140lb cold pressed)
- Brush: round #4
- Paints: Sap Green, Hooker's Green, Van Dyke Green
- Pencil, soft eraser, palette, water container, tissue, paper towels, clean cloth

Segmented linework technique

This creates a striking, graphic look through deliberate placement of varied wash values in adjacent linear segments. The careful control of edges produces a modern, clean aesthetic.

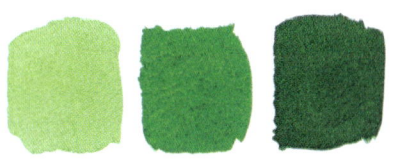

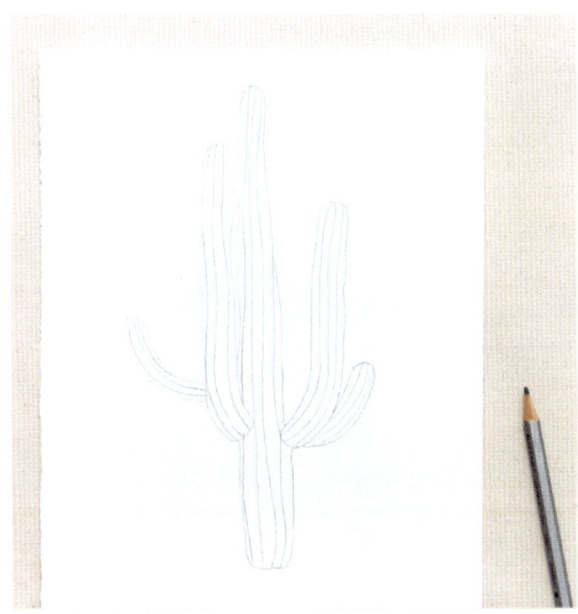

1. Sketch

Create a clear outline, including the main trunk and characteristic arms. Add the interior rib details as these will be a guide for your paint application. Keep your lines clean and deliberate.

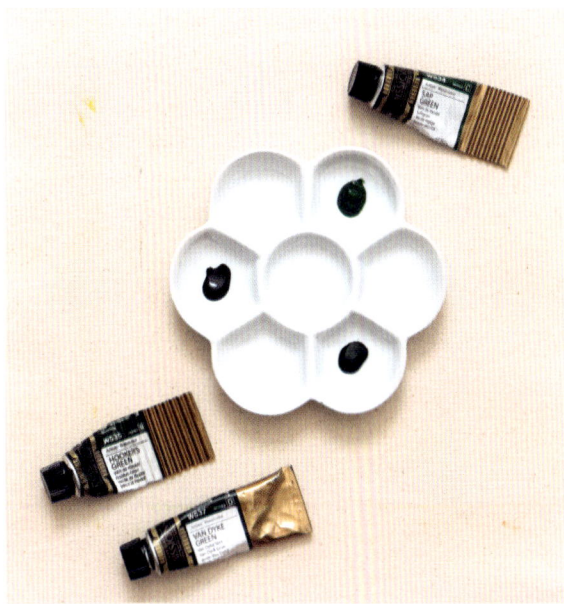

2. Mix your palette

Prepare several variations of green washes using Sap Green, Hooker's Green, and Van Dyke Green. Create a spectrum from very light to dark values for maximum visual interest.

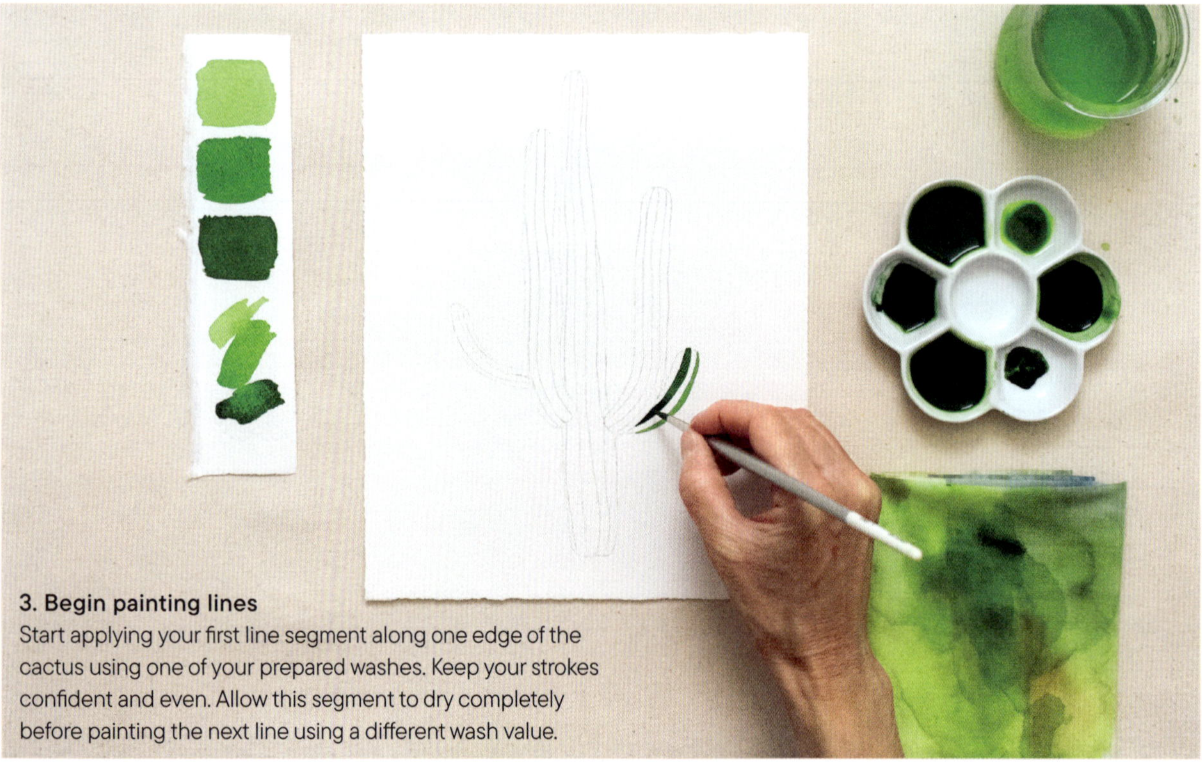

3. Begin painting lines

Start applying your first line segment along one edge of the cactus using one of your prepared washes. Keep your strokes confident and even. Allow this segment to dry completely before painting the next line using a different wash value.

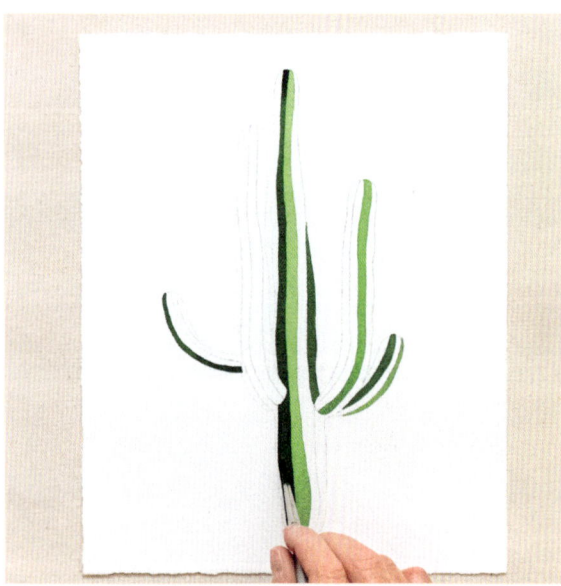

4. Build adjacent lines

Continue alternating between lighter and darker greens, creating a striped effect across the cactus. Keep your brush properly loaded with paint to maintain even line quality.

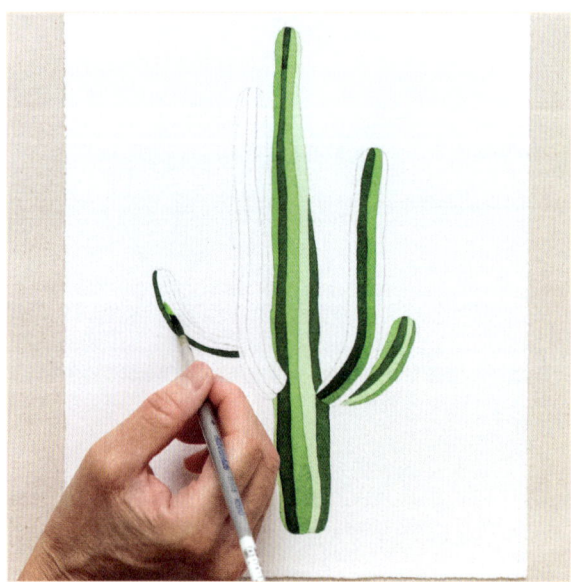

5. Pay attention to placement

Ensure each segment dries before painting neighboring lines and use minimal water to avoid color bleeding. If color does accidentally stray, blot it immediately with the edge of a tissue; if it has dried, try gently lifting it with a damp edge of a cloth.

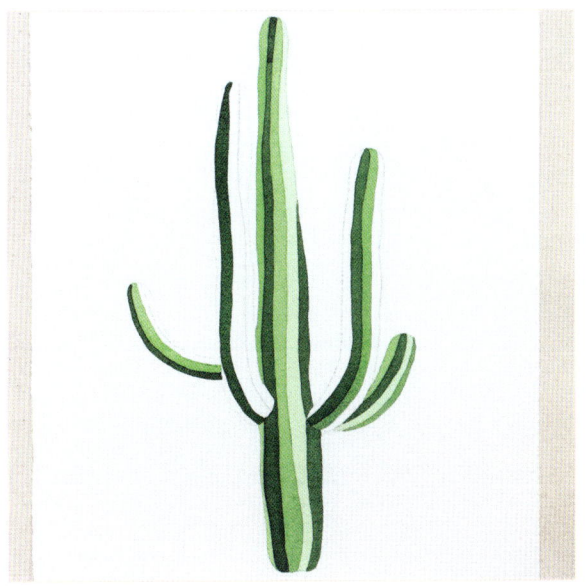

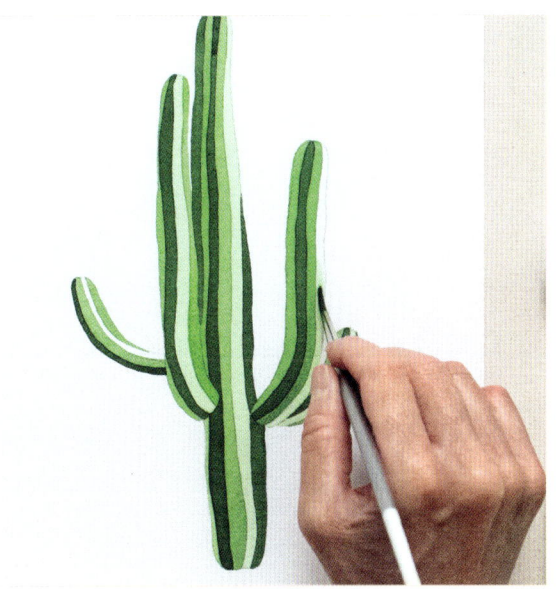

6. Create depth

Use strategic placement of darker and lighter washes to suggest the roundness of the cactus: darker segments can appear to recede while lighter ones come forward.

7. Play with color shifts

Vary your wash values intentionally for maximum visual impact. Darker tones on one side of each segment can suggest light direction and form.

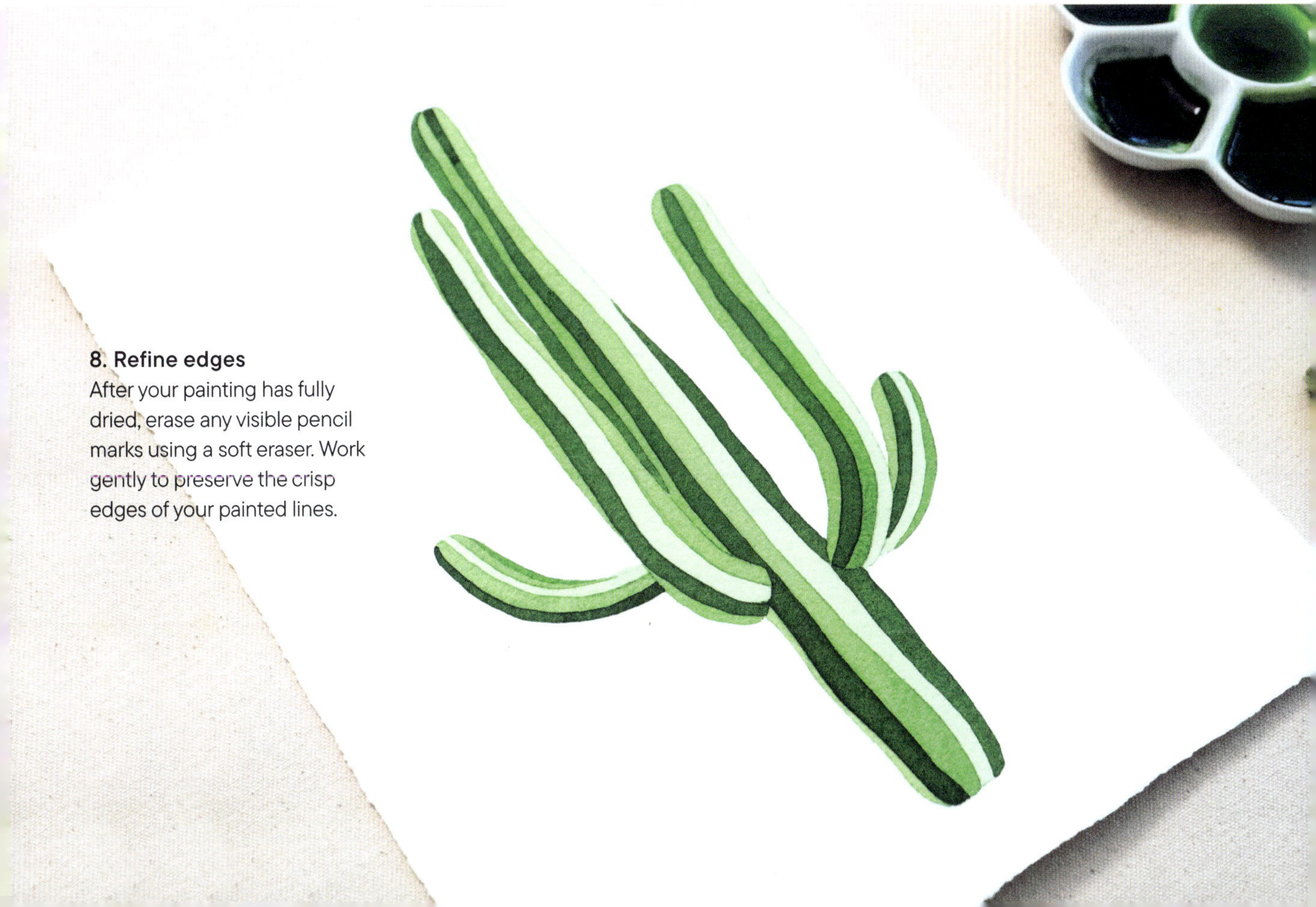

8. Refine edges

After your painting has fully dried, erase any visible pencil marks using a soft eraser. Work gently to preserve the crisp edges of your painted lines.

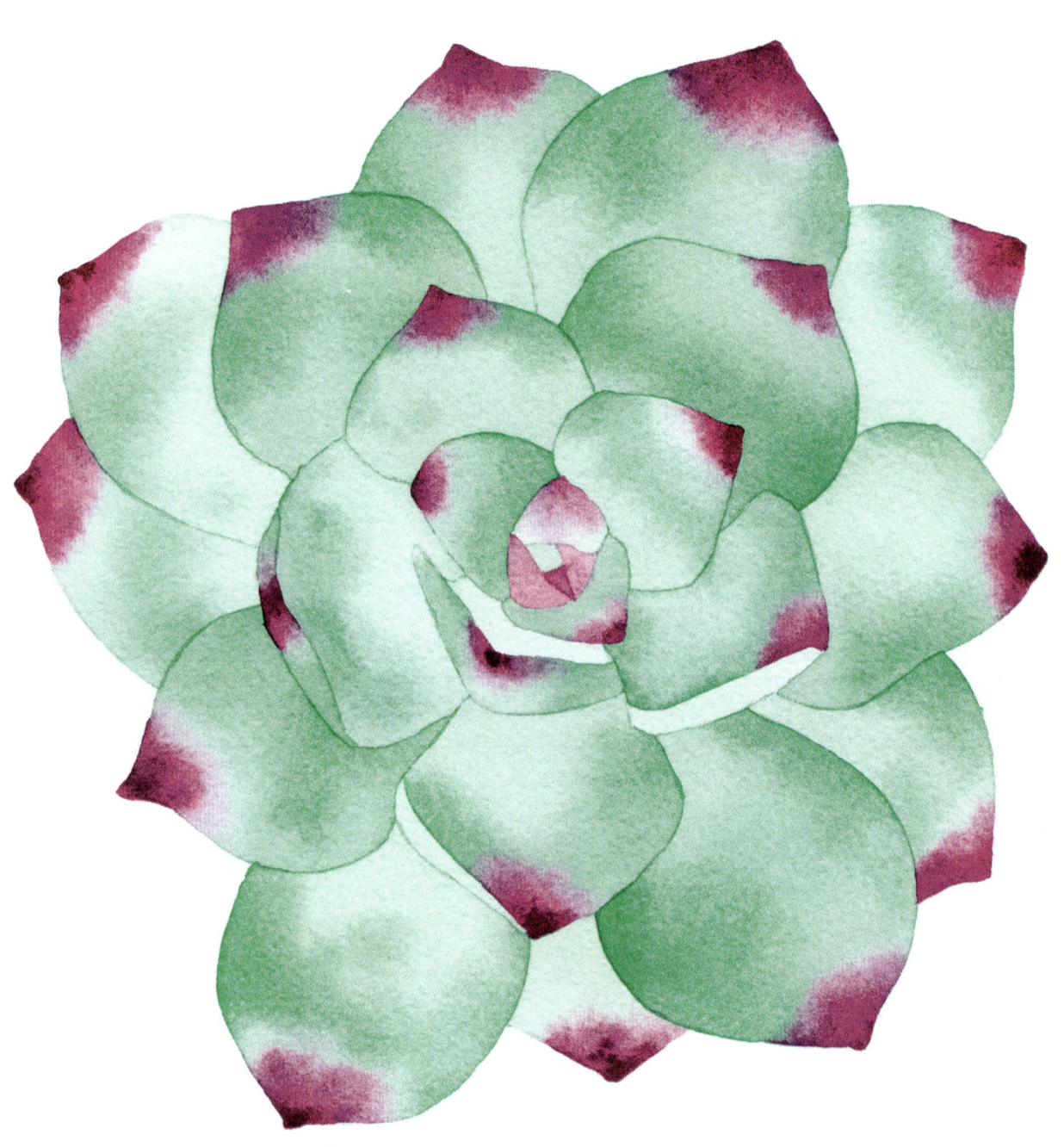

Echeveria

The echeveria's perfect spiral of leaves is a mesmerizing study in form and color transitions. These plants have a mathematical beauty, so let your systematic approach honor this natural precision while the controlled color bleeds add organic rhythm.

Materials

- Watercolor paper (140lb cold pressed)
- Brush: round #8
- Paints: Sap Green, Viridian, Red Violet, Jaune Brilliant No. 2
- Pencil, eraser, palette, two water containers, paper towels

Controlled color bleed technique

This utilizes precise application to create deliberate bleeds between colors. Manage water content and pigment load (see p.40) to determine exactly how much colors will interact while maintaining distinct boundaries.

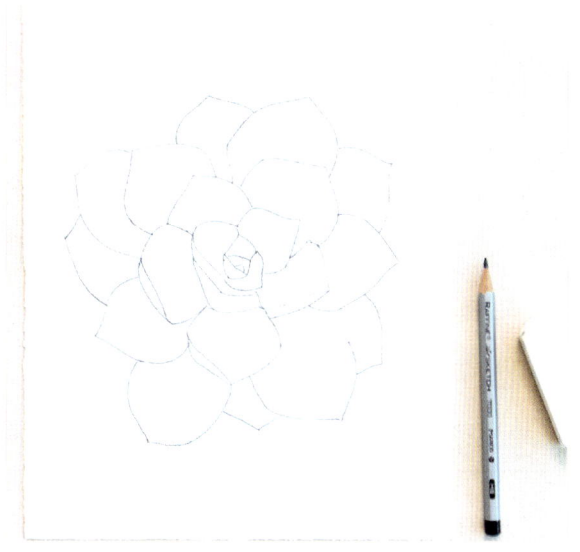

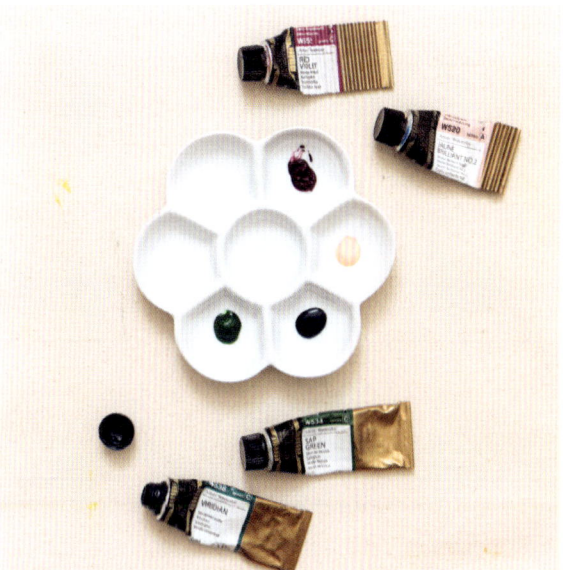

1. Sketch

Create a detailed spiral outline of your echeveria, marking each individual leaf shape. Unlike with more expressive techniques, this sketch should be fairly precise as it will guide your careful color application.

2. Prepare your palette

Mix Jaune Brilliant No. 2, Sap Green, and Viridian to create a mint-aqua base for the leaves. Prepare several variations of this in different intensities. Keep your Red Violet separate, in a rich, cream consistency. Keep separate water jars for warm and cool colors to prevent muddying.

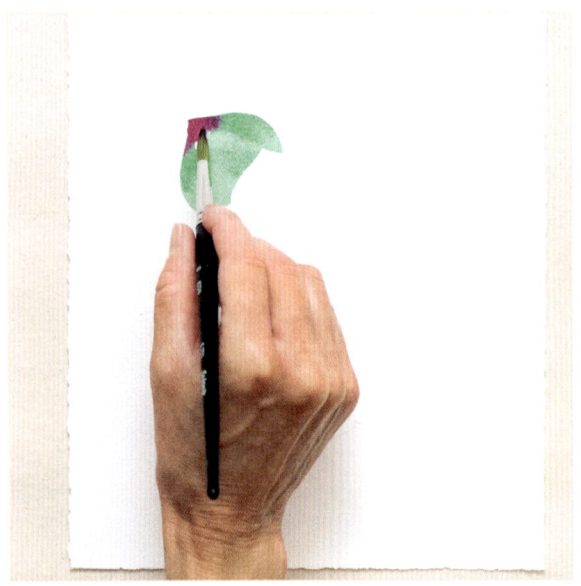

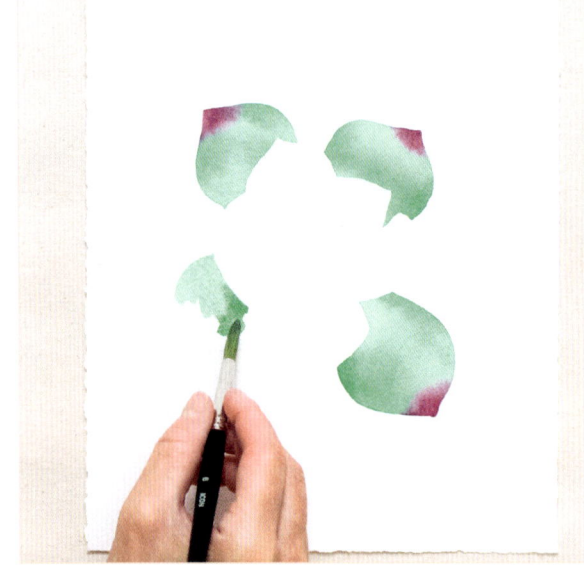

3. Begin the first leaf

Start with one outer leaf, applying your mint-aqua base. While the paint is still wet, carefully touch Red Violet to the tip of the leaf, allowing a controlled amount to bleed into the green.

4. Build systematically

Allow your first leaf to dry completely before painting adjacent leaves. Work in a methodical circular pattern (clockwise or counterclockwise), painting one leaf at a time and letting each dry before moving on to its neighbor.

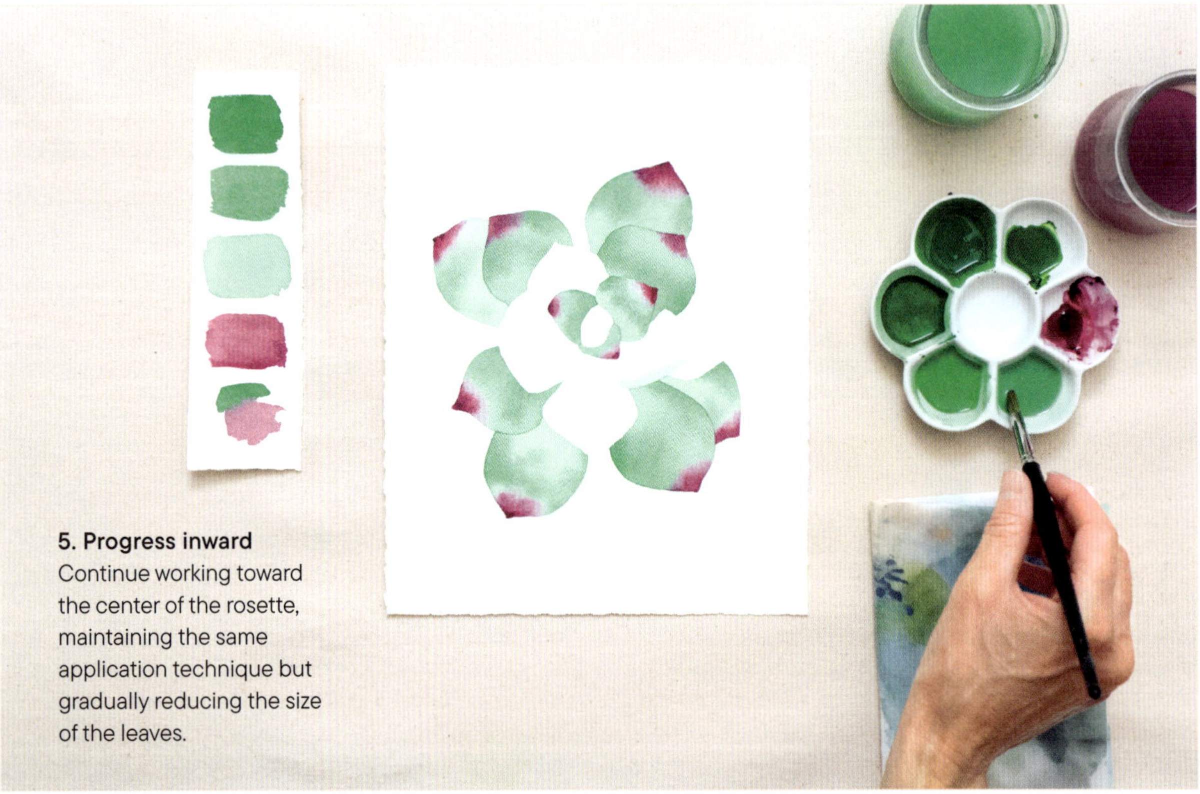

5. Progress inward

Continue working toward the center of the rosette, maintaining the same application technique but gradually reducing the size of the leaves.

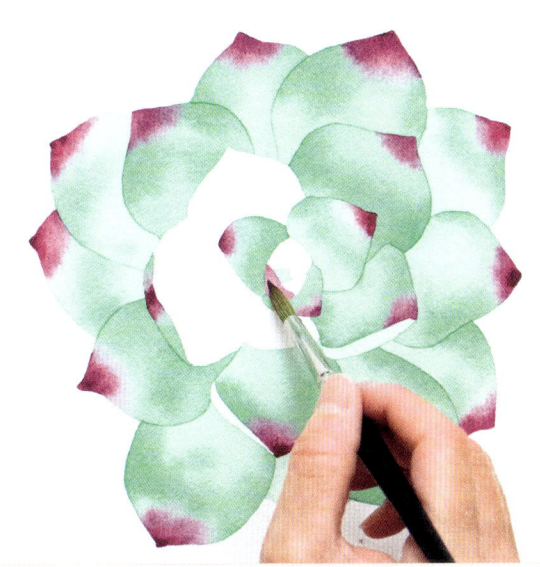

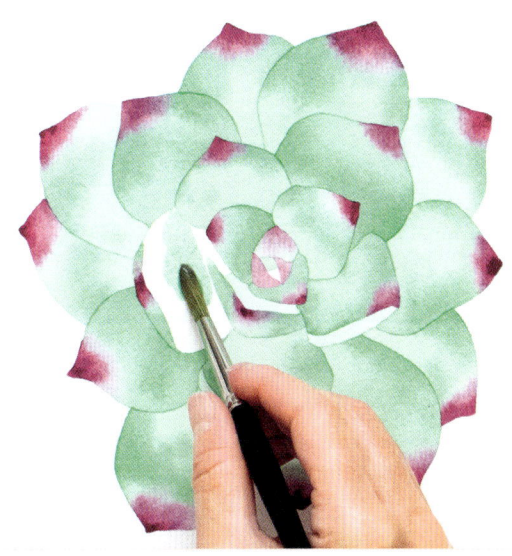

6. Central area
For the smallest central leaves, use predominantly Red Violet to create a rich focal point.

7. Focus on the spiral
Pay attention to the spiral pattern of the leaf arrangement for authentic succulent form, and create varying intensity in your color transitions throughout the rosette.

8. Final touches
Once dry, assess your painting and refine to enhance definition between leaves or strengthen color transitions.

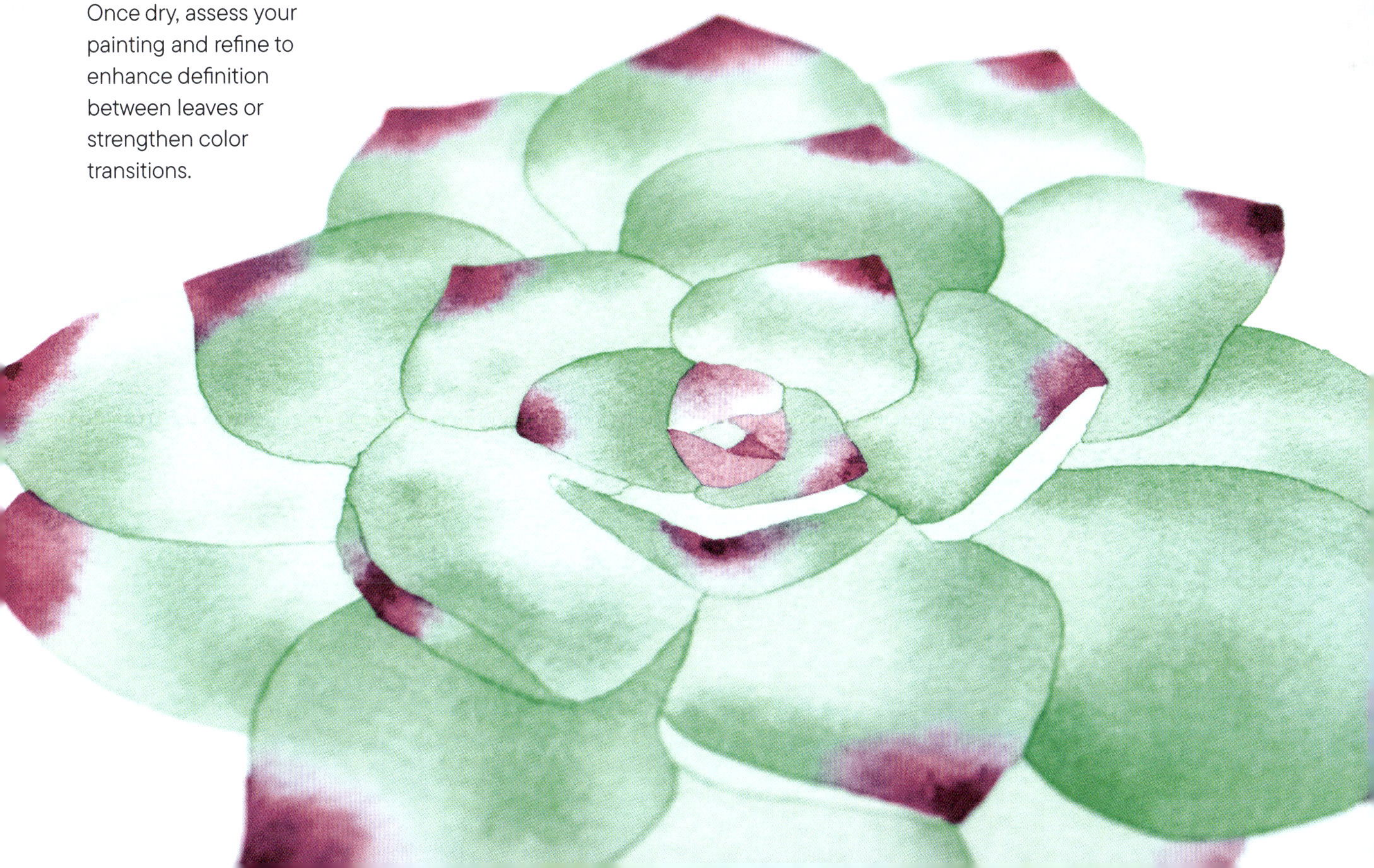

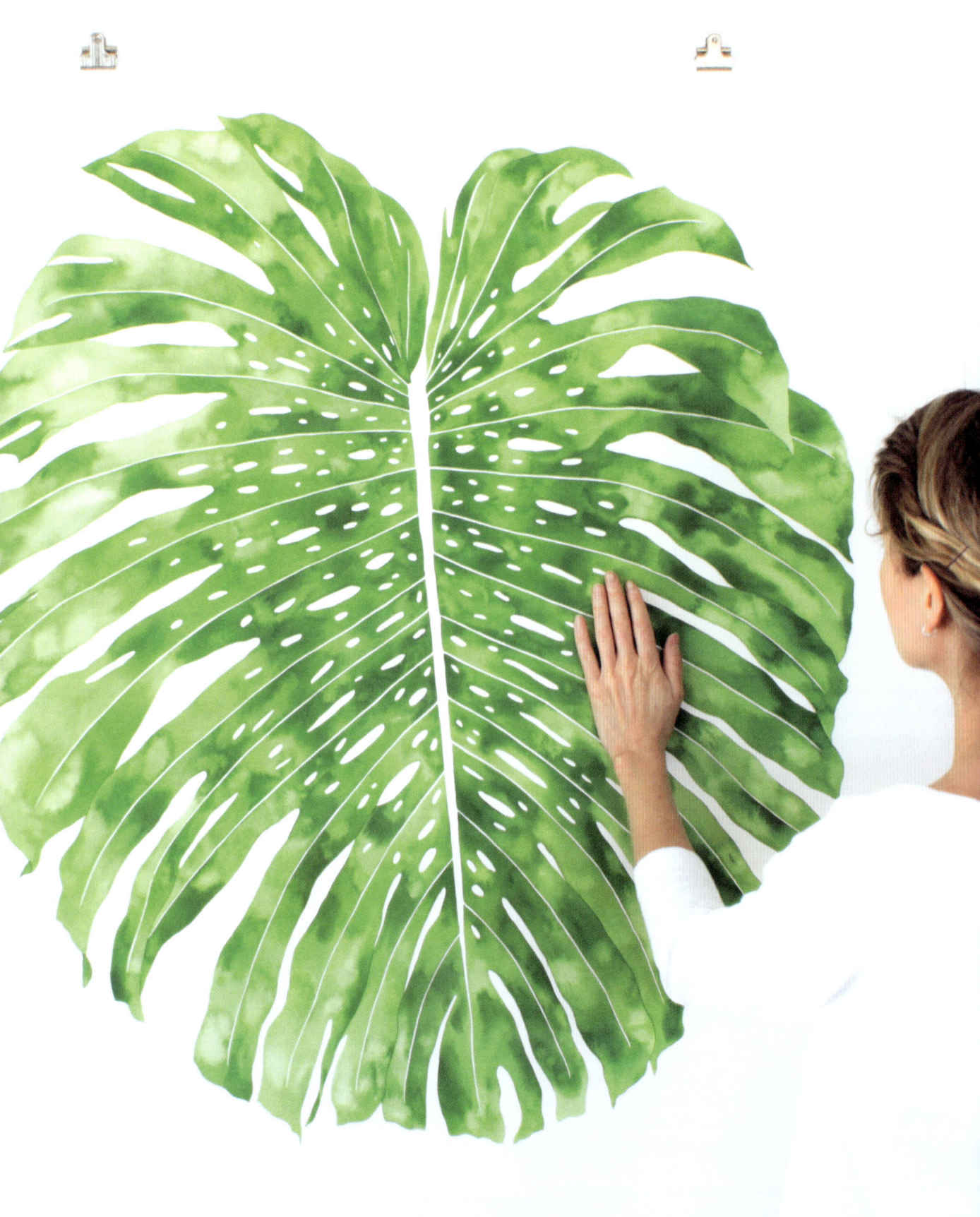

Continuing Your Botanical Watercolor Journey

This book has equipped you with a range of essential techniques, from color theory to specialized methods like gradient layering and controlled color bleeding. But your botanical watercolor exploration has only just begun.

The skills you have learned provide a foundation for producing botanical watercolors, but the real adventure lies in developing your personal artistic style. This will evolve as you progress on your journey, but the following strategies can help you along the way.

Practice daily or weekly goals

Consistent practice transforms techniques into intuitive skills. Rather than overwhelming yourself with ambitious projects, establish sustainable routines that build confidence gradually.

Smart strategies

Dedicate 15–20 minutes daily to focused botanical practice, painting a single leaf using delicate gradients or exploring color mixing with three pigments. Small, consistent efforts compound into significant improvement.

Weekly goals work well for larger projects, for example:

- Monday: brushwork techniques such as stippling and dry brush.
- Wednesday: color exploration using harmony principles.
- Friday: practice specialized methods like radiating color bleeds.

Structured progression

Try setting a timetable to progress particular techniques, for example:

Weeks 1–2: foundation building with basic washes and brush control.

Weeks 3–4: color exploration and mixing new combinations.

Weeks 5–6: technique integration, combining methods in small studies.

Weeks 7–8: personal style development with unique interpretations.

Progress isn't always linear. Difficult days often precede breakthroughs, and "failed" paintings teach valuable lessons about water control and timing. This is also when the "happy accidents" appear. Keep a practice journal documenting successful techniques and color combinations.

Expanding Your Practice

Throughout this book we've covered flowers, leaves, and tropical and desert plants, but the plant kingdom offers endless variety. Consider exploring fungi, aquatic plants, and seasonal documentation of the same location throughout a whole year. Each new subject will challenge you to adapt learned techniques.

As your confidence grows, experiment with combining techniques—layer controlled color bleeding with expressive brushwork or combine masking with wet-on-wet approaches. Push boundaries by asking "what if" questions about each method.

Building a community

Connect with other artists through local groups, online communities, or outdoor painting sessions. Sharing your work and receiving feedback accelerates learning, and teaching others can also deepen your own understanding of techniques.

Developing your voice

The techniques in this book are tools, not rules. As you become comfortable with fundamentals, make intentional choices about interpreting botanical subjects uniquely. Perhaps you're drawn to bold, graphic approaches like our segmented cactus work, or the soft, flowing methods from our rose studies. Your artistic voice emerges through hundreds of small decisions: color preferences, detail levels, brushwork style, and emotional expression.

Moving forward

Consider how your work might serve purposes beyond personal enjoyment—such as giftable art and cards, garden journals, or documenting local flora. Your paintings become both artistic expressions and botanical records.

Remember that every accomplished botanical artist began with curiosity, basic materials, and a desire to capture the beauty of the natural world. Be patient with yourself as your skills develop, and celebrate small victories: your first perfect wet-on-wet bloom, intuitive color mixing, or looking at a finished painting and thinking, "I created that." Every piece you produce is a celebration of nature's beauty. Whether it's the morning light on a single leaf or the vibrant energy of a flower garden, trust your brush to tell that story.

Resources

It's best to visit art stores in person to experience the look and feel of tools and materials, and where knowledgeable staff can offer a wealth of advice. The following brands and major retailers are recommended, so check them out online, and look out for them in your local area.

Watercolor paints
Daniel Smith Extra Fine Watercolors: danielsmith.com
Mijello Mission Gold Artists' Watercolors: en-mj.picpac.kr
Schmincke: schmincke.de/en
Winsor & Newton Professional: uk.winsornewton.com

Paper brands
Arches: arches-papers.com
Canson Heritage: en.canson.com
Fabriano Artistico: fabriano.com/en
Saunders Waterford: stcuthbertsmill.com/st-cuthberts-
    mill-paper/saunders-waterford-watercolour
Stonehenge Aqua: legionpaper.com/stonehenge-aqua

Brushes
Jackson's: jacksonsart.com/brushes/brushes
Princeton: princetonbrush.com
Royal & Langnickel: art.royalbrush.com
Silverwhite: silverbrush.com

Art equipment suppliers
Artist & Craftsman Supply: artistcraftsman.com
Blick Art Materials: dickblick.com
Jackson's: jacksonsart.com
Michaels: michaels.com

Further reading
Austin Kleon, *Keep Going*, Workman, 2019
Austin Kleon, *Steal Like an Artist*, Workman, 2012
Lisa Congdon, *Find Your Artistic Voice,* Chronicle, *2019*
Sonya Patel Ellis, *The Botanical Bible,* Abrams, 2018
Susan K. Pell and Bobbi Angell, *A Botanist's Vocabulary,*
    Timber Press, 2016

Acknowledgments

This book would not have been possible without so many wonderful people who have shaped my artistic journey.

First and foremost, my deepest gratitude goes to my family and friends, who have supported me with unwavering love and encouragement. A special thank you to my Nana, who filled my childhood with endless art supplies and patiently helped me through every craft project my curious hands wanted to create.

Thank you to my fellow artists and the vibrant watercolor community, both online and in person, who continue to inspire me daily with their creativity, generosity in sharing techniques, and support for one another's growth.

Special thanks go to my students and workshop participants who have taught me as much as I've taught them. Your questions, enthusiasm, and unique perspectives have made me a better teacher and artist.

Thanks to the gardens, botanical conservatories, and natural spaces that have provided endless inspiration for this work—from my local South Florida landscapes to the countless plants that have posed as patient models.

Thank you to the team at Skittledog who believed in this project and helped bring these pages to life, especially Zara and Gaynor for their guidance and patience throughout the process.

And finally, to everyone who picks up a brush and discovers the joy of painting plants—you are the reason this book exists. May your artistic journey be filled with as much wonder and discovery as mine has been.

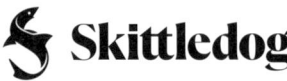

First published in the United Kingdom in 2026
by Skittledog, an imprint of Thames & Hudson Ltd,
6–24 Britannia Street, London WC1X 9JD

Modern Botanical Watercolor © 2026
Thames & Hudson Ltd, London

Text and photographs © 2026 Jenny Kiker

Senior Editor: Gaynor Sermon
Cover Designer: Alison Guile
Designer: Vanessa Green, The Urban Ant Ltd.
Production: Felicity Awdry

Distributed in North America by Abrams

ISBN 978-1-83776-085-5
01

Printed and bound in China by C&C Offset Printing Co., Ltd

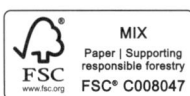

MIX
Paper | Supporting
responsible forestry
FSC® C008047

Be the first to know about our new releases, exclusive
content and author events by visiting:
thamesandhudson.com
thamesandhudsonusa.com
thamesandhudson.com.au